THE IRA AND ARMED STRUGGLE

Rogelio Alonso

Routledge
Taylor & Francis Group

LONDON AND NEW YORK

Spanish edition first published 2003
by Alianza Editorial, S.A.

English edition published 2007
by Routledge
2 Park Square, Milton Park, Abingdon, Oxon OX14 4RN

Simultaneously published in the USA and Canada
by Routledge
711 Third Avenue, New York, NY 10017, USA

Routledge is an imprint of the Taylor & Francis Group, an informa business

© Alianza Editorial, S.A., 2003
© 2003 Rogelio Alonso

This book was first published in Spanish with the title *Matar por Irlanda*
and has been translated by Andrew Read.

Typeset in Times New Roman by
Book Now Ltd, London

British Library Cataloguing in Publication Data
A catalogue record for this book is available from the British Library

Library of Congress Cataloging in Publication Data
Alonso, Rogelio.
[Matar por Irlanda. English]
The IRA and armed struggle / Rogelio Alonso.
p. cm. – (Political violence)
Translation of Matar por Irlanda.
Includes bibliographical references and index.
1. Irish Republican Army–History. 2. Political violence–Ireland–History–20th
century. 3. Guerrilla warfare–Ireland–History–20th century. 4. Political
violence–Northern Ireland. 5. Northern Ireland–History,
Military. 6. Ireland–History, Military. I. Title.
DA914.A4613 2007
941.5082–dc22   2006021639

ISBN10: 0–415–39610–7 (hbk)
ISBN10: 0–415–39611–5 (pbk)

ISBN13: 978–0–415–39610–3 (hbk)
ISBN13: 978–0–415–39611–0 (pbk)

THE IRA AND
ARMED STRUGGLE

Based on extensive interviews with former and existing members of the IRA, and a thorough analysis of primary and secondary sources, this book breaks major new ground in the understanding of the IRA and the Northern Ireland peace process. It also provides a rigorous evaluation of the personal and political consequences of the group's terrorist campaign.

Using a multi-disciplinary approach, with insights from political science, social psychology and history, Rogelio Alonso explains how the IRA came to end its long campaign without achieving its main political objectives. He analyses the motivations of IRA activists, and questions the efficacy of armed struggle by seeking to answer the question faced by many armed revolutionary movements: 'Was the war worth it?'

Most of the literature on Northern Ireland to date has failed to assess the political effectiveness of IRA terrorism. This factor must be examined properly if the yearned-for resolution of the conflict is to become a reality. This book analyses this vital issue through unprecedented access to the men and women behind the IRA's campaign of violence.

The IRA and Armed Struggle offers a provocative and new approach to understanding the IRA. It will be essential reading for students of Irish politics, the Northern Ireland peace process, and terrorism and political violence in general.

Rogelio Alonso is a Lecturer in Politics and Terrorism at Universidad Rey Juan Carlos, Madrid. He is the author of three other books on terrorism and several articles on the subject published in top-ranking academic journals.

THE PSYCHOLOGY OF TERRORISM
John Horgan

RESEARCH ON TERRORISM
Trends, achievements and failures
Andrew Silke (ed.)

A WAR OF WORDS
Political violence and public debate in Israel
Gerald Cromer

ROOT CAUSES OF SUICIDE TERRORISM
Globalization of martyrdom
Ami Pedahzur (ed.)

TERRORISM VERSUS DEMOCRACY
The liberal state response, 2nd edition
Paul Wilkinson

COUNTERING TERRORISM AND WMD
Creating a global counter-terrorism network
Peter Katona, Michael Intriligator and John Sullivan (eds)

MAPPING TERRORISM RESEARCH
State of the art, gaps and future direction
Magnus Ranstorp (ed.)

THE IDEOLOGICAL WAR ON TERROR
World-wide strategies for counter-terrorism
Anne Aldis and Graeme P. Herd (eds)

THE IRA AND ARMED STRUGGLE
Rogelio Alonso

CONTENTS

which myth was increasingly confused with reality with the ultimate objective of legitimising IRA violence. One of the activists interviewed confirms how lacking this education process was, revealing how in the first place republicans often assumed a series of beliefs that were later reinforced by an apparatus through which they justified their transgressional conduct: 'When I went into prison, when I was involved in the IRA, I was a very narrow-minded individual. When I went into prison everything was black or everything was white, or I could justify many things which today I could not do. And gradually, as you get a wee bit older, you get a bit of education. I've always turned round and said that it was very easy for me to be narrow-minded, it was very easy for me to see things black or white, do you understand the problem? But when you started opening up your mind and you start opening up your mind to different perspectives and you start seeing people as people and not just labels, it's then that things take on a different perspective.'[29]

The fact that, as the previous activist states, during his time as a member of the IRA he was able to justify acts which he could no longer either carry out or defend sheds light on the motivations for his actions and whether these were acceptable in the past. In other words, if he is no longer able to justify certain actions, why was he able to do so then, when the consequences were exactly the same? Through a process of personal transformation highly influenced by age, the relationship between the ends and the means chosen to achieve such ends experiences a fundamental change. In the same way, the expectations of success are lower when compared with those existing at the time that the decision to use violence was taken, as is clearly shown by the opinions of other republican activists. Jackie McMullan, who was born in 1956, considers that the reaction of young people of his generation should not be replicated by the new generation: 'I think the difference is that because of the thirty years experience that republicans are shrewd enough and intelligent enough to act only in ways that are going to achieve results.'[30] He then goes on to state that the violent response of thirty years ago did not achieve the results sought by the IRA. This view is backed up by other republicans, as summarised by the following testimonies:

'I've been involved in military conflict, right, but I also believe that war is futile.'[31]

'The combatants get older as well. As you know yourself, the way you think, very idealistic when you are a teenager or in your twenties is totally different to when you are in your forties. Your look at life totally differently. You have responsibilities, you have kids yourself. Nobody wants their kids to do, have the same kind of life as what they did. I know personally I don't want my daughter to have the same life, and she hasn't, that I grew up with. (…) I would say any *ism*, it doesn't give a damn what you are, if you are a Nationalist, Socialist, whatever, I think on the human level your views change in terms of you are getting older and your views on anything mellows. It is not as black and white and you are not as influenced by people as well. You just want to get on with life because life is too bloody short, you realise that. Again, as you mature as well you can empathise with other people, it doesn't give a damn where their politics come on a human level, we all go through the same things.'[32]

Brenda Murphy was sixteen years old when she received her first prison sentence, one year after joining the IRA. She is severely critical of the peace process in which the republican movement is now involved yet has no desire for her adolescent daughters to follow in her footsteps: 'In many ways I am glad it is over because that younger one would end up in prison the same as I did. You know you can see it in her, you can see it in her – the younger one is like, "this is just a sell out". And the older one "well, I don't care because I have a child here and wait till you have a child. I was born in prison and I don't want any of my children born in prison." So she's like that and the other one is the opposite.'[33] Her criticism of Sinn Féin is such that she refers to its acceptance of the Good Friday Agreement in 1998 as one of the most painful moments in her life, even going as far as to compare it with another extremely personal experience. On being released from prison in 1975 after four years behind bars, she returned to the IRA. She was arrested again in 1976: 'My baby was born in the prison. They told me if I came off the protest I could keep her for a year with me in the prison, but if I didn't I would have to send her out. So I refused and I had to send the baby out when she was six weeks old. They allowed me to breast feed her for six weeks and then I had to send her out to my family.'[34] Despite this, she admits that the objective of a united Ireland for which she joined the IRA is not worth spilling blood over. This opinion supports the argument of those who conclude that 'the war was futile'. It is worth noting that these former members advise those who are now at the same age as they were when they opted for violence not to follow that path. They implicitly doubt whether young people are mature enough to make the decision to join an organisation involved in murder since, as one of them put it, 'as you mature you can empathise with other people'.

'A very vulnerable and impressionable age'

As can be seen from the opinions expressed in previous pages, for many activists the nationalistic hope of a united Ireland was quite a vague goal, the traditional ideological principles of republicanism not being fully clear in their minds. 'I was a republican even at the age of thirteen. (...) You can't be fully mature at the age of thirteen.'[35] This is how one of the activists explained the limits of his ideological convictions. Traditionally republican ideology

Why didn't we ever try to get cross-community relations going and politics going through working class people who were suffering on the Protestant side? In fact we engaged in a nakedly sectarian apartheid movement where we only worked on the Catholic population and we never studied what it would take to unite Protestant and Catholic. We never used any prediction models to try and gauge what would happen if we started an IRA campaign, how it would fracture the communities in the North, how it would divide them for thirty, forty, fifty, sixty years. We clearly should have looked at probability models and so on to see what would happen here. We never did any of that. We just launched absolutely into a rebirth of the 1916/1918-style IRA campaign without any thought where it was going, just with a blind belief that in the bludgeoning forward of this armed struggle fruits would come for a united Ireland. But so far we've only had fruits for Sinn Féin political party and *only* when it gave up violence. There were no fruits for Sinn Féin movement, the fruits were all for the SDLP, largely on the grounds that they didn't take part in any violence.'[56]

'We were all young and it was the sixties'

As can be seen from the testimony of John Nixon cited above, while first-hand experiences of what was happening on the streets contributed to the social learning process of violence, television also played its part.[57] Violence in Northern Ireland reignited in the late 1960s, a time of global unrest and protest movements throughout the world which became an important influence for this particular generation of republicans. Volunteer Timothy, born in Derry in 1948 who joined the republican movement in the summer of 1969, sums up this atmosphere: 'Like most people at that time we used to listen to Bob Dylan singing protest songs and Joan Baez and we watched the American Civil Rights movement, the Black Civil Rights movement, the Vietnam War, the students in Paris and Germany, the Che Guevaras of the world, that were all our heroes at the time, so I think we were sort of a political generation.'[58] Despite this, the political philosophy of the generation described by this activist was very superficial, being characterised by vague idealistic political aspirations typical of youth. In addition, there were huge differences in the international contexts where the influences to which he refers developed, although this did not prevent republicans from using those models as useful examples of opposition and insurrection against the established order, as can be inferred from the following testimonies:

'This whole process of indoctrination started taking place and I was beginning to look at what was happening not just on a national context but an international context. For example every month or so the Cuban paper – the Granma – would come into our compounds and on our walls we would have José Marti. We would have Frank Ryan who fought in the Spanish revolution (sic). Our heroes were Malraux, Connolly and Che Guevara and Castro and there was this international dimension. And then of course we had all the works like Mao Tse Tung which we got stuck into – we read Frantz Fanon, Carlos Marighela – we had all these great debates, socialists. And then of course what was happening in the wider context, in Vietnam, the Khmer Rouges, what was happening in Africa, Angola, Mozambique and all the African struggles and we seen our own struggle as part of this ongoing process. As far as I could see these were people who had been exploited by imperialists for capitalist reasons.'[59]

'The armed struggle wasn't going to bring about the sort of victory that we would have been reading. The Algerian, the Vietnamese Revolution, the Cuban Revolution where it was sort of a straight cut, the people who were largely impoverished and living in appalling conditions fighting the popular struggle against an oppressive regime. We didn't have that here. You are on the edge of western Europe, you don't have their conditions, we are not living in sort of huts up a mountain with no running water, no electricity, we have fuckin' electricity, TVs, all the mod cons of modern day life and it is harder, you can't sort of let it duplicate a struggle from the jungles of Asia or the deserts of North Africa into this urban fuckin' jungle we live in.'[60]

It is important to point out that the readings they refer to were taken up by activists *after* joining the IRA and, in most cases, in prison. This allowed certain ideological limitations to be reproduced, resulting in political ideas that were simply 'reactionary'.[61] In the same way, another activist explains the motives which led him to take part for the first time in a pro-civil rights demonstration in Derry which ended in violence: 'It was politicisation through experience. I went on the first march on October 5th in 1968 and it was as much out of nosiness almost. I'd seen the demonstrations in London, Grosvenor Square, the anti Vietnam demonstration, civil rights was a buzz word and I went along on that, and then I saw that at first hand, and felt at first hand the violence of the RUC and I think it just created an awareness and an opening, everybody's eyes opened to what the hell kind of a state we were living in. It was from that point on that the real politicisation took place.'[62] In this regard, it is interesting to note how Joe Doherty, born on 20 January 1955 in north Belfast, describes what he calls his 'first political act': 'That was the Paris riots and what was happening in the United States with Dr Martin Luther King, that gave influence on young, the students movement and people within the community and we seen the birth of the Northern Ireland civil rights association and this was a non-violent association. It didn't really have any politics other than it was asking for reforms within the state. The response from the state was that the marches were banned, people were beaten on the street and people were taken into the police stations, and that had an influence on me as a child. I watched the TV, what was happening in the United States, Dr Martin Luther King, that the American government was responding to the civil rights marches there and to bring about reforms and we naturally thought that the British government would take the same path but what I seen on the streets was the civil rights marches being repressed by people being beat up on the streets and that's how I responded. And as a young boy of thirteen to fourteen years of age, that was my first political act when I picked up a rock and I threw it at a police jeep. They didn't have any politics really. A lot of people joined the republican movement then, all young men like myself. It was only once you went into jail, and then indoctrination, you had the self-indoctrination, you read books, you read Padraig Pearse and James Connolly and Wolfe Tone, you started reading all the history and then you developed your politics from that there. We were all young and it was the sixties, it was all John Lennon and Yoko Ono and Joan Baez and everything, Che Guevara, we were all into that there, you know, we were kind of naïve, we just realised later on that politics isn't black and white, it's more complex than that, it's more complex when you take over a government, you need investment in the country, you know, that was the sixties.'[63]

The lure of vague but attractive political ideals, so enticing during adolescence, was also evident in Feilim O hAdhmaill. Born in 1958, he decided to join the republican movement in the first half of the 1970s, acknowledging 'great international influences' such as 'the Vietnam War, the Palestinian struggle' and 'the likes of Che Guevara'.[64] Martin O'Hagan, born in 1954 in Lurgan, in Armagh, also joined the republican movement when still an adolescent in this same context, affected by the external influences referred to above. O'Hagan gives a very eloquent explanation of how the changing world scene really influenced his generation. In his case, it led him in the early 1970s to join one of the branches of the republican movement, the Official IRA, believing it to be more left-wing. As he himself explains, his decision to join was not really motivated by any serious ideological reasons, or the need to defend 'his people' which so many republicans referred to, but rather his 'fascination with a series of ideas':

> It was all a big game. The enthusiasm of youth. So when the civil rights came along, I hadn't a clue, I didn't need civil rights cause I wasn't discriminated against, I wasn't conscious of discrimination. The Troubles began. I became interested in the republican clubs as a left-wing alternative to what else was there, a sort of opening the hand of friendship to the majority population, rejection of sort of traditional Catholic values, and to a large extent it was exciting for me 'cause I'd never come across modern ideas, I'd never come across anything so exciting. I'd been reared as a Catholic, my world was very narrow and all of a sudden I came into this world of ideas and as a young fella of seventeen or

26

eighteen I was fascinated. I remember thinking it was very unfair, there was a newspaper called the *United Irishman*, which at that time was banned in the North of Ireland just as the republican clubs were banned. Now, it wasn't because of some sort of ideological principle but I think it was more to do with the devilment of belonging to a banned organisation and thumbing my nose at the system, at authority. I wasn't really conscious of Protestants and Catholics as such. So what happened then was in August 1971 internment was introduced. We all got involved in the riots, the riots were more fun than anything else, it was just young people out rioting.[65]

The role and the composition of the police in Northern Ireland meant that it was seen by republicans as a repressive instrument of control in the hands of unionists. This belief was confirmed by its excessive and violent reaction to the civil rights marches in the second half of the 1960s. However, as O'Hagan suggests, and as would seem logical, many young people did not fully understand what was happening and simply defying the police was reason enough for participating in many of these disturbances. As John Nixon points out, 'We didn't understand the political reasons for all this here but we knew they certainly were disliked. Who likes the police when they are young?'[66]

'A reaction to the brutality of the forces of the state'

One of the reasons many republicans give for joining the IRA was the need to defend a section of the nationalist community against the attacks that it suffered between the late 1960s and the early 1970s. On 14 July 1969, Francis McCloskey was found dead at a spot where the police had charged a group of people who had been throwing stones. Some sources consider that the police were responsible for his death, although others deny this. Two days later, Samuel Devenney died in Derry after having been beaten by the police some months earlier at the door of his house, when various youngsters who were being chased by the RUC had sought refuge. During the intense street violence of 14 August, 9-year-old Patrick Rooney died when he was hit while in bed by a stray police bullet fired from an armoured vehicle. An inquiry into the disturbances of that summer found that the shot fired was 'unjustified'.[67] On 14 August, two other people, Michael Lynch and John Gallagher, were shot and killed by the police in Belfast and Armagh respectively. The Scarman tribunal described Gallagher's death as amounting to grave misconduct on the part of the B Specials. The opinions of two former republicans who grew up in areas especially affected by the violent confrontations of the time, west and east Belfast, typify the sentiment expressed by other IRA members in relation to this matter. Jackie McMullan was born in 1956, and Jim Gibney in 1954.

'It was partly a reaction to the brutality of the state forces. The RUC at the time, they had not only facilitated loyalists in burning down nationalist streets and houses and putting people out of their homes, they had actually participated and had killed a number of people.'[68]

'When I joined the struggle in 1970 I would have been sixteen. I was born in August 1954. What was it that brought me into the republican movement? Very simple. I lived in east Belfast, a small place called the Short Strand, a very small nationalist community in the Short Strand. In 1969 that community like many others in Belfast were attacked, was attacked by loyalists, so I became, at fifteen years of age I became a vigilante, patrolling the streets where I lived. And what was I doing? Protecting my home and my family and my neighbours. We didn't have any guns so all we were, were eyes and ears to keep a watch, that was all. And what, then, between '69 and 1970? Well, there were many incidents of attack in the area, but June 1970, 27th June 1970 there was a concerted armed offensive by loyalists against the Short Strand during which they tried to burn the area to the ground, people were killed, homes were burnt, and there was a gun battle that went on for several hours throughout the night. So that was it as far as I was concerned. That was it! And that's when I joined the movement from that period onwards because you were there, I mean, by joining the republican movement it meant that you could properly defend the district.'[69]

As Gibney notes, during the intense gun battle that took place on the day he decided to join the republican movement, several people died. Robert Nelly and Robert James McCurrie, both Protestant civilians, thirty eight and thirty four years old respectively, died after being shot by the IRA. Two days later, Henry McIlhone, a 32-year-old Catholic, died after having been accidentally wounded by an IRA member on the night of the 27 June, during the same skirmishes.[70] As with many of the incidents that happened during that period when numerous clashes took place between Catholics and Protestants, opinions differ as to how things started. Each community blames the other. With respect to the specific events referred to by Gibney, it appears beyond doubt that, as the British army colonel Michael Dewar has written, 'the IRA had been permitted to play the role of defenders of the minority community', since the security forces were incapable of dealing with the various flashpoints across Belfast at the same time.[71]

In explaining his initiation into the republican movement, Robert McClenaghan, born in Belfast at the end of the 1950s, also referred to this need to defend his community as a key factor. Experiences of British army repression, which he considered unjustified, as well as the death of a childhood friend in the fateful month of August 1969 after being attacked by Protestants in the area where he lived and where soon after a wall known as the *peaceline* was built to separate the two communities, created in him a thirst for vengeance that led him to join the youth wing of the movement. McClenaghan's time in the *Fianna*, where he was submerged in a violent subculture, had a marked effect on him. As he himself noted later, this socialisation process motivated his decision to become involved in violence and the IRA. His testimony clearly explains the relevance of this violent subculture:

I would probably be a child of 1969 in that I lived in an area called Clonard which is just off the Falls Road, but it was one of those areas that came under loyalist and state attack in August 14th and 15th 1969. So that was my first experience as a child. I was eleven years of age when those attacks took place in Bombay Street – it was round the corner from our house. The person who lived in the next street to ours was a member of the junior IRA and he was killed. He was fifteen years of age and he was called Gerard McAuley. So he would have been a personal friend. So his death was like a big impact on me and our family, and that is if you like the first time as a child you start to say 'is there something wrong in this country?' Obviously then things developed. The British army came into the equation. By 1970 the British army were raiding our house. They were coming in the middle of the night and kicking the door in. Taking people out of bed and searching the house. Wrecking the house. So that is when you started to wonder or started to question. Then obviously we had the Falls curfew in June 1970. We also had the ongoing problem with Loyalism especially on the Springfield Road. I lived just off the Springfield Road. So we have always had that connection or that tie in, if you like, living on the *peaceline*. So by 1971 internment came in on August of 1971 and then it was about a couple of months after that ... it was about November of 1971 that I personally joined the junior IRA or junior republican movement at that stage. You didn't have a clearly worked out idea, you just knew that there was something wrong, that the British army or the RUC or the loyalists shouldn't be killing our people, that you had to do something to resist or something to fight against it. (...) And then it got to the stage where you wanted to use weapons to physically fight against it. So by 1972 you were involved in the junior wing of the IRA. We were the junior so we would have been out in front looking to see if there was any British army, looking to see if there was any RUC. The older volunteers in the IRA – they would have come out and done the shooting or whatever it was they were involved in. They would have given the weapons to us and then we would have took the weapons away and put them into a safe place. So that was my education on the streets and at that time by 1972 we were also starting to lose people ourselves in terms of losing volunteers from the area who were killed either in premature explosions, where they were trying to make the bomb. And in March 1972 we lost four IRA volunteers. So therefore then you had to go to the funerals. You were meeting the families. You were doing the guard of honour beside the coffin, for the three days of the wake and stuff. So all these experiences was what sort of motivated you and then by November 1974, well, technically you were supposed to be seventeen years of age before you could join the IRA, but because we had a good long introduction if you like from 1972 to 1974, myself and another volunteer we were actually inducted, or brought into the IRA about November 1974. So from November 1974 until I was arrested in November 1976 you would have been active within Belfast as part of the Belfast Brigade then. And then by 1976 your luck had run out. I had been involved in a bombing unit where basically our job was to take and plant bombs all over Belfast. And at one of those I left a palm print behind on one of the cars that we had hijacked and we were using and therefore I got arrested.[72]

As McClenaghan notes, the activities which he took part in as a member of the *Fianna* also 'motivated' him. It is clear that the acts described by McClenaghan, which meant coming into close contact with the IRA while still young and immature, were vitally important and influenced the decision of many to join. Another former IRA member recalls this process: 'I was asked if I would be interested in joining the republican movement and I went along. I just went along with the people who I felt had a more positive influence on me at the time. I was probably pretty naïve in many ways and I still felt at that stage my ideology would have been fairly simple: civil rights and Brits out, that simple analysis. I had no real in-depth political analysis to give, it was as basic as that.'[73]

There is no doubt that the direct experience of violence provided a crucial motivation for certain activists, who stress that a factor in their decision to join the IRA was the disproportionate stance of the British army from the early 1970s onwards, including the introduction of draconian measures such as internment without trial of those suspected of belonging to proscribed organisations. For example, Brenda Murphy decided to join the IRA when she was only sixteen years old following the dramatic events of 9 August 1971, when internment without trial was introduced and hundreds of people were arrested by the security forces, the majority of whom were totally inno-cent. The British Army raids on that day were followed by intense shooting carried by the IRA in different areas of Belfast. Three people died in the north of the city, one of whom was a member of the IRA and another one a soldier. Seven civilians died in west Belfast as a result of shootings by the British Army hours after the introduction of internment.

With me it was internment night what turned it from being just political to actually engaging in violence and becoming a member of what was then an illegal organisation – and still is. I was sixteen and the internment

30

started in Ballymurphy and soldiers just came down over the hill and raided every home, trailing people out. A lot of people were running about in confusion. There was nine people shot dead in a row sort of. After that I just thought: to hell with this! Because they are killing you if you try to contain you to civil rights only, and they are killing you if you don't, so the only way to beat these people is to fight back. And at that stage I got involved in the republican movement and shortly after that I was caught with a rifle, and I got four years in prison for that.[74]

Internment without trial had been used by both the British and Irish governments during the 1956–62 IRA campaign. This had devastating results for the republican movement, which found itself in such a weak position that it was forced to call a ceasefire. By contrast, the use of this measure at the beginning of the 1970s had very negative effects for British policy in Northern Ireland. Its indiscriminate use from August 1971 on deprived hundreds of their freedom, yet most had nothing to do with the IRA, since the security forces were acting on out-of-date information about its members. The poor coordination between the army and the police seriously hindered intelligence operations during this period. As a result, the multiple searches and arrests that occurred in areas where nationalists lived worsened relations between this community and the security forces. This is clear from the testimony of Breandan MacCionnaith, born in September 1957 in Aghagallon, county Armagh, close to the small country village of Lurgan, where he grew up. He describes how on one occasion the British Army came to arrest his grandfather, an old republican who had fought in the War of Independence back at the start of the century: 'Bearing in mind that my grandfather at that age was somewhere in the region of ninety four years of age, even the Brits were surprised when they came in.'[75]

The classic pattern of action–repression–reaction thus caused an escalation of violence in the first half of the 1970s. Violence spiralled out of control, with the consequences that two former IRA members describe:

'It became almost personal where you hated these people. There was a whole element, the mention of hatred and enmity between us. This became, I don't like to say a sectarian war, but sort of.'[76]

'Remembering when we were interned, it was, six or seven of the people who were with us, in our particular part of the ship, were actually all innocent, they had nothing to do with anything. And we were saying to the British soldiers who were sort of stationed around the boat, you know, "what you've got here are 60 per cent of the innocent", and they said, "but we've got 40 per cent of the guilty", you know, and that was their idea: "if we can lift ten men and get one IRA man in the middle of them, well, that's success for us", but what it creates is another nine IRA men out there in terms of the families of the people that they've arrested.

Similarly Bloody Sunday did the same. So, I, I would say that the campaign of violence by both the British government through the army and the campaign of the Provos actually intensified the sectarian situation that we had here in this part of the country.'[77]

Shane O'Doherty, born in 1955, joined the IRA when he was fifteen years old, influenced by youthful idealism and patriotism, fed by his perception of the unjust way in which the British had historically treated the Irish and which, in his opinion, went back to the potato famines of the nineteenth century. He was inspired by the republican tradition and the heroes of the 1916 Easter Rising against the British. Reading about such events ignited in him 'a passionate patriotism and an equally passionate desire to emulate the heroic deeds recounted therein'.[78] In 1971, he decided to leave the organisation. There were two reasons for this. The first was the death in August of that year of his friend and fellow IRA member, Eamonn Lafferty, during a gun battle with the British army. The second occurred in November, when an IRA leader reproached him for throwing a grenade off target, an act which almost killed a woman and her two children.[79] He returned to the movement as a result of Bloody Sunday:

> I left, and it was only on Bloody Sunday that I thought 'ah, fuck, we got to meet violence with violence here, even if I am going to be killed on the streets like Eamonn at least I am defending my people'. So it was the defence thing again that drove us back, what drove us back into the IRA in 1972. It was: 'fuck, you are better to die defending your people than just be killed on the street because you are a Catholic or because you are a Nationalist or you are a civil rights marcher, fuck that. I don't want to be killed as a civil rights marcher walking down the fuckin' street after my Sunday dinner, I want to die as an activist.' So that's the fuel of going back into the IRA was Bloody Sunday again, and if Bloody Sunday hadn't happened, I have met many people who told me that they wouldn't have been in the movement if Bloody Sunday hadn't happened. One famous Sinn Féin councillor in Belfast told me ten years ago, just after I got out of prison, that he joined the IRA after Bloody Sunday and didn't imagine joining if Bloody Sunday hadn't happened. So things like Bloody Sunday and the hunger strikes and stuff are sort of critical, crucial moments, defining moments. But Bloody Sunday is a fucking defining moment for the IRA because like after Bloody Sunday they had complete legitimacy, before Bloody Sunday they didn't have any at all.[80]

The security forces were accused on numerous occasions of torturing and abusing those arrested to the point that some of them were paid compensation by the British authorities, as is the case of one of those interviewed for this book, Seamus Lynch, who was interned between 1971 and 1972 after having joined the IRA in the 1960s. The techniques used in the exhaustive questioning sessions were ruled to be illegal in 1976 by the European Commission of Human Rights, which declared that the United Kingdom had breached the European Convention on Human Rights by torturing prisoners. The methods used included sleep deprivation, only providing a bread and water diet, applying noise in order to cause disorientation, covering the head with a hood, and requiring prisoners to stand spreadeagled for long periods of time. Two years later, the European Court of Human Rights disagreed with the use of the word 'torture', stating that the prisoners had received 'inhuman and degrading treatment'. Nevertheless, experiences of violence and sectarian strife, as well as abuses by the security forces, differed according to geographical areas. Therefore the importance of these factors as a motivation for membership was not the same in all cases, as Paul Little, a former member of Sinn Féin and the INLA (Irish National Liberation Army), a splinter group from the IRA, who was born at the end of the 1950s in Antrim, in the north of the region, explains:

> I was originally from Antrim town which is approximately twenty miles from Belfast. In the sixties, certainly it would have been a unionist, very much a unionist town. We were a Catholic family who lived in Antrim, a fairly small Catholic population. In the sixties we basically just got on with our lives, politics probably wouldn't have touched very much into our lives at all. My experience would have been different say than people who were living in the Falls Road or Ballymurphy or somewhere else. See the experience of country people was different than the experience of Belfast people. We didn't experience the same oppression on a day, nearly on an hour to hour, day-to-day basis as people were experiencing in Belfast. And I think in a sense, I would say that helped assisting me in homing in on my politics because it meant always you were looking at a political reason or justification for what you were doing and what actions and the way you thought and all those type of things. Whereas I think on a day to day basis if you were walking out your front door and tripping over soldiers all the time and you were getting into rows and fights and they were stopping you in the street, often your anger would have overtaken. I experienced that when I got out of jail and I lived in Belfast because I couldn't go back home because it was a loyalist town. So I experienced that then and I know it didn't leave you an awful lot of time for working things out politically.[81]

'I became involved to unite the working class'

For some activists, socialism was a fundamental part of the nationalist ideology and one of their main reasons for joining the republican movement. This was the case of Paul Little, who, after an initial period selling Sinn Féin's newspapers, chose to join the INLA at the end of the 1970s, a time when he was increasingly involved in demonstrations supporting the republican inmates in the Maze prison who were demanding recognition as political prisoners. After being active in the INLA for less than a year, Little was arrested and sentenced to nine years in prison, finally being released in 1984. He opted for the INLA rather than another republican group because he saw in it a means of pursuing a 'class struggle alongside the freedom struggle' but also for the following reason: 'The other thing was, and I don't make any secret about it, I had a relative who was a member of this movement and opportunity plays a lot, I knew where to go. For many people living where we lived, the whole mechanism of trying to join the organisation probably was a lot more complicated or difficult than it was in Belfast. So there would have been a certain amount to do with opportunity as well.'[82] The combination of opportunity with an ideology which saw the sole aspiration of a united Ireland as insufficient would determine this activist's path. Another example of putting socialism before nationalism is found in Mickey McMullan, born in Belfast in 1951, who joined the IRA in 1971 on returning to Northern Ireland after having spent a year in London. He dismisses the idea that his decision to join the IRA was motivated by any desire to defend 'his people', a factor so often mentioned by other republicans. Instead, he focuses on the following aspects:

I came back to Ireland in 1971, January, where again I was in conflict as to which organisation to become involved in. The split had occurred in the republican movement between the Provisionals and the Officials. The Officials appeared to be much more left-wing whereas the Provisionals were much more militarily inclined. At that point in my life I felt that the only way to resolve difficulties with the British State was through armed conflict, so I opted for the Provisional IRA, became involved with the IRA, became active. (...) I became involved to remove British imperialism from Ireland, to unite the working class in Ireland into a unified country, and the struggle for a socialist republic in terms of James Connolly. In saying that, that's not to say that I was politically articulate in 1970 or '71, I was very immature politically. I had a gut feeling in terms of where my politics should lie. I was from a working-class background. (...) I never really considered myself a nationalist. I suppose because of partition, because of the way I was brought up, I had an understanding of Irish history. Whilst at school one of the few subjects I was actually good at was the Irish language and Irish history.

I had an interest in the Irish language from early days but I suppose the more politically aware I became the less nationalistic I was. Encountering people from Belfast in London in 1970 was like a breath of fresh air because I was introduced to Marxism, socialism. Again I wasn't greatly educated. It was only through jail that I became educated, I done a lot of reading. So I never really considered myself a great nationalist.[83]

The 'gut feeling' to which McMullan refers, coupled with a vague left-wing philosophy, are the features with which Brendan Holland also identifies. At the age of eighteen, Holland started to participate in the marches organised by the People's Democracy after the attacks suffered by demonstrators from that organisation in Derry in 1968: 'Before that I wasn't in any way political. Within the People's Democracy I became radicalised quite a bit because it was a left-wing organisation. It was a mixture of all sorts of different kinds of Marxists, anarchists and just republicans. But it always had a left-wing attitude. Different from the left-wing attitude of say the republican movement at that time, which was left-wing but Stalinist. So it was that critique of the republican movement from the left within People's Democracy, which was a primarily student movement. And it just went on from there. It just continued to get radicalised. Then there would have been periods where I would have gone to London to work. I wasn't a student, I just worked. And politically there was quite a few things happening in London at that time – the whole Vietnam thing. Generally a revolutionary culture. So I didn't come from a traditionally republican background.'[84]

This radicalisation of the People's Democracy which he refers to led its leaders to hold demonstrations that were criticised by other leaders of the civil rights movement on the grounds that they were 'provocative'. These other groups exhorted their followers not to become involved in such demonstrations then, convinced that they would lead to violent disturbances between demonstrators and unionists taking part in counter-demonstrations.[85] This was the atmosphere in which Holland continued his activism, which constituted a very good 'ferment of ideas' although he states that it was 'more middle class' and a 'fashionable left-wing' movement, in contrast to his greater identification with the 'working class'. Ultimately, it was this last factor which caused him to abandon the People's Democracy joining the IRA: 'As a matter of fact I actually joined the Officials first. At that time there was a lot of searching going on. And actually after the split in January 1970 in the republican movement, I briefly joined the Officials. But what I carried with me into the Officials was that culture of PD which was critical of left authoritarianism but at the same time it was an ambiguous position. You were trying to be far more serious than the middle class students of the People's Democracy, so therefore you joined the republican movement which was a working class organisation – so therefore I felt more at home and much more attracted to it. But also what I had was the critique of authoritarianism. So very rapidly within less than two months, I became disillusioned with the Officials. It was quite obvious you were moving into an organisation with strict military control and you had to follow the party line. Some of the political lectures that were given were pretty authoritarian, they were expressing support for the Soviet Union and Eastern European socialism in general, which I had big problems with. You are young, it was a period of confusion and a lot of your actions were not completely rational, you followed your gut instincts.'[86]

After a brief period in the Official IRA, he went to work in London, where he continued in contact with friends with whom he debated which organisation best suited his political stance. Finally, he decided to return to Ireland and join the Provisional IRA for reasons that can hardly be described as ideological or the fruit of mature thought: 'So I think leaving all the ideology aside and theory and so on, as much as we knew about it, I think the determining factor was that one of my mate's father, the father of one of my mates reckoned the Provos were the way to go. So when internment broke out then, we left London and joined the Provisionals.'[87] This confirms that, as he himself notes, the crucial decision to join the IRA cannot be described as 'completely rational'. Despite this marked lack of political maturity, activists like him would later underline the political nature of their violent acts within the IRA.

One of the conclusions that can be extracted from the testimonies gathered is the incompatibility of the socialist ideals to which certain activists aspired and the violent methods that they used on joining the republican movement. Socialism was a goal included by the IRA in its Green Book: 'Our task is not only to kill as many enemy personnel as possible or to cause as much economic damage as possible but of equal importance to create support which will carry us not only through a war of liberation which could last another decade but which will support us past the "Brits Out" state to the ultimate aim of a Democratic Socialist Republic.'[88] Similarly, James Connolly, who took part in the Easter Rising in 1916 and was one of the first writers to analyse the Irish situation from a Marxist perspective, was a mythical figure for the organisation, constantly eulogised in the republican discourse. Yet IRA violence did not contribute the slightest bit towards achieving socialism and the declared aim of uniting Catholic and Protestant working classes. Paddy Devlin, nationalist politician and one of the founders of the Social Democratic and Labour Party (SDLP) who had belonged to the republican movement in the 1940s and was interned for his activities then, emphasised this point: 'How could republicanism be compatible with socialism if those responsible for it give orders to kill Protestants for no other reason than that they need a number of Protestants murdered to make a political point to the British government, to the security forces, to Ian Paisley and to the SDLP? Can republicanism be compatible with socialism if it is identified with the blowing up of factories mainly owned by Protestants, to multiply the numbers of workless and deter new industry from coming in to set up in the worst-hit areas for unemployment in these islands?'[89] The IRA has never been able to answer these questions adequately, despite the fact that socialism is one of the reasons that activists often provide for joining. The explanation may lie in the excessively simplistic way in which the IRA has interpreted the term 'socialism', and which Gerry Adams himself sums up in the following terms: 'You cannot be a socialist without being a separatist. You cannot be a socialist if you condone, support or ignore the colonial stronghold which the British government maintains over this part of our country. There can be no socialism in Ireland while the British connection divides workers in the Six Counties and while partition prevents a national unity of working-class interests.'[90] In 1987, the Sinn Féin Department of Education published 'Questions of History', a history of the Irish republican movement until 1922, written by a group of IRA prisoners in the Maze prison, on the outskirts of Belfast. A second part was to be published, but Adams, displeased that some of the prisoners involved in its writing questioned their leader's view of socialism, prohibited it.[91]

By making socialism subject to the national question, Adams failed to explain where those working-class Protestants fitted in, since they would define themselves as both unionist and socialist while being forced to distance themselves from possible joint action with groups like the IRA which was advocating the murder of members of their community. In contrast to what many activists have claimed, it is possible to show that republican violence was sectarian, its logical effect being the increase of antagonism between the Northern Irish communities, deepening the division between nationalists and unionists, a matter that will be examined further in later chapters.[92] The overwhelming rejection of IRA terrorism by Protestants and unionists exposes the weaknesses in the republican analysis with respect to socialism. In fact the IRA was guilty of the 'exploitation' of the Catholic and nationalist working class, as one of the interviewees recognised when he stated that 'the biggest exploiters of our people are often people who come from within our communities'.[93]

2

DEFENDERS?

'It just gave added justification for killing soldiers and policemen'

'Traditional republicanism didn't motivate me'

'I never considered myself a great nationalist,' declared Mickey McMullan, expressing an opinion shared by many of those who joined the republican movement. Yet the relationship between violence and nationalism was to affect decisively the membership of those who joined the movement. One member explained this by highlighting the ineffectiveness of the armed struggle in achieving the socialist objectives that motivated certain republicans, generating instead counterproductive effects which would worsen the conflict and damage the nationalist cause: 'I don't think it [the armed struggle] was an awakening of the working class. And I think that is probably one of the reasons that for Ireland and the Irish people and the working class in particular it is probably as well that it came to an end. What it did was it awakened a latent nationality within republicanism or within Irish people and that then became the reason [for using the armed struggle].'[1] This 'latent nationality' plays a major part in traditional republican ideology and it was a factor which motivated certain members, especially those that joined the IRA before the 1969 split and the outbreak of violence that is usually considered to mark the beginning of the Troubles. In most of these cases, the family atmosphere in which future members grew up and were educated was an important means of transmitting the traditional ideals of Irish republicanism to a new generation. The contrast between those who joined the IRA in these different periods can be clearly seen if we compare the testimonies in the previous chapter with those of former members who joined in the 1950s and the early to mid-1960s, before the Troubles began. John Kelly is typical of the latter group:

> I was born 5th April 1936, in north Belfast, and most of my adult, teen-age life has been devoted to the republican movement, to the physical force elements of the republican movement. My background is and always has been a republican background, my mother and father were republicans and their parents before them were republicans. If I could

just explain what I mean by republican. Republican for us in Ireland means the unity of Catholic, Protestant and dissenter under the common name of Irishman, so it is non-sectarian, it has nothing to do with the sectarian conflict that sometimes epitomises the conflict in Ireland and in the North of Ireland, so I have been a republican for as long as I can remember. I joined officially the republican movement, that is the IRA, when I was fifteen years old. I was imprisoned in 1956 until 1964 for eight years for what was called then the Border Campaign within the Six Counties. I came out of prison and then we took up the agitation of civil rights and then we had the events of 1969 which caused the reactivation of the IRA. After the campaign of 1956 to 1962 the IRA had, of its own volition, put weapons beyond use, but now the circumstances were that the state or the security forces of the state within the Six Counties unleashed their forces against the nationalist population.[2]

On being asked of his reasons for joining the IRA at the beginning of the 1950s, Kelly answered as follows: 'Because it was traditional within my own family background that the only way to oppose British rule in Ireland was through the use of physical force and that is a longstanding tradition within Irish political life.'[3] This ideology was broadly shared by Bob Murray, born in Belfast in 1941, who also participated in the 1950s campaign and later joined the Provisional IRA after the schism in the republican movement, becoming Gerry Adams' bodyguard until the second half of the 1980s. He was also responsible for certain matters related to the financial administration of the organisation.[4] The same can be said of Ruairi O'Bradaigh, born in 1932 in county Longford, in the south of Ireland. In 1950 he joined Sinn Féin, and a year later the IRA. He came to hold an important position during the campaign which ended in 1962, and was also one of the founders of the Provisional IRA some years later. In 1986 he left to set up Republican Sinn Féin, of which he has been president ever since.[5]

Other republicans of this same generation who joined the IRA, albeit slightly later, in the mid-1960s, largely because of 'their family heritage', have the same traditional ideological references as O'Bradaigh, Kelly or Murray. At the same time, however, these factors are complemented with others of a social nature which they identify as having a profound effect on their views, and which mean that they had a slightly different picture of republicanism. The influence of this factor on these activists perhaps helps to explain the way their views evolved after the split in the republican movement, which resulted in them staying with the Official IRA instead of opting for the Provisional IRA, as two former members now explain.

Johnny White was born in Derry in 1947 and after joining the movement in 1965, he became Chief of Staff of the Official IRA in that city at the beginning of the 1970s: 'From the mid-sixties until 1969, until the split, you would have had a very traditional attitude within the leadership of the republican movement. There was no split. But the attitude was basically, "we want a united Ireland, that's it", there was no social aspect to it, there was no socialism, and there was a lot of people within the leadership at that time who would have considered our involvement on issues such as unemployment, homelessness, bad housing conditions, as being nothing to do with republicanism. There were some people within the leadership who believed that we were stepping outside the realms of republicanism, that we shouldn't get involved in that type of thing. But in the mainstream of the republican movement there was a shift in direction away from traditional republican's standpoint to this more social orientated policies and activities. That we shouldn't be sitting back waiting till the opportunity for when the gun was produced and we were in a war with the British army, that there had to be an involvement of the people, and we had to be representing the interests of the working class people of the areas that we were supposed to be representing, that we could not ignore that, that we were part of the community, that these issues had affected us as members of the community, and as republicans, we should reflect this, and we should work on it. On the other side, there was people who believed that this was completely wrong and that the total emphasis must be put on attacking militarily, like, the British army and the Orangemen, and that the whole emphasis should be put on attaining weapons. At the same time, apart from the social issue, we realised that there was a definite need for armed struggle and armed resistance to the British army, and any other elements who would pose a threat to our communities. And because of this, at that particular time, there was a lot of training, acquiring of weapons and things like that, and developing a military struggle, a military organisation capable of either defence or attack if necessary on the British forces.'[6]

For his part, Seamus Lynch, born in Belfast in 1945, became involved in the republican movement about 1964 due to what he describes as a strong family connection with republicanism. He remained in the Official IRA after the split with the Provisionals until, at the beginning of the 1970s, his opposition to the armed struggle as a 'political weapon' grew to the extent that he definitively abandoned the organisation shortly afterwards.

[Republicanism] was an important issue in our family, that's not to suggest for a moment that it was an important issue in the area that we lived because it wasn't. Over the years there would have been a small number of families that would have seen themselves as republicans as opposed to nationalists, but they would have been a fairly small number, and that would have been noticeable in the different military campaigns, the military campaign that I would have kind of had knowledge of a little bit would have been the 1956 to 1962 military campaign, when I would have known people in my area that would have been imprisoned, a very small number of people, so it wasn't as if republicanism was a very popular concept or a very popular organisation to join at that particular time. At that time when the 1956–62 military campaign finished very quickly, it was when people started to get out of prison. Around 1962 apparently there was a little debate in the prison about, 'well, we've had another glorious failure, where do we go from here?', and there was many conclusions they had reached and many different analyses and there had been a history in the republican movement of people coming out of prison, being demoralised. On this occasion the general consensus of those who were interested was that, 'look, we've been engaged in a military campaign with little or no support of the masses of the people and the people have many other issues that they're confronted with on a daily basis that they don't really relate to the need for violence, or understand the need for physical force'. So the general consensus was, 'we need to try to develop an organisation, a mass organisation that would involve the participation of more and more working people', and there was always, always at the back of their minds the issue of the potential sectarianism in Northern Ireland. Now, when I say 'potential sectarianism', it always existed but the potential for it to accelerate therefore when you're talking in terms of physical force in Northern Ireland and the British being seen as the kind of the imperialist enemy, one had always to bear in mind that you had the police who were the RUC in the main who were maybe 95 per cent, 96 per cent Protestant, therefore the Protestant community seen them as their police and that was always going to lead, and of course you had what was known as the B Specials which were the reserve police, were a highly sectarian force.[7]

Lynch goes on to explain the importance of social issues in his decision to join the IRA:

I lived in poverty, my family lived in poverty for many years and there was much poverty around us, so we could certainly see the inequalities and the injustices in the society we lived in, we didn't always know the best way to handle them or to counteract them or whatever, so there was perhaps joining for the wrong reasons from the point of view of what you wanted to do, because when people feel angry in how they've to live, the immediate reaction is not always necessarily the best reaction or the most constructive reaction. So there was a fair bit of romanticism, to be quite honest and frank, there was a romantic thing as well, perhaps an emotional thing, because you were talking about a working class lad who was big and strong and felt maybe angry at the situation that he watched his family growing up in the circumstances and how the state had discriminated against people around the areas of jobs and housing, because there was twelve of us lived, twelve and my parents which was fourteen, that lived in a one-bedroom house. And at night most of the family went, had to go out and sleep with aunts and grandmothers and all of that, so it wasn't a good quality of life. And having said that, Protestant people lived on our street that lived the same way, hence the reason that I could never see the Protestant people as the enemy the way many of the republican, well, what I call the Provos republicans, but many of the people in the latter day would see, and over the years they would see the Protestant community [as the enemy].[8]

The weakness of the republican movement was patent in the second half of the 1960s. As has been mentioned, it was the specific events that took place at the end of that decade that contributed to reactivating a republican ideology which, until then, had lacked sufficient force to attract the support and sympathy of a considerable number of fellow citizens. Johnnie White, a prominent leader of the Official IRA in Derry at the start of the seventies, states that before the Troubles started in 1969, the republicans had only about twenty activists in Northern Ireland's second biggest city.[9] Their situation was not much better in Belfast, as Seamus Lynch, who held a similar position in the capital of Northern Ireland to that of White in Derry, describes: '1966 was a fairly important year, because that was the anniversary of the 1916 Rising and it created a bit of enthusiasm within the republican movement and there was a few more recruits and all of that. However, nothing substantial as such. I can give you an example, in the whole of north Belfast stretching across to areas of south and east Belfast we would have had maybe fifteen members, and our newspaper then was the *United Irishman*, and if we sold three dozen we were doing well and many of the people that we had approached with a view to joining turned us away. The sectarian situation developed in 1969, it was clear to us then that we could see people coming out to defend their homes which was quite natural, so you had then the formation really of the defence, a defence mentality, and everyone was looking for guns to defend their areas.'[10]

John Kelly, one of the IRA's main leaders at the end of the 1960s, describes in similar terms the crisis that the organisation suffered before and after 1962. This was the year in which the IRA announced the end of its armed campaign, and the statement containing this announcement clearly reflected the group's failure to achieve its republican objectives: 'The decision to end the Resistance Campaign has been taken in view of the general situation. Foremost among the factors motivating this course of action has been the attitude of the general public whose minds have been deliberately distracted from the supreme issue facing the Irish people – the unity and freedom of Ireland.'[11]

After the Border Campaign of 1956 to 1963 there was a growing realisation within the republican movement that the armed conflict was not succeeding, it hadn't succeeded in the forties and it hadn't succeeded in the thirties, now we're into the fifties and again into the sixties and it had failed because the support of the people was not there on the ground. So the republican movement, I think wisely, decided then that we would embark on a socialist republican agenda to politicise the struggle in that sense, to try and influence the Protestant working classes in the North to unite with Catholic working classes and to see that there was a common enemy, i.e. imperialism, capitalism, whatever *ism*, and so that notion took hold within the republican movement. It was opposed by the more traditional elements within the republican movement like Ruairi O'Bradaigh and Sean MacStiofain, but Cathal Goulding and those who were following Cathal Goulding on the politicisation element succeeded and so arms were put beyond use by the IRA, by the republican movement. And then unfortunately the events of 1969, the whole sectarian attacks on nationalists within the Six Counties reawakened the more traditional elements within the republican movement and those who had pursued the politicisation mind were seen to have failed because they hadn't provided the weapons to defend the nationalist population within the Six Counties which was always part of the republican philosophy. The traditional republican attitude to Britain's occupation of Ireland was to remove England from Ireland by the use of physical force. That changed in 1969, in the context of defending nationalism, of defending Catholics within the Six Counties, but out of that conflict grew, or reawakened the notion of traditional republicanism, that we would continue the ideological concept of removing England from Ireland that was through physical force and that's how the 30-year war evolved.[12]

Therefore, the influence of traditional factors on the decision to join the republican movement appears greater in the pre-1969 period, as has been confirmed by Anthony McIntyre, when pointing out that events rather than ideas were what motivated those that joined the Provisional IRA: 'Defence fed into a psyche. In 1974, in Crumlin Road jail, Friday night looking out the window from my cell, I was thinking of all my mates, Franky Rea, Mark McAllister all at the disco and me stuck in a cell, and I said "well, Pearse would have done it". And I thought about it for five minutes and I was no happier, and I says, "well, I don't really give a fuck what Pearse would have done". It didn't motivate me, Pearse did not motivate me. That sort of republicanism in 1916, traditional republicanism did not motivate me. I was motivated by provisional republicanism which was post 1969.'[13]

Nevertheless, others insist that ideology was important. For example, Marian Price, unlike other activists, categorically rejects the possibility that her decision to join the Provisional IRA was motivated by the need to defend her community because of the situation on the ground: 'Not at all. I joined the Irish Republican Army to get the British out of Ireland, to establish a thirty-two county socialist republic. I had never any intentions of joining the IRA to become some sort of Catholic defender. It was not something that I considered. My one and only motivation was to remove the British presence from Ireland because I believe that things here will never be, there is no chance of getting things rectified, all this nonsense about cross-community stuff and all that. While there's a British presence here that won't happen.'[14]

In March 1973, Marian Price, who in February of that year had celebrated her nineteenth birthday, was arrested and sentenced to life imprisonment after being accused of taking part in an IRA car-bomb campaign in Great Britain. Her father and mother had been active members of the movement in the 1930s, and in 1938 one of her aunts, Bridie Dolan, lost both her sight and her hands when the grenades that she was carrying exploded. Following in the footsteps of these family members and her elder sister, Dolours, Marian decided to join the IRA just before her seventeenth birthday.

> I've always been involved in the republican movement, my family come from a long line of republicans so I was brought up with republicanism my whole life. My father had been in the IRA before me, my mother was a member of *Cumann na mBan* [an IRA's women's organisation], all my aunts were in *Cumann na mBan*. My grandmother was a republican who served time for the cause. So I come from a long line of republicans, but in saying that I don't feel I was brainwashed as a child. Certainly I was aware of my history and of republicanism but it was never forced down my throat. And I think there comes a time in everybody's life where you have to make choices for yourself. I was brought up a Catholic but there came a time when I made choices for that myself, sort of my mid-teens, and of course I chose to go against Catholicism, although my mother was a devout Catholic and I had always been brought up as that. But I mean I asked questions and couldn't get the proper answers so I cast that aside. With republicanism I asked questions too but I certainly got the answers that I wanted within republicanism.[15]

This mentality is typical of the republican leaders of that era and the founders of the Provisional IRA in 1969, but it does not appear to prevail in the majority of young people who joined later on. It is significant that Andersonstown, the west Belfast area where Marian Price was born and grew up, and which in the 1960s became one of the best known focal points of resistance to the British presence, had no republican tradition whatsoever.[16] Martin McGuinness has confirmed that exactly the same can be said of Derry, where prior to 1971 republicanism was only supported by 'less than a dozen families', which were isolated from the rest of the nationalist population.[17] At the end of the 1960s, then, when the influence of 'traditional republicanism' had waned so much, even in those cases where family tradition and republican ideology were important motivational factors, it can be observed that the specific events on the ground taking place at that time were equally or more important reasons for joining. In this regard, the testimonies of two other women, Rose McCotter and Margaret McKearney, as well as those of Margaret's brother – Tommy – and Liam McAnoy illustrate this point well.

Rose McCotter, born in the mid-1950s, defines her decision to join the IRA when she was about fifteen years old as a 'natural progression', whose origins can be found in her family's solid republican tradition: 'My father had been in jail himself in the 1930s campaign. My grandfather, my paternal grandfather had been in the IRA in the early 1920s. My aunt had been in jail in the forties as well. In my immediate family, apart from my father, there was myself, my sister, my three brothers were all in jail in this campaign and various people who we've either lived with or got married to people that have all been in jail as well. My father would have been a very prominent republican. My uncle was Seamus Twomey, he'd be the chief of staff of the IRA, he's dead now, he was very well known too. So it is kind of long, probably carrying on the family tradition. We were very young, not indoctrinated but being made aware, politics was a thing in our house, my mother as well, even though she was very young and had ten kids, she would have been caught up in it herself. So it is a kind of natural progression.'[18]

McCotter goes on to explain her main reasons for joining the IRA: 'Obviously at fifteen you are still a child, you don't have any kind of political philosophy or whatever. Literally what was happening at the time on the streets of Belfast, people were actually being burnt out of their houses and stuff and I actually helped when I was fourteen or fifteen to actually move. And then when people did get involved they developed their philosophy. I don't think I would have been politically aware until I actually got out of jail as well. I went to jail just before I was eighteen, that was Armagh jail in 1972 and I was sentenced to six years for a botched armed robbery. There was myself and three other people, two boys and a girl and we were three 17-year-olds and a 16-year-old.'[19]

Similar factors can also be found in the case of Tommy McKearney, born in 1952 in the small town of Moy, County Tyrone.

I joined the IRA in late 1971 in the months after the internment, beginning of internment in August of 1971 and I imagine that that was the incident above all else that would have propelled me into the IRA, in common with hundreds if not several thousand others at the time. When I joined the IRA I had just turned nineteen and it would be wrong to see it as a situation where I joined because of one reason alone, that was probably, internment was the incident that propelled me, it was the one that really convinced me that I should then make a commitment. But a number of circumstances would have come together to cause me to take the final decision to commit myself to the IRA in those years. One would have been the fact that my personal background, my family background would have provided a historical connection with the IRA, both my grandfathers had been IRA members in the 1920s. Both my paternal and maternal families had a strong Irish republican identity, a long and strong history of participation in radical, physical force republicanism and radical political republicanism as well, not just purely confined to the physical force element. So with that in my family background, the decision to join the IRA wouldn't have been a huge political leap that it may have been for others or it might seem to be in terms of those looking at it from a distance. Secondly, there was the fact that circumstances in Northern Ireland at the time made us very conscious of being discriminated against, that we occupied a position in some ways it seemed to us to be a hopeless position and one in which we were seriously disadvantaged. Then in 1967 and 1968 we attempted to resolve the problems through political, non-violent action on the streets. We attempted it in parliament, were denied any type of hearing, we took our protests to the streets, it was a political, non-violent people's movement on the streets and it was met with, not with a reasonable response but with a violent opposition from both the official forces of the Northern state and the unofficial supporters of the Northern state.[20]

Although McKearney attaches great importance to those street protests, he states that he did not take part in these demonstrations that motivated him so much. His sister, Margaret, who was born in January 1954, describes her activism as a 'response to national and international events in the late sixties'. Her republican 'romantic idea' of joining the IRA materialised once her brother Padraig was arrested in 1972 and shortly after another of her brothers, Thomas, left the family home on the run. Both were active members of the IRA at that time.[21]

Liam McAnoy was born in 1953 into what he describes as a 'very republican' family. His father had been a member of the republican movement who had participated in 'military activities', while his mother was 'a very strong supporter in terms of collecting finances for them, organising social functions to raise money, keeping firearms, explosives, and stuff like that'.[22] At the beginning of the 1960s, McAnoy states that at such a young age he had 'been drawn instinctively towards the republican movement', although he did not actually join the IRA until 1969. On 15 August of that year he received a shot in the leg while trying to attack a police station throwing stones and petrol bombs. It was after leaving hospital following treatment for his injuries that he decided to join the IRA, although up to that point he had always viewed its violence as 'detrimental'. He therefore recognises an apparent contradiction in his behaviour, which he explains in the following terms:

At that particular time the police had withdrawn from Catholic communities and the army was policing the area, and the army being an army and being trained killers rather than policemen acted in a very heavy-handed way, kicking in doors. My mother was a very devout religious woman, for soldiers to come in and get her out of bed and stand and watch while she dressed was a form of mental rape for her, you know, there was no legal redress, they had the power to do it under the Special Powers Act, so the only way in which we could actually get back was to fight back. Of course that was part and parcel of the whole idea, removing Britain anyway, but it just gave added justification for killing soldiers and policemen as well. So I actually joined the IRA, did a series of training exercises with them and then I was caught, interned on the prison ship out on the harbour which was called the Maidstone prison ship.[23]

This 'added justification for killing soldiers and policemen' to which McAnoy refers is revealing. Some authors consider that the effect of emphasising the republican tradition has been to minimise the role of the state in the 'construction of insurgent identities' and in the 'formation of republican identity'.[24] Yet while it is true that personal experiences can generate 'collective political meanings',[25] such a factor must not be used to disregard completely the influence of traditional republican ideology, particularly in those who were leading the movement at that time since they were able to 'resuscitate' an ideology that gave a central role to the 'incomplete Irish national liberation' and the need to use violence to achieve it.[26] Placing the emphasis on the role of the state can lead to the mistake of arguing that the sole reason for people joining the IRA at that time was the actions of the British state and army. In fact, when McAnoy joined the IRA, the British army was enjoying what has been called a 'honeymoon period' with the Catholic community, which initially saw the soldiers as there to defend them from Protestant attacks. Many of the new IRA recruits shared this view of the British Army before the relationship with the Catholic community deteriorated as a result of measures such as internment without trial in August 1971 or the Falls Road curfew in July 1970 which resulted in massive house searches, serious disturbances and the death of five people. For example, Danny Morrison, who would later become a prominent figure in the movement, has admitted that he did not understand the predictions of a veteran republican, who stated in November 1969 that 'very soon we will attack the British'.[27] However, this definition of the enemy was a key part of the IRA's ideological apparatus, which it made use of to justify its existence and actions in the following decades. Many republicans agree that this ideology was 'very nationalist' and 'simplistic', and lacked any real political content beyond the mere 'Brits out of Ireland'. In this way, presenting the IRA

campaign as an inevitable defensive reaction to what was seen as the disproportionate and repressive actions of the state supplied 'added justification
for killing soldiers and policemen'.

It should be recalled that while the IRA has frequently justified its campaign in terms of defence needs, this was not its main task, as can be clearly
seen from Eamonn MacDermott's explanation of his reasons for joining the
IRA in 1973: 'There was obviously an element of tradition, my grandfather
was republican, my grandfather was in prison in 1916 and there was always a
republican strain running through the family, but that wouldn't be enough.
It wasn't even defence, it was more a proactive thing: this problem has to be
solved and at the time you believe the only way to solve it was to force the
British government to withdraw from Ireland and the only way they could
be forced was through the use of violence, so that's what you do. I didn't
have a defensive notion or anything else, I wasn't defending the community,
I was proactively attacking the British state.'[28]

In considering this idea of defence, it is worth remembering that the
intense confrontations between the Catholic and Protestant communities
that caused masses of people to be displaced from different parts of Northern
Ireland, especially Belfast, were at their worst in the summer of 1969.[29] But
the changed scenario following the deployment of the British army was
welcomed by Catholics, as is clear from the mid-1972 statement made by the
parish priest for an area badly affected by the sectarian violence, which
condemned in no uncertain terms the IRA campaign.[30] One year later, the
same priest published another vehement attack on the IRA, refuting
categorically that they were 'defenders' or 'protectors', recalling that the
community demanded the presence of the British Army in 1969, whose
presence, he stressed, they still needed. For this reason, he accused the
members of the IRA of having lost all notion of the difference between good
and evil: 'to kill, to bomb, to shoot down soldiers as they guard your
schoolchildren, to torture men and women and even children, to hand guns
to youngsters and teach them to hate – is "good" because it is done in the
name of the people and for Ireland'.[31]

The nature of the republican movement obliged it to make use of the
ideological apparatus of nationalism in order to homogenise its members
and the direction in which they should go. As one of its former members
points out, the IRA was quite disparate and took people in from different
orders in order to survive.[32] Normally, when differences arise between
individual and group interests, attempts are made to resolve such conflicts
by encouraging aspirations to converge as regards aspirations.[33] This also
happened with the republican movement. It should be recalled that for
many of those interviewed, political reasons were not the most important for
joining the IRA. However, once recruited, these youngsters defined their
membership differently, as is shown by one activist, who stated that 'they
used the excuse that it was a political war' waged by people for many of

whom the important thing was the 'military: bombs, bombs, bombs, guns, guns, guns'.[34] Thus, republican ideology was used 'to point them in the right direction' and as a justification for killing for Ireland, as declared by a 1973 editorial of the newspaper *An Phoblacht* entitled 'Republican tradition' which emphasised that republicanism would kill British soldiers while they remained on Irish soil.[35] In this way, the traditional ideology was used to construct a collective identity, a key part of which was the armed struggle. Questioning the commitment of the organization to the nationalist cause and its use of violence as the means of achieving it amounted to casting doubt on this identity, which was so important for activists. As will be seen in the following chapters, the republican leadership took advantage of this useful ideological tool to reinforce internal unity, eliminating any threats of dissidence that questioned their power over the group.

In the summer of 1972, during the commemoration of the death of the volunteer Eamonn Lafferty which had occurred one year earlier, Martin McGuinness, at that time already one of the IRA's main leaders, promised that the battle against the British occupying forces would continue until Lafferty's dream of a united Ireland came true.[36] Only two years after the Provisionals had come into being, the traditional republican ideology and the legacy of past heroes already had a prominent position in the mentality of the movement. Although many who joined the movement in the late 1960s–early 1970s highlighted the importance of events on the ground which led them to stress the defence of their community as their main motivation, thus playing down the role of ideology, the latter became used in conjunction with the former. As one of the activists referred to noted, 'defence fed into a psyche', but this apparent defence need was in itself incapable of becoming the motor of a violent campaign that ended up being purely offensive lasting thirty years. Given this, as the sociologist Frank Burton has shown, many in the Catholic community perceived that far from being their protector, what the IRA really wanted to do was create the conditions in which they could then present themselves as the only organization capable of offering such protection: 'They blow the fuck out of the city centre, madden the Orangees, bring down the Brits on our backs and then claim to be our protectors!'[37]

A constant feature of the republican movement in recent decades has been the commemorations of those considered heroes and firm defenders of the traditional ideology. In April 2003, Martin McGuinness commemorated the death of the 'martyrs of Drumboe', a group of IRA members executed by their former colleagues during the civil war that took place between 1922 and 1923. McGuinness, who has admitted that he himself did not join the IRA for ideological reasons, once again used traditional republican ideology in an attempt to establish a link with the past in order to give a veneer of legitimacy to the acts of the terrorist organisation by identifying them with the tradition of those who fought for the independence of the Irish state in the early twentieth century.

'Poverty didn't jump in and out of Protestant houses'

Some authors have considered deprivation an important causal factor of collective violence. For Davies, a group of individuals is affected by deprivation when, on comparing its situation with that of another group, it finds itself in a disadvantageous situation.[38] Ted Gurr has suggested that not just real deprivation, but also the perception that deprivation exists regardless of whether or not this is actually the case, is a factor which affects the behaviour of those who resort to violence. Gurr thus defines relative deprivation as the perception of discrepancies between the aspirations that a group has as regards the social conditions which it is capable of attaining and maintaining in relation to the means at its disposal. In his opinion, when these aspirations do not materialise, the readiness to respond with violence is greater.[39] This approach has been used to explain the origins of violence in Northern Ireland, linked to the widely-held belief that Catholics were traditionally in a much worse position than Protestants.

During the fifty years of existence of the Stormont parliament, the Northern Ireland government engaged in various anti-democratic practices. In this way, the Ulster Unionist Party, the governing party throughout this period, tried to maintain Protestant unity by discriminating against the Catholic minority in certain areas. As a result, when violence erupted at the end of the 1960s, Northern Ireland could not be said to enjoy anything resembling what has been termed 'consensus democracy'.[40] Today, the question to be answered is not whether discrimination existed, but what was its real extent. In 1968, the United Kingdom's economic indicators showed Northern Ireland to be among its poorest regions with one of the highest rates of unemployment. Hopes were raised among the Catholic community by the modernisation programme introduced by Terence O'Neill after becoming Prime Minister for Northern Ireland in 1963, yet these reforms proved to be insufficient. As Bew and Patterson have pointed out, the policies implemented by the unionist premier did not tackle discrimination against Catholics, and he would have been successful only if the reforms in local government and housing had been introduced sooner.[41] Rolston has also criticised these reforms, stating they were deeply sectarian albeit dressed up as liberal.[42] This approach is reflected in the well-known words of O'Neill in an interview published in May 1969, after his resignation one month before, in which he stated the following: 'It is frightfully hard to explain to Protestants that if you give Roman Catholics a good job and a good house they will live like Protestants, because they will see neighbours with cars and television sets. They will refuse to have eighteen children. But if a Roman Catholic is jobless and lives in a most ghastly hovel, he will rear eighteen children on national assistance. If you treat Roman Catholics with due consideration and kindness they will live like Protestants, in spite of the authoritarian nature of their church.'[43]

There is no doubt that the massive civil rights demonstrations which took place after the Northern Ireland Civil Rights Association (NICRA) was set up in 1967 reflected the existence of a system which Lijphart has termed 'pseudo democracy'.[44] However, it is not that clear that deprivation and the perception of deprivation were factors that led to violence. Birrell showed that relative deprivation was of relevance within the Northern Ireland conflict and established a relationship between some of the economic, social and political grievances and certain manifestations of violence, mainly those that led to civil disturbances in the streets of the region.[45] He also argued that the increase in violence by Protestant extremists in the second half of the 1960s can be explained in terms of 'inverted deprivation'. These extremists reacted violently to the perception that the poorest sectors of the Protestant community, which were not receiving the help that the Catholics were obtaining at that time, were being placed at a relative disadvantage.[46]

In a later work, however, Birrell admitted that although deprivation may be a factor that contributes to people becoming involved in violence, very little research supports this proposition with respect to Northern Ireland.[47] In fact, academics largely agree that the economic factors in themselves are insufficient to explain the conflict.[48] Birrell himself has recognised that, with hindsight, the allegations of discrimination against Catholics in the allocation of housing at the end of the 1960s were overstated, since they were not sufficiently backed up by statistics.[49] This problem led to erroneous conclusions being reached in a particularly complicated area, since although there was a difference in the economic status of the main Northern Irish communities, the gap between them was 'surprisingly narrow', there being, as Rose shows, 'many poor Protestants'.[50] Given this, many authors consider that political rather than socio-economic factors were more important in causing the violence.[51] For example, Thompson has shown that in Northern Ireland the escalations of violence do not have a direct relationship with increases in the level of unemployment and suggests the need to look elsewhere for explanations for the outbreak and perpetuation of violence.[52] The fact that most terrorists are recruited from deprived areas does not in itself conclusively prove that deprivation motivates those who use violence, despite the fact that the absence of social expectations may lead certain individuals to join violent groups because of their perception that membership will provide them with a status which they would otherwise lack.

Another example may show that the accusations of discrimination to which some refer to explain the motivations of IRA members have frequently been exaggerated. Between 1950 and 1951 Joe Cahill, member of the IRA who had a death sentence for the murder of a Northern Irish policeman commuted, worked in the Harland and Wolff shipyards, traditionally considered by many Northern Irish to be an exclusively Protestant enclave. In an interview in 2003, he stated that despite being Catholic and a prominent republican activist, he was not treated with any hostility whatsoever by

Protestant employees. Cahill recalled that at that time there was little difficulty in finding work in the shipyards due to the great demand caused by the
Second World War. He also pointed out that he only considered himself to
be discriminated against when he was refused promotion after being identified in a photograph of the annual commemoration of the Easter Rising in
1950 attended by IRA sympathisers and members in the Milltown cemetery
in Belfast. With respect to those republicans interviewed for this book, most
of them did not personally suffer discrimination of a level to lead them
to join the movement, although they do reflect a general perception that
their community was at a disadvantage and treated unfairly. Among those
injustices that they most directly associate with their decision to join the
IRA, social and economic issues were not as important as the violent actions
of agents of the state.

Cathal Crumley became involved in the republican movement before he
was eighteen years old. In 1976, when eighteen, he was imprisoned for being
a member of the Provisional IRA, being released in August 1980. In his
view, people became involved for the following reasons: 'When Ireland was
partitioned in the 1920s we had a one-party system based at Stormont, a
unionist parliament for the unionist people that gave no regard at all to
a considerable minority. And it's often the case that those people felt
partitioned against their will, they felt like prisoners in their own country.
Sometimes people don't understand the psychology of partition. We were
partitioned into what, in effect, was an invented British state in north-east
Ireland which consisted of six counties, which consisted of the maximum
amount of space that unionism could control and it was militarised and it was
run almost on a basis of apartheid for nearly fifty years.'[53] Like Cathal
Crumley, Tommy McKearney does not provide any examples of personal
discrimination, although he does state that before joining the IRA he was
very conscious of the fact that his community was in a disadvantageous
situation. He illustrates his point by indicating that the BBC had 'very
sketchy reports of Irish football', that they 'couldn't get official recognition
for Gaelic football, Irish music', or that they were not able to see on local
television 'films made in Dublin' which 'were not too many at the time'. In
his view, these were 'a number of small but aggravating episodes which when
all put together left us of a mind frame and myself and the community, that
we were disadvantaged citizens within that Northern Irish state'.[54]

The sister of this former activist, Margaret McKearney, answers the
question of whether she suffered discrimination before joining the IRA in
the following manner: 'Where I grew up there wasn't the deprivation that
maybe was experienced in other parts of the North. We lived in a little
village, there wasn't extremes of wealth or poverty in it. Everybody was sort
of the same socio-economic level. OK, somebody maybe had a better car
than we did or, something like that, but there wasn't a huge, or at least it
wasn't in our face, huge deprivation. As a society we didn't have, I didn't

grow up having to bring turf to school to light the fire, we didn't have to cut our nibs, you know, do you know what I mean? There's people roughly the same age as me in the South of Ireland had to, you know. We had modern schools.'[55] It is significant that McKearney compares the situation with that existing in the Republic of Ireland at that time. This point of reference was also commonly used when the Troubles started. As the sociological study carried out by Richard Rose shows, most Northern Ireland Catholics did not feel themselves to be in a disadvantageous position compared to their southern counterparts, while only 13 per cent felt that the ending of partition would improve their situation.[56] Further, the study shows that relations between the Catholic and Protestant communities had experienced a marked improvement during the sixties. Those who lived through this era agree that where the two communities lived together relationships were peaceful until the outbreak of violence at the end of the 1960s which led to increasing segregation.[57] In this sense, Margaret McKearney states that relations with the other community were 'very good on the surface': 'It's only now that I can in hindsight look back and realise that we were a fairly comfortable society, we were a modern enough society, we had a reasonable standard of living. It was only when little things like I talked to people who were brought up in the equivalent background, but down in the South of Ireland, and they'd say, "Do you not remember having to, you know, use inkwells and things like that?" "No, we had biros", you know, little things like that. Dad was a local shopkeeper, he was a butcher and people would come in and he would have a mixed clientele, it wouldn't have mattered. But there was a "them and us" mentality, like they didn't buy our land and we didn't sell it to them. They were quietly confident in our area that they were the superior race and that's it.'[58]

Pat McNamee grew up in the south of Armagh, right on the border with the Republic of Ireland, an area with a long tradition of opposition to the British during previous IRA campaigns. As he explains with reference to the period immediately before being recruited, he joined the IRA in the first half of the 1970s not as the result of socio-economic deprivation: 'As I was growing up in the early and mid-sixties Crossmaglen was a very quiet place, there was a little police station which had four or five members of the RUC stationed there. The sergeant lived there with his family, it was a fairly open building, and for the most part it was a quiet little country village. However, at Easter each year the temporary fortifications, sandbags, would be erected and the RUC would patrol outside the barracks with submachine guns and this was because of a perceived threat from republicans across the border and that was the first, I suppose, visual sign of, you know, that I lived in a country of conflict because Crossmaglen is very much a nationalist area, as is South Armagh, and we lived close to the border and we would frequently shop south of the border, socialise south of the border, indeed the border would have had little significance in social terms.'[59]

In the opinion of other former IRA members, given such normality the 'fight against injustice' that so many activists have referred to as their motivation for joining could equally have justified violence against the Irish state, given the relentless repression of republicanism in the preceding decades by, amongst others, key IRA figures such as Eamon de Valera, who became Irish Prime Minister in 1932. The IRA was declared illegal in the South in 1936 and between April 1939 and May 1949 twenty-six members were executed or died while on hunger strike. During the Second World War, more than five hundred people were interned without trial, and the extremely strict Offences Against the State Act was applied to more than six hundred.[60] For the IRA, de Valera was 'Judas'.[61] The 'ruthless repression' of the Irish state against republicans included the internment without trial of more than one hundred people during 1957.[62] Despite the criticism of the IRA for what its members saw as the 'tyranny' of the Irish government, including internment, such measures continued until militant republicanism in the South was left in tatters.[63] Pat McNamee, who was arrested in 1982 for his involvement in the IRA and spent six years in Portlaoise jail after having been found guilty in a trial without jury in accordance with the antiterrorist legislation of the Republic of Ireland, did not see many differences between the laws on either side of the border, defining those existing in the Republic as 'very repressive': 'The special powers in the South were at times more extensive than the powers in the North and indeed the state forces had the power to arrest and detain people for seven days in the South and did so routinely prior to those measures being taken in the North and, not only the availability of the powers, but they were enthusiastically applied by the Garda in the South.'[64] As former activists suggest, under those circumstances if some of the political grievances which were said to motivate IRA violence were considered in relation to a reference group such as the Irish state rather than the British or Northern Irish state, the perception of deprivation and the response thereto could be similar.

The republican movement has frequently compared the situation in Northern Ireland with South African apartheid and the institutionalised and systematic racism existing in certain areas of the United States. Neither of these comparisons stand up to serious analysis.[65] As Purdie has noted in his analysis of how the NICRA, the civil rights association, looked for inspiration in the black movement, the discrimination suffered by blacks was undoubtedly much worse and much more patent than that complained of in Northern Ireland. Adopting the style and the inflammatory rhetoric of the black movement therefore fuelled a natural tendency towards exaggeration and increased the tension between the Northern Ireland communities.[66] Danny Morrison, one of the activists interviewed, made use of such rhetoric in his comparison between the situation of Northern Irish Catholics and that of black citizens in the United States: 'I have no problem with them being unionists. What I have a problem with is that the price of their unionism is that I have to remain a second class citizen, that I have to travel at the back of the bus, that we're only allowed to walk up the right hand side of the street.'[67] However, both the testimony of Margaret McKearney given above and her answer to the question of whether the comparisons between the situation in Northern Ireland and elsewhere are exaggerated help to understand the real connection between the allegations of deprivation and the decision to use violence. In her recollection of her relationship with the other community while she was growing up she can only find two events which she terms as 'insidious rather than hostile'. One of them refers to the nuns at St Joseph's Convent deciding to change the traditional scarf of the girls' uniform because it had green and yellow stripes which, according to McKearney, were seen by Protestants as a 'symbol of nationalism'. The other event refers to members of the Orange Order singing when passing by her home the song entitled *Dolly's Brae*, which recalls the battle fought on 12 July 1849 in which Protestants defeated Catholics.

The choice of reference group is crucial in maintaining a perception of relative deprivation, as another republican stresses when establishing a close connection between the social context in Northern Ireland and South Africa, ignoring the obvious differences between the two situations which require those who make such comparisons to put them into perspective. In his view, 'If you feel you're on the bottom rung of the ladder, you're on the bottom rung of the ladder. It isn't about what you have really, and that's the reality.'[68] By contrast, former IRA member Seamus Lynch rejects any analogy between the socio-economic situation under the unionist regime with that existing in South Africa or the USA in the 1960s. Lynch gives the following opinion about the conditions of deprivation in an urban area such as Belfast before the critical upward spiral in violence: 'In my street poverty didn't jump in and out of houses, which was a mixed street. We always lived in an area where there was Protestants and Catholics, and that poverty didn't jump houses, it was the length and breadth of the whole street, and these was the Protestant people who were afraid to speak out. OK, there was advantages for Protestants, there were Protestants [that] got better opportunities for the shipyard and places like that, that's all well documented, but there were many Protestants that didn't get those advantages, and it hurt them even more to be told that "you're better off than the Catholics", when they were living next door to the Catholics and having to endure the same standard of living and having to queue up for their dole money every Tuesday alongside them. I know these people, I was born and reared with them.'[69]

Another republican paints a similar picture when criticising the republican arguments linking IRA violence with the alleged privileges enjoyed by the Protestant community: 'The statistics would prove that there was discrimination in terms of employment and in terms of housing, and I have no qualms about that. That's why the Civil Rights Movement had a solid base, because those things were real. But very many Protestants will tell you that they were discriminated in terms of jobs, that they were discriminated in terms of houses, not by Catholics but by the state. For example, very many working-class Protestants who are unemployed would say they lived in atrocious conditions on the Shankill or Taghmona or The Village or Sandy Row or Donegall Pass round here [in Belfast], but no one ever acknowledged their disadvantage and they certainly didn't either because they believed that to do that would be an attack on the state, it would be an attack on their government, so they never highlighted it and as a result of that the impression was given that only Catholics suffered disadvantage and discrimination. But they suffered it every bit as much.'[70]

When referring to the connection between violence and relative deprivation, Martin McKevitt highlights his own naivety and lack of political analysis at the time he joined the IRA which led him to certain flawed conclusions about discrimination. As he states now, discrimination affected working-class Catholics and Protestants.[71] Another member of the Provisional IRA put things similarly in relation to 'the perception of privilege, because you had a lot of people on the Shankill Road, for example, who were unionists but who were just equally as bad off as Catholics in the Falls Road, but there was a perception of privilege'.[72] In fact, until the outbreak of violence at the end of the 1960s, as with the rural area where Tommy and Margaret McKearney grew up, other republicans from urban areas which would later be focal points of the sectarian conflict describe the relationship between the two communities as relatively normal without any significant inequalities between them: 'The area I was living in at that time was a mixed area, it was Catholics and Protestants, and never really had a problem among them because at the time I was young, but when internment was introduced the street just sort of divided, Catholics, Protestants.'[73]

This relaxed environment and the existence of interaction between the two communities is also mentioned in the following testimonies of two other former IRA activists. The first one, Tom Kelly, was born in 1955 in the south of Belfast and the second, Feilim O hAdhmaill, three years later. Kelly worked for a while in a pub owned by a Protestant landlord and regularly frequented by the British Army. He left his job after the IRA planted a bomb nearby demolishing the bakery which was located a couple of doors from his workplace. It was then that for the first time he felt fear for his safety 'because people were calling out for a backlash towards Nationalists, Catholics, and they knew I was a Catholic and a Nationalist'.[74] For his part, O hAdhmaill admits that in the Sixties most of his friends in the area of north Belfast where he lived were Protestants. As he points out, 'I didn't regard them as Protestants, I just regarded them as friends.' The only time when certain tension between them would arise was around the Twelfth of July celebrations. O hAdhmaill saw the traditional bonfires as a game although some of the Protestant children would then call him 'Fenian', a term whose meaning he didn't fully understand.[75]

However, the conclusions that can be extracted from this apparently normal co-existence make difficult reading for those who believe that an inextricable link exists between IRA violence and social deprivation in the Catholic community. As the following testimony of a former member of the IRA who grew up in north Belfast shows, constant comparisons are made between the situation in Northern Ireland and the United States. Joe O'Doherty remembers how he grew up in a mixed area where 'everybody got on', the reason being in his view that at that particular period, 'we were not a threat to Protestants': 'It's like when you go to the Southern States of America, Alabama. There was times there when life just went on, it was only when, it's what the whites said, that the agitators came in and told them, "you have a right to vote, you have a right to education, you shouldn't be in a segregated school", that it created a panic within whites down there and actually that panic manifested itself in violence and that's when the churches were burned down, black churches. And that's what we had here, everything was going good, when the civil rights movement came, we seen the change in the attitude of people who lived on that street, they got panicky because of change, I mean this is the Protestants, because we kind of knew our place in society.'[76]

In the 1940s, the introduction of the welfare state in Northern Ireland undoubtedly benefited one of the poorest regions of the United Kingdom. Among the social and economic improvements made, those concerning education must be highlighted, since they made it possible for increasing numbers of Catholics to attend university, which in turn led to a substantial improvement in life conditions.[77] To this must be added a new social security and pensions system, as well as the creation of an organ for allocating housing, whose efficient functioning kept it mostly free of accusations of discrimination. Despite this, the Catholic population continued to be under-represented in sectors such as the civil service, local government or the judiciary, having a greater presence in unskilled work. Sectarianism had always affected Northern Ireland to a greater or lesser extent and the decades prior to the Troubles were no exception, resulting in the appearance and consolidation of specific social identities that could be seen in group attitudes. One of the republicans interviewed illustrates this point when he recalls the example of a relative, a Catholic like him, who had worked in the linen industry, particularly prosperous in the nineteenth century. 'I was reared on this idea, I don't know if it's a mythology or not, that he was so smart that the Protestants had to give him a job as a tinter. I don't know if that's true or not, you know what I mean, but that was just part of the mythology that fed into my world outlook, my perception.'[78] In his opinion, although it was obvious that fanatical loyalists with 'a racist attitude towards Catholics' existed, prejudice and the tendency to pigeonhole influenced decisively the controversial question of discrimination:

I remember my father showing me in the Sixties, as a child, a thing in the paper, saying, 'no Catholic need apply'. That wasn't on the same scale as the blacks in America, they tried to draw a parallel, it's not the same as that there. There was a certain amount of discrimination, people would have preferred to have employed their own, if they had the opportunity. But let's be realistic, there was more Catholics unemployed. But that's because a lot of the sectarianism wasn't conscious. For example, if over there was the shipyard and I lived in a wee terraced house, a wee two-up-two-down, coming up from the shipyard, and my son's getting to the age of worker, I'd go to the foreman and I'd say, 'look, any chance of getting the young fella in as an apprentice?', and the foreman who knows me well, is a friend of mine, would say, 'aye, I'll get him in'. That's not a conscious sectarianism, I'm not going over and saying to him, 'any chance of getting him in? We'll keep the Taigs out.'[79]

Social stereotypes have often been fed by myths which have constructed a society and a conflict at odds with reality, as can be seen from the words of a former IRA member: 'Because of the high levels of Catholics within the six county state and the state being run solely for Protestants, every ten to fifteen years they had a state sponsored pogrom against the nationalist communities that drove tens of thousands of Catholics either across the border down South or they left and went to England where because of the massive population they could be absorbed quite easily – two generations down their children would be completely anglicised and would see themselves as English. So normally they would have drove up to a one hundred thousand Catholics out of the State in any one of these pogroms – and there has been a pogrom every ten to fifteen years in the history of the state, and that kept the numbers down.'[80]

In order for this version of events to be correct, Catholics would have had to reproduce at that time and since then at breakneck speed in order to maintain the current levels of population. In addition, the state would have needed sufficient resources to enable it to carry out a systematic policy of ethnic cleansing. The state neither had such resources, nor did any ethnic cleansing take place. Such a glaring misrepresentation of the facts obviously cannot be found in any history book or census, yet the belief in the existence of such pogroms has become one of the most celebrated myths of certain sections of the nationalist community.[81]

There are many examples of IRA members politicising the past in order to legitimate the campaign of violence that took place from the end of the 1960s onward, as has been exposed by contemporaries of these republicans who grew up in the same communities. Thus, for example, the journalist and author Jack Holland contradicts the version that senior members of the IRA, like Danny Morrison and Gerry Adams, have offered of their experiences of what they have described as their 'nationalist youth' prior to the outbreaks of the Troubles.[82] As Holland recalls, 'I grew up in the Falls Road area, a rebellious youth, but I was not aware of myself as a young nationalist, nor were any of my friends. We were working-class Catholics, and fairly representative. But our rebellion was against the moral oppressiveness of our society, especially the Catholic Church, which had more of an impact on our lives than the Special Powers Act. What Morrison and other Provisional writers such as Gerry Adams have done is in fact a kind of revisionism, which has politicised the past (in a slovenly romantic way) in order to justify the Provisional political agenda to portray the Northern conflict as merely the continuation of the 1919 War of Independence.'[83]

In the light of what has been said so far regarding relative deprivation, if the search for social justice was accepted as the main motivation for those who joined the IRA, it would be normal to find recruits with a considerable degree of ideological conviction. Yet the reverse is in fact the case, recruits usually being politically immature, an argument backed up by the age of those recruited. In addition, if we consider the initial period of violence, it was actually another group of individuals, and not those who finally joined terrorist groups, who could legitimately claim that their aspirations had not been met. If relative deprivation was applied to Northern Ireland during this period, those most directly and actively involved in the civil rights movement should, in theory, have been the ones most likely to join groups like the IRA once they had become convinced that other peaceful forms of action, such as those that they had employed, were no longer effective. Having been able to obtain certain political concessions, their hopes of a longed-for radical structural transformation should have been much greater than those of young people who, in most cases, had neither their age, their experience gained through participation nor their understanding of the situation.

'These men are dying for Ireland'

Despite the political and social transformation that Northern Ireland experienced after the outbreak of violence, the IRA still continued to recruit young people. As has been seen in the previous pages, those who joined the organisation in the late 1960s and the 1970s did so because of certain factors, some of which continued to motivate young people in the 1980s and 1990s. After violence erupted at the end of the 1960s, a dramatic intensification of violence took place; in the first half of the 1970s, the number of deaths and incidents was higher than at any other time during the conflict. The statistics show, however, that in the second half of the 1970s violence decreased considerably and progressively until the IRA's ceasefire declaration in 1994, which was followed by a truce declared by the main loyalist terrorist organisations. Over this long period of time, one can also observe a reduction in the number of arrests, detentions and house searches, which had been especially high when the Troubles began.[84] In a context which also saw various attempts to put into practice different political initiatives to stop the violence, the IRA continued to attract young republicans who shared some of the motivations of their predecessors. It is significant that the way that young people came into contact with and then joined the IRA, as well as their subsequent indoctrination, was largely the same for those who became members in the 1980s and 1990s. During this period the hunger strikes of 1980 and 1981 which concluded with the death of ten republican prisoners contributed to a new wave of activism, adding to other trigger factors, as the following testimonies of certain activists show. In general, those joining during this period continued to see their involvement in terms of 'a necessary response to state violence'. The main declared motivation for joining was, then, a desire to 'remove the British presence from Ireland', with very little else in ideological terms beyond that generic claim.

Like many republicans, Gerard Rice, who was born in 1962, also saw joining the Provisional IRA in the 1980s as a reaction to events at that time: 'For me personally, my first reaction was about defence. For me it was about, if it does break out into a civil war, who is going to protect me? It certainly isn't the British government, I didn't believe it, it wouldn't be the Irish government either, and it certainly wouldn't have been the RUC, so it was a matter of how do you protect yourself and are you in a position to protect yourself, and at that time I didn't think I was, so I joined the IRA. My first reason to join the IRA was the protection of my family and my community.'[85] By contrast, volunteer Carl Reilly, born in 1975 and who joined the group before his eighteenth birthday, utterly rejects the idea that the need to defend one's community, a motivation referred to by many republicans, was the IRA's *raison d'être*. Reilly argues that IRA activists insist on that role because 'they had to justify their existence and what they were about':

> Put it this way, throughout the seventies, eighties, nineties, loyalists just killed Catholics randomly, left, right and centre. While loyalists were assassinating Catholics on an almost nightly basis the IRA were con-centrating on trying to blow up city centres and attacking the Brits, very rarely did they retaliate against the loyalists. I'm not saying it never happened, they did retaliate but not to the same scale and effort that the loyalists were putting into attacking Catholics, so this idea that, 'we were there and the UDA [Ulster Defence Association] came into west Belfast and killed two Catholics this evening, so we'll make sure that it doesn't happen again', no, what they were doing is while the UDA was coming in and killing two Catholics, they were up the road looking at an army base, worrying how to get a mortar into it, or a car bomb into it, or how to shoot someone coming out of it, not worrying about the two Catholics down the road because those two Catholics weren't IRA personnel. If you killed an IRA man then all of a sudden you got retaliation. So 'are you the people's army?', 'no', 'what you're saying is you fuck us about,

then we'll crack you. If you kill a Catholic, then that's no problem, we'll just carry on doing what we're doing.' It got them off the ground, it got them power, got their foothold in nationalist areas, and they created the myth that the people needed them, that, 'we need yous to exist, to be here for us, 'cause if you aren't, we'll get murdered, we'll be trampled on, but if you are here it won't happen'. A myth. A myth. If people only but knew, it's a myth![86]

This criticism of the IRA's alleged defensive role was backed up by other members of the organisation interviewed. Some of them confirmed this role by referring to the so-called 'Top Man's Agreement', the name given to the pact between the UDA, the loyalist terrorist organisation, and the IRA, according to which neither group should attack the other's main leaders. Nonetheless, this pact was broken on various occasions, such as the attempted murder of Gerry Adams in 1984 and the murder of John McMichael, a leading member of the UDA, in 1987. Raymond Wilkinson, who was born in May 1973 and joined the Provisional IRA at the age of twenty, shares Reilly's viewpoint in relation to the group's inability to defend the nationalist community because of the nature of the threat: 'loyalists would have drove in the car maybe and shot somebody and away again, which was sort of something you couldn't really defend against'.[87] A raid by loyalist terrorists similar to this type of attack ended the life of Laurence 'Larry' Marley, a prominent member of the IRA in north Belfast, when he opened his front door on 3 April 1987.[88] This caused disturbances in north and west Belfast for several days. In addition, Marley's funeral had to be postponed when the police stopped his coffin from leaving his home in an attempt to prevent paramilitary symbols from being displayed. Wilkinson points out that this murder was a very important factor in his subsequent decision to join the IRA, since the children of the deceased were neighbourhood friends.

Although defence continued to play an important part in republican rhetoric, Wilkinson, Reilly, and others who joined in the 1980s and 1990s, play down its importance for the IRA, highlighting instead other motivations. Given that Wilkinson grew up and lived in north Belfast until his arrest and imprisonment in 1997, his opinions about the alleged objective of protecting the community are particularly enlightening. Known as BT 14 because of its postcode, more murders per square metre have taken place in this area than anywhere else in Northern Ireland.[89] When Wilkinson decided to join the IRA, he did so with the sole objective of 'expelling the British' and then 'seeing what happened', because 'instead of standing in the background watching other men doing it, and other men going to jail, and other men dying and things like that, I thought, "well, you have to stand up and be a man yourself and go out and do it"'.[90]

Thomas Cosgrove, who comes from the same area, also rejects being motivated by any notion of defending his community. Born in Germany in

1965, before his first birthday his family moved to a house that his father had bought on the Shankill Road in Belfast. In 1969 the family were forced to abandon their home after receiving threats, and they moved to Estelle Gardens, in Ardoyne, north Belfast, where he grew up. In the mid-1980s he decided to join the IRA. One of the events that had a particular impact on him during his childhood was the death of Danny Barrett, a childhood friend. In July 1981 Barrett, who was only fifteen years old at the time, was shot by a British soldier from an observation post in Ardoyne. Barrett was sitting in the garden of his house a few metres from where an IRA unit had just fired on a police patrol. Cosgrove explains his reasons for joining the republican organisation in the following way:

> I started to read more into republicanism, and found out facts, and I started to listen to republican music and ballads and got educated from them, asking questions, 'who was this fella?' and 'who was this girl?', martyrs', and 'what did Bobby Sands and Francis Hughes and the boys die for?', and then it just awoke my consciousness, so it did. I wanted to join because I got educated, I educated myself about republicanism and felt strongly about an occupying force in my country and I felt that I was right in what I was doing, I had right on my side. When I read up and learned about Ireland's history, it embittered me towards Britain and to see Britain still on our streets, British soldiers still on our streets enforcing their laws on our people, it just made me conscious, decide that, 'right, enough is enough'. I became involved in the movement at the age of twenty. I was engaged to be married, but I made the conscious decision, I actually left it. I wanted to join the IRA earlier at the age of eighteen, at that stage that the IRA let you join but I felt that I wasn't ready, I felt that I wasn't strong enough to give the commitment that the IRA were after, secrecy, and if you were arrested being able to stay silent in the barracks and be strong in the barracks, so I felt that I wasn't strong enough just then, so I waited till I felt the time was right. Then I joined. I was engaged to be married but I felt so strongly about joining the movement that it was interfering with my life and my way of thinking towards a normal life, I would have liked to have got married, but I just felt so strongly about joining the movement, and my girlfriend at the time, she didn't really appreciate what was going on around her. She, like a lot of other people, which I don't blame them, just couldn't understand what motivated people to join the IRA, so she gave me an ultimatum: 'leave the IRA or call off the wedding'. So I called off the wedding. But I don't regret it, never ever regret. I regret the missed opportunity but I don't regret ever joining the IRA, 'cause I believed, I still believe to the day that it was the right thing to do.[91]

Like many other volunteers, at the time he joined the organisation Cosgrove had no professional training or fixed income. It was at this time that he took the 'conscious decision' to join the IRA. However, he also admits the decisive importance of 'emotions' in leading him to take a decision that would involve breaking up with his fiancée: 'My emotions over the IRA and the conflict were too strong, I just couldn't walk away, I couldn't. I kept thinking about it every day and I kept getting a bit depressed about it that, "I'm sitting about and I want to do something, but I know that I'm going to lose my fiancée."' At the same time, the process which he describes, which provided him with his 'education about republicanism' and ultimately resulted in him joining the IRA, was highly flawed and very much conditioned by factors that do not appear to have been very well thought through at all. As he himself admits, he lacked any profound political awareness; instead, he had a complete fixation that was 'interfering' with his 'life' and his 'way of thinking': 'My main objective at the time was nothing mattered to me, I wasn't really politically aware, it was just Brits out, I want Brits out, that was my main objective at the time, and I'd have done anything in my power to get them out.'[92] His testimony reveals elements that are typical of a fanatical personality type, such as the absolute conviction of the correctness of one's own ideas, to the point that such ideas have complete control over one's conscience. Violence therefore becomes defined as a necessary evil, and as a 'personal sacrifice'.[93] Similar elements can be detected in the process by which volunteer Carl Reilly, who joined the IRA before he was eighteen, came into contact with the group. His socialisation at a young age took place in an environment which contributed to endorse an influential culture of death through different events, the hunger strikes among them, as he sums up:

> I was only young, I was watching all the big funerals, the IRA colour parties leading, and the riots every single night after it, and then I remember speaking to my parents and saying, 'what's all this about?' even though I was only a child, they were going: 'these men are dying for Ireland, they're dying for what they believe in', I suppose I just went, 'aye, right, right, right', and carried on as normal, which was great. Then we moved on and then I started coming into the teenage years, and then, basically when I was coming near secondary school stage I found myself going down a more republican road whereas some of my friends were going down a road which was to do with maybe careers and moving off to America and Australia, that was their destiny, even though at twelve or thirteen, that's where they were intending to go, and I knew in my own head, my own goal was to get involved in the republican movement.[94]

It must be pointed out that many young activists like this one did not undergo a coherent politicisation process before they were recruited. Their decision to join cannot be said, therefore, to be mainly a result of the conclusions they had reached following the consistent political education process to which some of them claim to have had, which essentially consisted in reading history books about Ireland. Their testimonies suggest that, for them, the correctness of their decision to join the group, one of the main reasons for which was their community's experience of the violence at the time, was confirmed by a very deficient politicisation process. Such behaviour recalls that of members of German terrorist organisations studied by Fetscher and Rohrmoser. These authors concluded that ideology may have been part of the rhetoric of these groups used as a means of justification, but it was not what truly motivated them.[95] The interviews carried out with those who joined the IRA as youngsters during the 1980s and 1990s reveal common ground, in that certain emotional factors typical of this stage of personal development constitute quite an important variable. As one interviewee put it: 'It's habit, yeah. It's like some guys I know when a woman sticks her ass in the air they'll fucking stick their dick in it. Just for the hell of it, you know. For no other reason just to fucking do it. I think with a lot of people, yes. And they used the excuse of a political war. Well, why do you stick cocaine up your nose? 'Cause it gives you a buzz maybe. Why set off bombs in fucking London? Or Belfast? It gives you a buzz, so it fucking does.'[96]

In relation to the testimony of Carl Reilly given above, it is also worth noting that while his youthful curiosity led him towards the IRA, other friends took a radically different path. Other alternatives did, therefore, exist, in contrast to those who claim, deterministically, that the armed struggle was the only way. Family background also appears to be an important motivational factor, as he suggests when telling how six members of his family – three uncles and three cousins – were murdered as a result of the violence of loyalist terrorist groups. However, although he stresses the importance of this matter, he is unable to remember any of the deceased's names. In fact, some of them he never even knew. Although the effect of violence on his family should not be ruled out as influencing his decision to join the IRA, we must weigh up the importance of this factor in the light of the relationship between the interviewee and the family members referred to, whose names he does not remember and who, in some cases, he had only heard of through the stories told by other family members. Having done so, we can reach the conclusion that his family background affected his behaviour in the sense that he formed part of a family 'that was always republican' and in which one of the members died in 'active service' during 'an IRA operation'. Thus he joined the IRA 'because the British presence in Ireland was wrong', since, as he puts it, 'they were the reason behind my family being killed, they were the reason behind my family members going to jail, they were the reason behind my house being wrecked at six o'clock in the morning. They were treating us differently from the way they were treating loyalists or unionists. And you went into the unionist areas, it was all fancy houses and nice clean cop cars, you went to west Belfast and it was all downtrodden areas, unemployment was high and the military presence in the area was at unacceptable levels. So for all those reasons coming in together, the only one route that was left open to me was to come in and join the republican movement.'[97]

It can be seen, then, that this activist refers to the situation on the ground together with a rudimentary traditional ideology in order to explain his activism. His description is typical of that of other volunteers, although later on in his testimony, he doubts its accuracy, admitting that to a great extent many of those grievances are simply the result of the manipulation carried out by republicans themselves, who are particularly interested in adopting the role of victims in order to reinforce their justification of the existence of the IRA as a necessary response to the British presence. It is of great significance that he himself recognises that the claims for economic and social justice that formed such an important part of the republican discourse had begun to be satisfied some years beforehand, between the end of the 1960s and the beginning of the 1970s. Despite this, however, demands for action on such issues continued to be made, because of their powerful symbolic value.[98] As Reilly puts it:

> Sinn Féin, the Provisionals have always had this, if there's not a situation there which can create the conditions that they need, Sinn Féin have the art of creating one, it's a smokescreen. The problem isn't really there, it's a small maybe minute problem, if you tinker with it, it can be worked with, but they make it look as if it's really bad, I mean, 'look what these ones are doing to us, we need all these things, you know what I mean, I mean, let's be honest, the whole equality issue, it was different when it was a case of one man one vote, that was different, people had the right to have a vote and they weren't getting it, but they now have it, people were living ten and twelve people to one house, that's another case, the case now is that people are now living in, in sort of reasonably good houses, the case of the Catholics couldn't get a job, they had to go across the water to England to even get a job, and they were getting £20 a day, that's not the case now, Catholics are getting jobs in sort of high businesses and sort of good positions, so where is this equality that they say we need, you know, is it that we need the unionists stripped of some of their powers to boost ours up or is it because that we are so downtrodden that we need to be brought up on a par with unionism? It's a myth.[99]

The interviewee illustrates his criticism of the manipulative attitude of the republican movement citing several events which were exploited by the IRA for propaganda purposes, because, in his view, 'Republicans love to play the role of victims, "poor us". But most of the "poor us" they create themselves.'[100]

When referring to the rationale behind his decision to join the IRA Reilly acknowledged the need to develop his very elementary political ideology, which caused him to reflect on the reasons used to justify the resort to violence leading him to recognise its limited effectiveness: 'It wasn't just about going out with an AK and shooting a Brit. That wasn't going to be the answer to my problems because when you hit that Brit there's going to be another one walking down the road a half an hour later. Armed struggle was limited. However, armed struggle was never going to free Ireland, it was never going to get a united Ireland that we hoped for, everyone was aware of that, volunteers were aware of that, I was even aware of it even then. That wasn't going to be the aim, we had to go into negotiations, at some stage of the game we had to negotiate and we had to bring an end, we had to call a ceasefire.'[101] Although he admitted that the 'effectiveness of violence was minimal', Reilly continued to be active in the armed wing of the movement after reaching such a conclusion. This highlights the true nature of the politicisation process to which he refers when assessing his motivations, also exposing relevant weaknesses, as he confirms when explaining how in 1994 he initially accepted the IRA's ceasefire believing 'the myth that the British had been defeated', in spite of the limitations on the effectiveness of violence which he himself acknowledged.[102]

As will be explained later, republicans generally believed that, after decades of violence, it was impossible to defeat the British, which made it necessary to look for alternative solutions, such as a peace process whose first step had to be an IRA ceasefire. The 'myth' of the British defeat referred to by this interviewee and others was totally at odds with the political reality of the time. From the mid-1980s onwards, the debate within the republican movement had centred on the ineffectiveness of the armed struggle, a debate which intensified at the start of the 1990s. As with other clandestine organisations, there was no sophisticated politicisation process in place prior to the use of violence. Nor did this happen earlier, between the time when individuals first came into contact with the group and the moment when they actually joined. In the case of the IRA, the initiation phase of those who ended up becoming full members did not comprise a series of clearly defined stages in which their political education took place, if by political education we mean that an individual obtains a broad, balanced and rational understanding of the different interpretations of the conflict, and the possible responses thereto. In fact, the politicisation which occurred can best be described as 'homogenous indoctrination', rather than a truly plural and open process aimed at stimulating an individual's critical faculties with a view to making it possible for him or her to take the most rational decision after having studied various possible alternative courses of action. As will be seen in the next chapter, when young recruits are 'politicised' in such a way it is unsurprising that the effect on the rest of their activism is so profound.

3

THE CAPTIVE MIND

'Have you not got the balls for the
armed struggle?'

Groupthink

The interviews carried out for this book suggest that new recruits to the republican movement did not have an in-depth understanding of the political structures existing at the time of their joining, as can be deduced from the analysis in the previous chapters of how they became members and the motivations with which they rationalised this decision. This is unsurprising if we take into account the nature of the relationship between factors as important as age, ideology and membership. This significant connection explains the extent to which political objectives can be regarded as motivational factors for IRA members. It is worth recalling some of the expressions used by young activists when referring to their personal conduct at the time that they were recruited: 'I was a hot head'; 'It was an emotional response'; 'I was a very narrow minded individual'; 'I was very intolerant'; 'Mine was a gut reaction'; 'I wasn't politically conscious'; 'Politically I was very immature'; 'I was very pro republican without knowing what republicanism actually was'; 'I had very romantic ideas about Ireland and the IRA'; 'My entry into the struggle at that very young age would have been instinctive, it would not have been based on any sort of real understanding of the politics.'

These statements help us to understand the state of mind of recruits at the time they took the crucial decision to join the IRA. In addition, they did so in a political and social context typified by violence and revolt and it would therefore be logical to expect that rational assessments as part of the response mechanism would considerably change over time. Despite this, many republicans still continue to argue that their decision to enter the IRA was both right and necessary. To some extent, such an attitude is logical since once an individual is committed to a given decision, objectivity will diminish leading to biased behaviour when examining and weighing up the alternatives. It is frequently the case that when confronted with the negative results of the decisions taken, IRA members attempt to evaluate them in a positive manner, concluding that the suffering was worth it. As Aronson and Mill have shown, it is quite normal for people to evaluate those choices that have had prejudicial consequences in a more benign manner, since otherwise they would experience a feeling of uselessness that would be difficult to deal with.[1] As we will see, this phenomenon is present in some of the activists interviewed. It is no coincidence that an IRA publication of 1973 should stress that 'It is the duty of all to ensure that the suffering and losses of families and friends of the dead, injured and jailed is not in vain.'[2] In 1978, a senior leader of the IRA who was asked whether the cost of the campaign of violence had been worth it answered in the following manner: 'Of course not. Virtually nothing has been achieved. We can't give up now and admit that men and women who were sent to their graves died for nothing.'[3]

The testimonies of IRA members contain many attempts to reduce what Leo Festinger defined as 'cognitive dissonance',[4] which occurs when the effectiveness of their involvement in the movement is questioned, particularly in the context of the peace process in which their main objectives have not been attained. The following comment of one of the activists interviewed is typical of the doubts that arise regarding their membership in such a situation: 'I, like a lot of other people, I'd say: I spent the best years of my life full-time working for a political objective. And now, at 54 years of age, I say, what the fuck was it all about? And I saw a lot of great fucking people, great men, dead. Seriously, great people. And I say: what the fuck! Wild.'[5] Another former IRA member expressed his disappointment when the organisation accepted the Good Friday Agreement signed in 1998 in the following way: 'My God, I've done twenty one years in jail for this! This is not what I fought for!'[6]

In the desire to avoid the cognitive dissonance and the resulting stress that this causes, recourse to 'groupthink' is very common. Unanimity of opinions emerges as a dominant characteristic of groups influenced by groupthink, as evidenced by the IRA. The group thus strives to achieve cohesion, since it depends on this for its survival.[7] The IRA itself has recognised the need for this unity, claiming that 'Taken together, the people and the IRA are invincible. Apart, they can be defeated – and then God help us.'[8] This exaggerated idea of the group's infallibility is another element of the groupthink model developed by Irving Janis, a model which can perfectly well be applied to the Irish republican movement.[9] Its activists require certainty and dogmas, since from their perspective it would be inconsistent to risk their own lives and take those of others if the motivations for doing so were not based on solid and consistent ideas. This certainty is provided by the interpretation of events given by the group, which is accepted by activists as part of the requirement of commitment and loyalty to the cause and its leaders. The main elements of groupthink identified by Janis are as follows: illusion of invulnerability which leads to group members being convinced that their behaviour is always correct; constant use of stereotypes, particularly when referring to rivals, in order to justify the group position taken; group members believe in the rightness of their cause and that they are morally superior – in this way, the negative consequences of the group's acts can be justified as necessary; self-censorship and pressure on dissidents that could threaten the group's certainty and cohesion so leaders are protected from criticism and any questioning of their leadership.

The presence of these elements facilitates a *post hoc* rationalisation of the decision to join a terrorist group, once this choice has been made in circumstances that show that this was not the best possible course of action available at the time. The reason for this is that IRA recruitment took place in most cases without young activists having considered other alternatives, concentrating on a single idea and without paying any attention to others. In the absence of consideration for other alternatives their decision was not compared with other possibilities, reinforcing the conviction that the behaviour was not mistaken. As has been seen, immaturity, impulsiveness, emotional dependency and the search for strong emotions are all part of the make-up of IRA recruits. This means that the search for information carried out by these young people was mostly superficial or non-existent, without properly assessing the costs and risks of a whole range of options. As a result, there is a tendency to ignore or minimise the consequences of decisions, particularly negative ones, and a search for instant rewards.

This *post hoc* rationalisation which tends to validate previous acts is crucial since it determines the legitimacy or otherwise of killing for Ireland.[10] According to this process, IRA violence could be interpreted as rational on the grounds that its use was necessary and correct in order to achieve republican goals. By contrast, it could be seen as irrational if it is concluded that the decision to use violence was reached without previously having properly weighed up the possible alternatives and their consequences. The opinions that IRA members interviewed gave about the way they came into contact with and ultimately joined the group suggest that, unlike those that participated in other forms of collective violence, many republicans did not consider the advantages and disadvantages of engaging in violent actions before engaging in them, nor did they properly assess other alternatives. This does not mean that the IRA campaign lacked any rational basis, if by 'rational' we mean the existence of an intentionality and an objective expected to be achieved through the so-called armed struggle, since it is clear that both existed. Yet for many activists the decision to use violence was highly influenced by emotional factors that were bound to affect decisively how rational their decisions were.[11] The real extent of the rationality of their acts must be questioned if we consider the surprising lack of conflicts in their decision-making at crucial moments, as is also revealed by the limited amount of time between the moment that they joined the group and when they first became involved in violent acts. Such an important decision, which requires much careful thought, was instead taken following a deficient or non-existent analysis of the relevant facts. As the activists interviewed for this book and cited in the next section show, their membership was very much influenced by groupthink.

'Who wants to kill anybody? Only a psychopath'

Let us examine how a former IRA member explains one of the murders he committed when he was fifteen years old. Born in 1958, volunteer Bobby was only twelve years old when he first took part in IRA activities. Three years later, he was accused of being involved in an attack in which four British soldiers were killed. On 5 March 1973, two IRA members killed Gary Barlow, a 19-year-old British soldier, shooting him in the head:

I was only fourteen and I was with another member of the IRA D Company. Another volunteer and I executed this soldier in Lower Falls. He was left behind by his patrol in an alleyway, in a broken down scrap yard, like for old cars and things like that. And this foot patrol were getting stoned and he got left behind, they ran, jumped into their armoured cars and left him. And he was standing, I remember him standing crying, vividly crying in front of me, he didn't know that we were carrying firearms, didn't know who we were, he was disorientated, he was only a child, he was only a teenager from England. And that's one memory that really sticks out, very vividly, probably till the day I die, actually, there's no question about that. And I remember that young soldier crying, tears running down his face, and myself and the other volunteer with me shot him dead, point-blank range. (...) So, when I look back on that and I say 'good God, he was only a child!', and I do feel very sorry. I feel deeply sorry that anybody has to die, because if you didn't have feelings then you'd have no politics behind you, it would be immoral and you'd be just a pure psychopath, you'd be doing it for the kicks, there'd be no principles, no political principles or morality or nothing. No, I feel deeply sorry that anybody died, from any side, all sides in this war. Of course I do, yeah.[12]

The way in which volunteer Bobby brings together political, emotional and moral criteria is striking. He thus avoids any feelings of guilt to which his actions could give rise by justifying his conduct on the basis of the conditions which caused his actions. The activist himself returns to consider this point when explaining his attitude towards those who died as a result of his actions:

There was no sympathy then, 'cause I was only a young kid. But in later life, for example, sitting here now, as a man in my forties, I think back of all the thirty years and I think about them and I can visualise how they were killed and I watched them die and I remember their names and I seen their tears, some of them before they actually died and I do have very deep sympathy for them, of course I do, if I didn't I would be a psychopath. I deeply regret that any of them, soldiers or policemen or

UDR men ever had to die, deeply regret it, but unfortunately there was a war going on and it was getting fought from both sides, there was brutality all round, it was a brutal war, a dirty war and I participated in it and there is lots of things that happened that should never have happened. They had mothers and fathers and brothers and sisters. Of course I feel sorry that any of them had died, but they came over and they participated in the oppression of the Irish people and all I did as a nationalist and a republican was defend my community.[13]

The contrast that emerges between the terrible consequences of his actions – the death of human beings – and the part he played in this is significant, since in his opinion all he did was to defend his community. In this way, responsibility is diluted and becomes a group rather than an individual concern; he only did what any other republican would do,[14] transforming choice into an obligation, namely the defence of his community. His acts thus acquire absolute legitimacy, being seen as necessary and justified, since otherwise he would be forced to consider himself as a psychopath, something which he totally rejects. He therefore needs to provide a rational explanation for the murders he committed, a point which he underlines when answering the question of whether the killing was worth it:

That's a question I ask myself on a regular basis. I've asked myself that dozens of times to be quite honest with you, dozens of times, within my own mind. I've questioned my conscience and questioned everything and I've said 'was this worth it, was all these deaths, destruction, misery worth all this, all the imprisonment that you've done in jail, times you've been shot, people you've killed, the children you've left behind, the fucking misery that you've left behind and their families, was it all worth it?' and I can't really reach a conclusion there because, I can't find an answer to that, because I've said to myself, 'I wish to God that I never had to ever lift a gun and kill any human being in my life, politically in any, in this war, six county war.' And then I say to myself 'well, I had to do it 'cause I was defending my community and I was fighting for a legitimate cause, to get the oppressors and a foreign nation out of my country'. So the answer really is yes, it was worth it, it has to be worth it, morally, principally, and ideologically and every way, of course, it was worth it, absolutely, but it hurts me deeply when I think about the tragedy that it entailed, the misery and the suffering. I just say to myself 'I wish there had been some other way of resolving this, without anybody ever having to be killed', which is a natural thing to come to because, who wants to kill anybody, only a psychopath, or who wants to take people's lives, nobody, do you know what I mean? So, I have human feelings, I do feel for them people.[15]

His testimony reveals a state of denial which is very common in other republican activists and which is used to deal with adverse or negative feelings,[16] whereby psychosocial mechanisms of neutralisation or moral disengagement and guilt transference are activated.[17] Note how he continually rejected the label of psychopath, and chose instead to link his feelings with political motivation, insisting that without this his acts would have been 'immoral' and without 'principles'.[18] Like other former members of the IRA, this activist also casts doubt on the effectiveness of the use of violence which, as he notes, generated more violence, and in doing so he effectively questions his belief that people 'had to die to resolve the conflict'. As with many other republicans, he admits that his 'politicisation' did not take place before he joined the organisation or even before he committed murder, and it is therefore necessary to question the true nature of his 'political motivation' and the objective of the latter. Again it can be observed how ideology was not a main motivational factor but rather a part of the member's self-justifying rhetoric, which in fact was acquired *after* joining the group. This is the context in which we must analyse the belief prevalent in republican circles that the use of violence was the only possible form of action, a belief that is shared by this activist, despite his questioning its effectiveness in recognising that it simply led to more violence. His contradictory rationale also emerges when he wishes that 'there had been some other way of resolving this without anybody ever having to be killed', while at the same time admitting that he 'didn't have a clue about politics'. All of this reveals a highly deficient political education or politicisation, since, as Fields has concluded, violence and terrorism do not politicise children; rather, they lead them to choose violence over politics.[19] It therefore seems appropriate to focus our attention once again on the way in which these young people were recruited by the IRA since such an analysis shows that many of them joined the group, as one of them put it, for 'the wrong reasons', because 'when people feel angry in how they've to live, the immediate reaction is not always necessarily the best reaction or the most constructive reaction'.[20]

A similar conclusion was reached by Eamon Collins, a member of the Provisional IRA, who, after leaving the organisation, was murdered by his former comrades in 1999 after seriously criticising the republican violence which he himself had used in the past: 'The important question is "Was violence the best, and most effective, way of combating that discrimination?" The answer to that question is: "No. The Provisionals' so-called war of liberation has been a long drawn-out scourge that has failed to defend or advance the cause of Catholics in the North."'[21] The correct assessment of the motives put forward by republicans for choosing the IRA instead of an exclusively political and peaceful alternative which they argued did not exist requires an examination of the *post hoc* methods of rationalisation mentioned above. As some republicans recognise, many activists feel the psychological need to find a meaning for their negative experiences and the results of their actions. In other words, 'it has to be worth it'. The testimonies which follow show the importance of this process and how it has seriously distorted their view of the past.

'I spent so much time thinking of ways of how to take life and destroy life and to see your child born in front of you, it opened up something in my mind and I suppose an awful lot within my heart. Then I began to feel very guilty for things I had done on people.'[22]

'Yes, a lot of people need to believe it was worth it. If they didn't, they'd go insane with absolute guilt that they actually killed human beings, horribly killed them, kidnapped them, tortured them and brutally murdered them or blew them up in bombs, blew their bodies apart, their limbs apart, and they'd go insane. So they're hanging on to the moral side that they were justified. I think there's a lot of people like that. [Either that] or "I'm a criminal and I've killed all these people for absolutely nothing and I deserve to die or I'll go insane with guilt", of course, there's a lot of that, believe me.'[23]

'I think if I was to turn round and say "no it wasn't worth it", I think it would be a massive impact on me. Don't get me wrong, I often sit and think: I'm forty-two years old, I have absolutely fuck all to show for my life. I could say "no it wasn't worth it", and then your next step is, well, what are you going to do? Kill yourself or something? Throw yourself into the doldrums that way. But it was worth it in some ways, it wasn't worth it in other ways, we got nothing out of it.'[24]

'If some guy is to go in and say, "everything I did was wrong there", what you're doing then is challenging the whole raison d'être of that there person, do you understand what I mean? A person doesn't become involved in something for the sake of becoming involved in something, a person doesn't go out and take a human life not unless they think in taking that human life it is going to make things better. (...) You have to live with yourself, I have to go home here and sleep, I have to go home and get on with my life. (...) A lot of people have a lot of ways of coping with things and maybe people are capable of turning round and saying, "I'm really sorry, I've done this here or I done that there", but there's other people going to turn round and say, "well, if I start doing that there then all them years I spent in the republican movement, what was it for?", they start questioning themselves, and that's the problem.'[25]

Having made these observations, the next section contains testimonies that confirm that the way in which many young people were recruited had the precise potential ingredients to cause them to 'start questioning themselves' about their real reasons for choosing an organisation that advocated the use of violence, as well as the usefulness of this decision. Undoubtedly, this process can prove to be quite a complex one.

'I didn't think, I was a soldier'

Tom Kelly was born in south Belfast in 1955. Five years later, his family moved to an area west of the city known as Turf Lodge. When he refers to the motivations that led him to join the IRA, he explains: 'I was just a young lad who became wild, easy influenced and, if you like, used and abused by those who were directing the violence. I had no concept of republicanism or socialism, I just seen myself as being a soldier and thrown into the deep end, fighting the British Army and anybody who stood against the principles of republicanism.'[26] As can be seen, this former activist recognises his willingness to kill for principles about which he admits that he knew nothing. The socialisation process through which he learned to use violence clearly shows the highly defective republican 'politicisation' and 'education' to which he was subjected in the republican movement. In his testimony below, he describes how, following a 'very normal childhood', he found work in a pub run by a Protestant, a job which he was forced to give up after the IRA placed a bomb next to this establishment. This event fundamentally changed relations between the two communities, which, until then, had been cordial.

> We began to hang around street corners and round the barricades where there were armed men and eventually I joined in the rioting. We started throwing stones and bottles. After a while a lot of my friends had actually joined the junior wing of the IRA, which was called *Fianna Éireann*, and it was through a wee bit of peer pressure that they asked me to join it and I did. It is the type of organisation you are not allowed to open your mouth or say anything and I just joined in what was going on and they began to train people like me drill and how to use weapons where you break them down and put them together again, etc. Eventually I was asked to join the main ranks of the IRA because they thought I was ready and my turn came and I joined. I was still fifteen. So I got involved in the IRA and the first weapon I ever fired was a 3-0-3, that was my introduction into the IRA. And the more that I got involved the more training I got and learnt how to snipe and make different types of bombs, booby traps. I got that involved, eventually security forces got to hear about me and I was being arrested every week or so and eventually I was interned when I was seventeen, and I spent two-and-a-half years in Long Kesh.[27]

His decision to join an organisation where 'you are not allowed to open your mouth or say anything' was partly a result of 'peer pressure' exerted by his friends. Once again we can observe how the very vulnerable period of adolescence conditions an individual's conduct; leading the interviewee to stress the need to pay attention to young people, a group that is particularly prone to being sucked into acts of violence: 'To me the youth are very important. I can tell them what happened to me when I was fifteen and how my life went downhill at fifteen. I can take them ones for where they are, what pressures they are under and whatever peer pressure it may be, whether it is republicanism, whether it is drugs or alcohol, etc. It is important for me to tell them that it is important to respect their own dignity and their own values and what they want out of life, not what people tells them that they should have.'[28]

Joining the group at a young age and the subsequent experiences of imprisonment, which involves coexisting in extreme conditions, is complemented by an increasing dependence on the group. The inevitable consequence is that the individual has less opportunity to make independent decisions, since he or she is part of a structure where the group monopolises the selection and interpretation of ideology, thus permitting the nurturing of ideas that justify the use of violence.[29] Tom Kelly associates the time he spent in prison with a complete lack of debate with other inmates about political issues, something which he justifies in the following manner: 'I wasn't a thinker then, I was a soldier, at that time I was just a soldier. I would have done what I was told to do, that was it. Now it is totally different, I think for myself.'[30] He accepts the description of the IRA as a totalitarian organisation which repressed debate, his attitude at the time being one of 'immaturity' and lack of interest in politics because 'politics is for the politicians'.[31] The important consequences of the activist's submissive attitude to the group is revealed by his own words: 'Sometimes if you think too hard when you are a soldier, you confuse things. A soldier just does what he is told to do: do it and that's it. That is what soldiers are there for. I always said to myself: "Right, there is logic in it. I'm asked to do this, so I have to do it." I think every army, you tell your soldiers what to do, they are expected to take orders, if they don't take orders they are disciplined. If they don't take orders they are not going to win their war.'[32]

The manipulation of young people and children was described by sociologist Frank Burton when, at the beginning of the 1970s, he interviewed members of a Catholic community in Belfast. He concluded that 'a frequently voiced criticism of the Provos concerned what people considered to be a cynical use of children and adolescents in their campaign'.[33] The opinions given by republicans interviewed for this book corroborate this point, as the following testimonies reveal: 'At one time we would have put five hundred kids out there throwing petrol bombs and bricks at Brits and *peelers* [policemen] but they shot loads of them with plastic bullets. We actually stopped it when they were shooting them dead, not because we thought it was wrong to attack them with it but because tactically it was damaging our community.'[34]

When they [the British] started shooting people here in the streets, we knew it was coming because for weeks we had been agitating, we had been causing street riots day after day. And during the street riots there was petrol bombs, nail bombs and stuff getting thrown. And we knew there was coming a point, they were going to open fire. (...) Things have always been manipulated, always. In 1971, the first Derry people [that] got shot was Cusack and Beattie and for six weeks or possibly two months every single night we were out agitating, we were out throwing petrol bombs, nail bombs, we were stirring, we were really putting the Army under pressure. (...) When Cusack and Beatty got shot dead they opened fire on crowds of ordinary people. But we knew the situation was going to happen, right? If we provoked them enough, if we attacked them enough, at some point it wasn't just us they were going to be shooting at, it was the people. It didn't matter. There was a difference between somebody getting shot in a gun battle and some innocent people getting shot in the streets. And we knew the situation had to come to escalate the war. That they had to shoot civilians and we knew that. And we agitated and agitated until we got to the situation.

We had to move the violence to a new level, right? And the only way that we could do that was causing thems to commit the outrageous, to shoot innocent civilians. But this was inevitable because if you are going out and there's riots going on and some people are throwing stones and they're throwing bombs, at the end of the day they are going to retaliate. As soon as they shoot somebody, you cry, 'Foul, they are shooting innocent people.' Which, in a sense they were, but the situation was engineered. All it takes is one soldier on the ground to lose control and open fire and suddenly you can come up and 'Look what's happened they're shooting people here, they're shooting ordinary people!' And we knew that situation was going to happen. In fact we had information that when they opened fire we knew they were going to open fire and we took our [IRA] people off the streets. Simply because of pragmatic reasons: we had so few people that we couldn't afford at that point to lose any volunteers. So we took them off the streets knowing that innocent people were going to be killed. If we had wanted we could have cleared all the streets to stop all the rioting. But we needed the whole situation to be escalated. The thing was always planned.[35]

Similarly, in 1971 the IRA decided to intensify its campaign of violence, despite the consequences that this would have for civilians, in order to provoke the British into the drastic response of introducing internment without trial. This strategy was based on the view that the premature introduction of such a controversial and repressive measure would benefit the IRA, since the British lacked up-to-date information about group members. Republicans therefore decided to 'force' the British to introduce internment before its intelligence services could gather improved information, which led to a large number of people who had no connection with the IRA being deprived of their liberty.[36]

'Quite considerable moral pressure'

Many of those who ended up joining the IRA were first drawn towards the movement in violent circumstances such as those described by the republicans quoted above. Unsurprisingly, young people were particularly prone to becoming involved in the disturbances, which decisively affected their immediate future. David O'Donnell was born in 1954 in the lower Falls Road area, in west Belfast. Before his sixteenth birthday he joined the Official IRA and was sent to a young person's detention centre, having been convicted for possession of an explosive device. He managed to escape, and immediately went into hiding in Cork, in the south of Ireland, where he took part in various activities for the group. Shortly afterwards, following the Official IRA's ceasefire declaration in 1972, he distanced himself somewhat from the republican movement, although he became fully involved again as a result of what he describes as 'quite considerable moral pressure'.[37] This 'moral pressure' to which O'Donnell attributes his renewed involvement in the Official IRA after having been inactive for a year was exerted by other members of the movement. A decisive factor was the strong ties established among the group of activists with which he had come into contact when in hiding in the south of Ireland even before he reached his eighteenth birthday. This stopped him from breaking totally with the violence, despite the internal contradictions which, according to O'Donnell, 'haunted' him:

> That was a wee community ready to accept me and embrace me and, you know, nurture me, help me out and give me advice and assistance and give me a social framework within to work, and it was very welcome. I remember at the time thinking these people are reaching out, they know it was very difficult for me, I was only sixteen at the time. And that's a very strong bond and you try and pull away from that in what is still quite a strange environment, it's actually quite difficult. So whenever those people who you have come to be very close to, share a lot of time with and have a lot of respect for, then begin to question ... and people who were involved in republicanism much longer than I ever was, individuals who were much older than me, people whose views, political views that I had a lot of respect for; certainly people whose analytical skills I thought I was very impressed with, because my analytical skills at that point were not particularly good, so when people like that begin to sort of argue against your quite unsophisticated analysis it's very, very difficult to counter that. So rather than just say fuck off, I disagree with you, I got my view, okay your view might be stronger than mine, I've got my view and I'm going to stick to it, that's a silly position anyway. So what I found was that people were talking to me and I suppose felt they were doing what was in my best interest and I just felt that the pressure to get involved again was very difficult to resist at that time.[38]

O'Donnell admits that the intense socialisation process that took place with the IRA activists who had 'welcomed' him during the difficult early years of his membership prevented him from acting on his desire to definitively break with the organisation, a desire which, he says, was partly due to his aversion to violence. In fact, it was only when he was imprisoned again in the second half of the 1970s that he found himself sufficiently distanced from the group that had so conditioned his behaviour, and he was able to sever his links with the movement:

> But I suppose once I went into prison and had all of that time to reflect and read and educate and think and analyse, it was much easier to put those feelings into a political framework. And quite quickly within three or four years I think I developed a personal political philosophy or attitude that was quite easy to live with. It meant not having any association with former comrades because that was untenable. And so that was when I finally made the break. But I think that was that constant unhappiness, unsettled feeling with being involved in this stuff but then once that was reinforced by a greater political sophistication and understanding of the conflict and the nature of it and how it could possibly be resolved, then calling a halt to my involvement in that organisation was quite easy apart from the social difficulties and ex-comrades turning their back on me and so on, that was difficult. But at least I think that I had arrived at a position whereby my abhorrence for violence met a better political understanding and the two sat quite well together, and I've been there ever since. I think I was much more able to begin the process of analysis and I think that many foot soldiers if you like within the republican movement don't have that capacity, they wait for instructions to come from above and then follow them and that's probably evidenced with the peace process. There's no doubt that there are many, many members of the Provisionals that are deeply unhappy about that, but because the leadership dictates that that's the way the process is going to go then they follow that.[39]

'You have to stand up and be a man yourself and go out and do it'

Such a challenging process was influenced by another type of 'pressure' which one activist describes in the following way: 'I was nineteen and had given my whole life to the IRA, and saw no way out of the IRA because I was wanted for a lot of bombings and stuff, and I saw no other life than the IRA life.'[40] Therefore, belonging to the group could satisfy important personal interests. The power that a group has to influence its members depends to a large extent on how they evaluate their membership.[41] As has been seen in the fairly typical cases of Tom Kelly and David O'Donnell, these individuals were attracted to the IRA for reasons that were very closely related with the satisfaction of certain needs that had little or nothing to do with the alleged political objectives of the republican movement. In addition, while such reasons were what initially attracted activists, membership was also maintained due to individual motivations based on the search for self-esteem, something which was satisfied within the group by choosing to stress certain positive elements that would derive from activism in the organisation.[42] Personal interests selected by the individual to assess the convenience of remaining a member of the group were also influenced by emotional factors, as the following activist suggests:

> I don't think that the nationalist community is the most politically sophisticated community in western Europe at all. I think a lot of it is based on hatred, a lot of it is based on a very, very romantic notion. You go along to the Felons Club or any of the republican clubs in west Belfast on a Friday or Saturday night, when everybody's got a few drinks in them and somebody gets up and starts singing, 'Kevin Barry', and there's tears in everybody's eyes, and the anger wells up again and you've the anti-Britishness and the anti-unionism wells up within all of that emotionality and, 'Tom Williams murdered when he was sixteen' and all of this, 'the hunger strikers!', 'oh my God!', and it's very emotional. I don't go to those events any more because I find myself getting sucked into the whole emotion and I recognise that in the very early days whenever I got involved, an element of that was emotion. And that inspires a lot of people.[43]

Some of those who ended up joining the movement were also attracted by the idea of a certain status which they would enjoy in their local community. Many republicans deny that this was a factor which motivated their own membership, arguing that they were warned before joining that one or two years later they would either be dead or in prison. However, it does not seem very plausible that this warning would have been given during the 1970s, a time when the IRA was making constant public declarations about the imminence of its victory, claiming, for example, that 1972 was 'the year of victory'. Two years later, they were announcing 'Victory for the IRA in 1974' while proclaiming 'the British are getting ready to leave'. Three years later, the IRA leadership trumpeted that victory was certain as they had entered the 'final phase of the war with England'.[44] This was also a time when the IRA required a larger number of recruits than in later years, when a different operative structure based on cells was introduced, which required less activists. This organisational change, coupled with a greater realism which led them to replace their initial triumphalism with a new strategic approach known as 'the long war' and based on trying to wear down the British, meant that the future perspectives of new recruits were somewhat different, as one of the republicans who joined the IRA in the 1980s pointed out: 'They were told quite plainly from the outset that your future is either prison or the graveyard. You weren't told "your future's bright". You weren't told "you're going to see a united Ireland tomorrow" or "you're going to see a victory tomorrow", you were told "if you choose this path, then the path means that in a relatively short period you're going to either end up in prison, incarcerated or in a graveyard".'[45] This is without doubt a different perspective than that which existed in previous years, as is shown by the following representative comments of various activists with reference to the 1970s:

'When I first went into jail everything was so black and white, we were going to fight the British and the British were going to leave, as simple as that. And we were watching the whole situation with the United States and Vietnam, the Portuguese and Angola, you thought everything was black and white. I think we realised after a while that there was an impasse, that we couldn't force the British out.'[46]

'In 1971, 1972, I was 16, 17. I thought "it will be probably be over in a year or two". I remember when I was 17 being told there will be an amnesty, you know this will all be over in nine or twelve months. It reminded me of the poor bastards going out in the First World War. I went in the second time and the same thing was being said, and by that time I was in my twenties and there were kids at 17 the way I had been and people were saying "this will be all over" and I was saying "don't fucking even go there, this is a long haul".'[47]

'We really believed that a 2- or 3-year struggle would unite Ireland. It was idealistic, teenage, childish, puerile, uninformed, uneducated and it was just the youthful idealism gone wrong, but we really believed it would only take two or three years because we had nothing to go on.'[48]

Some interviewees recognised that the influence of selective and personal interests as a motivational factor should not be underestimated; moreover, as they indicate, it is something which is not normally admitted in public since to do so would mean devaluing political aspirations. As one of the interviewees points out, it must be borne in mind that not all of the positions within the IRA's organisational hierarchy had the same level of risk and responsibility. For example, those members who were in what republicans describe as the 'security department' were in charge of the internal investigations within the movement. Such functions allowed them to 'have a good life-style without many risks' while also allowing a 'certain status out of respect or fear in the ghettos where the IRA gets its support'.[49] It is not at all strange that certain individuals' membership of the IRA was known within the social circles in which they moved and that the 'feeling of power' and 'capacity of control' which this entailed were attractive for some,[50] although at the same time they were criticised by others. The ethnographic study of one such community carried out by Frank Burton offers many examples of this phenomenon, as the following quotation illustrates: 'Pat considered himself a republican but disagreed almost completely with the Provos. He condemned the clubs as places where too many decisions were made under the influence of too many drinks. He deplored the fact that the IRA tolerated such behaviour from its volunteers: "These Provos have ruined the ideal of republicanism. They're gangsters ruling with guns and if you say so you get your knee-caps blown off. These drinking clubs are an evil ... There are too many young men having a good time without working; they won't want to give that up ... It's people like these who have created informers; and what have they done? Got rid of Stormont? I don't believe they did ... they've done nothing but create seven hundred empty chairs." Pat's extensive and vitriolic criticisms of the Provos were frequently voiced.'[51]

Another former member of the organisation recognised that the social reinforcement that belonging to the group provided to 'many people with nothing else' or to 'youngsters with few expectations who simply wanted to be like the lads', that is, IRA members, were undoubtedly more interesting and attractive objectives than defending the community: 'If all the Catholics who have lost somebody had joined or supported the IRA, it would have been big. But they didn't because they knew that was not going to guarantee their defence. If you are nobody and suddenly you get into a group like this, you feel different, you feel power, a sense of direction in your life.'[52]

The support that the republican movement and the IRA's actions received in the ghettos of Northern Ireland may be defined as ambivalent and changing, despite the fact that attempts have been made to present them as practically total and unwavering. Burton has demonstrated clearly the numerous criticisms made of the IRA's approach in those communities where it received significant levels of support, and the serious difficulties that this created for the organisation.[53] His is a more rigorous approach than that of Sluka who, in his study of a nationalist community in Belfast, stated that the presence of the IRA was largely accepted as necessary and that fear and intimidation were not factors that conditioned such support.[54] As Mallie and Bishop also concluded, the level of IRA intimidation in the ghettos of Belfast and Derry show that rather than 'admired', the group was merely 'tolerated'.[55] This obliged the IRA to make constant efforts to maintain its presence and influence in such areas, for example by making use of republican culture that has venerated the 'sacrifice' of volunteers through constant rituals and commemorations of the past, as well as funerals and other public events which formed an essential part of the movement's ideological apparatus. Remembering the dead heroes of the republican cause has nurtured a martyrology which has been used in an attempt to obtain the sympathy of the nationalist community, and, in this way, to provide a source of collective identity.[56] For this reason, being an IRA member was sometimes seen as something to be proud of, something that strengthened an individual's self-esteem, as the following testimonies show: 'Instead of standing in the background watching other men doing it, going to jail, and other men dying and things like that, I thought, "well, you have to stand up and be a man yourself and go out and do it".' This activist also recalls how when he was imprisoned his mother 'was more proud than anything'.[57] Echoing a similar pride, another activist pointed out: 'I believe nobody has shown more courage than IRA volunteers, given that from the outset you're told you're going to jail, you're going to die. It's the truth. I've buried many friends, I've watched many friends get incarcerated, but I believe there's nobody more courageous.'[58]

This favourable image that some activists have of themselves is very closely linked to the way that they describe their decision to join the IRA as a kind of duty. It is a means of rationalisation that reinforces the decision, interpreting it as worthwhile despite the costs that it entails. In other words, the risk of prison or death is accepted if it is compensated by a feeling of pride or recognition, since joining the group does not in itself provide any guarantee at all that the political objectives of the group will be attained, whether in the short or long term. In this respect, the words of activist Thomas Cosgrove when he referred to the decision to join the IRA as 'simply a personal sacrifice'[59] are worth recalling. Such declarations also allow activists to avoid responsibility for the negative consequences, which may be socially repugnant, associated with the choice taken claiming that it is a force over which an individual has hardly any control: 'It was awful that people were put in that position, people who would never break the law if they were living in England or in any fair and decent society.'[60] This interpretation is based on the delusion that those who joined the IRA had no freedom to choose a given course of action; instead, this was effectively imposed on them by forces beyond their control, as the following testimonies show:

'The armed struggle was not a campaign set out and strategically worked out. It was something that was forced onto us. That struggle came about by accident rather than design, it wasn't probably until the end of the seventies into the 1980s that we started, that republicans started to design what the struggle was about, to take control of the struggle rather than responding to events on the ground, which is how this whole thing started initially, through people responding, not dictating the circumstances.'[61]

'The armed struggle aspect of it was forced onto people. It wasn't a case of people just saying "we'll have an armed struggle". It wasn't. It was a hard decision to take and people agonised over being involved in it.'[62]

'I don't think there was any other way we could have went. Armed struggle was forced upon us in the late 1960s. It wasn't something that the IRA went out to create. It was something that happened, we were products of the sort of political climate that we were living in.'[63]

'Using armed struggle is the last resort option, it's not the first one, and in some cases you don't even have an option to be able to consider whether you use armed struggle or not because it's forced upon you, forced upon you by your political opponents.'[64]

As can be seen, it is within this framework that activists engage in a process of guilt transfer, as demonstrated by the words of Thomas Quigley, who was imprisoned for the first time when he was sixteen years old. He was released in 1975, after spending three and a half years in prison, arrested again in 1983 and finally released in 1998 after having been accused of being involved in various attacks carried out in London. In Quigley's opinion: 'It is not just a case of "we were to blame also". We didn't, the war came to us, we didn't go looking for a war. Armed struggle actually was forced upon people, it wasn't a choice. I didn't see that we had any choice.'[65] The constant need to make this point derives from the fact that, as noted above, the inconsistencies between past actions and subsequent reflections about them cause problems for the individual, as can be seen by comparing the last quote with the following one from the same activist:

We all made choices, people in the RUC made choices to join the RUC, they knew why they were joining the RUC, they had very clear reasons for it, people in the British Army did the same, people in the UDR did the same, people within Loyalism did the same. And we made choices. We know that in the course of this war suffering was inflicted on both sides and we are prepared to accept it, our choices led to some of that suffering but we are certainly not prepared to accept that it was all our fault, that the people who were killed by the British Army, by the RUC, by loyalists, they weren't real victims.[66]

If, as Quigley himself went on to mention, choices were made and decisions were taken, one could ask whether these choices and decisions were not the right ones. However, the mere questioning of such decisions could shake the apparently solid republican discourse, and is therefore seen as a threat which must be rejected, as the following dialogue between the author and one of the interviewees reveals:

Author: 'You talk about learning from the mistakes of the past as well, so in order to do that I suppose you have to look back and assess whether armed struggle was the right tactic or correct course of action. Is that sort of thing going on?'

Paul O'Neill: 'I think it is a wrong premise. Armed struggle came to us. People didn't just all of a sudden decide "let's engage in armed struggle", people say often "oh, these people had a choice". When you are fourteen, fifteen years of age and you see your streets being burned by the people who are supposed to be protecting you, the police, and they are coming into your areas, they are wrecking your homes, they are shooting people. When you see mobs coming in, backed by these people, what options have you got there? A lot of people would have said there was only one option, you had to defend, you had to fight fire with fire basically. So therefore people gravitated naturally towards republicanism and the whole armed struggle business. So in that sense I think it is a wee bit purposeless to reflect on, was armed struggle a good thing? Should people have engaged in armed struggle? I think armed struggle actually was forced upon people, it wasn't a choice.'[67]

It is clear that violence was not imperative, since other exclusively peaceful means of action were available, as have been seen in Chapter 1. This denial leads to frequent contradictions in the republican narrative, as corroborated by Eamon MacDermott's explanation. Although he emphasises that he 'didn't have a choice' but to join the IRA, when asked about the consequences of the actions that he carried out, in particular for the murder of a policeman for which he was imprisoned, he states: 'I took a side, he took a side. He picked a side in this war, I picked a side. We were on opposite sides. He was not some sort of innocent, he had taken a side, you take a side in a war and you suffer for it. I don't complain about my fifteen years in jail, I don't say "oh, I'm terribly hard done by", I took my side, took my chance and lost, I got caught. That's my problem, that's my decision. Someone who joins the RUC, they made a decision, somebody who joins the UDR made a decision, somebody joins the British army made a decision, so, I mean, you make these decisions, you take what comes. So you take your choice.'[68]

Similar contradictions can be found in the discourse of Jim Gibney, another former member who saw the campaign of violence as an 'imposition'. The contrast which he makes in comparing the options available in Northern Ireland at the beginning of the 1970s with those existing elsewhere, such as Zimbabwe in 2002, are highly revealing. Despite the huge differences between the two places in terms of structural inequality – Zimbabwe having much higher levels of violence and deprivation, this former activist was against using violence in the African state and instead advocated the use of political pressure in response to the extensive and prolonged human rights violations committed by the Zimbabwean state. By contrast, however, Gibney ruled out the possibility of political action in 1970s Northern Ireland, despite the fact that it undoubtedly would have had much more chance of success there:

In 1970 republicans had no options. They had one, either to close your door, pretend what's happening is not happening or stand up and fight. Many people closed their door and pretended that it didn't happen, many other people stood and fought. Republicans stood and fought. So similarly, if you're in the Basque country you have to decide, if you're in Palestine you have to decide, if you're there in Zimbabwe you have to decide, if you believe passionately that you are living in an unjust society, then you have to bring about changes, you have to be the instrument of change and the pressure that you can apply and then you decide whether it's political pressure or armed pressure and what's acceptable and what's more likely to win, and it's clear cut. In Zimbabwe, as we speak, what should the opposition movement do in the face of Mugabe rigging the elections? Should they resort to armed struggle? Remove him from office? No. Why? Because it's not going to work, that's why. What should they do? Build a mass movement among the people? Yes, that's precisely what they should do and they should harness international support to isolate Mugabe, that's what they should do. So from area to area the circumstances change. Liberation movements, especially those involved in armed struggle, they're not powerless. In some cases they can be very effective, so they have options to consider when they're employing their armed individuals, they have options. You don't have to, if you don't want, to put a bomb down in the town. You don't have to, if you don't want, to shoot a politician. You don't have to, if you don't want, to shoot somebody who works in a military installation, there are other options other than that.[69]

'The immaturity and rebelliousness of youth contributed to propelling the conflict'

Therefore, in contrast to what some activists claim, there were options and alternatives yet many republicans still avoid addressing this issue. As one of them put it: 'The republican movement was not a very analytical movement for a long time, so they never looked at the question of armed struggle. This is what they had always done. Once you have an armed struggle, there's people dying, it takes on a certain momentum of its own, you keep on going because you can't give up.'[70] However, there are other former IRA members who consider that a more critical analysis on why the path of violence was taken is absolutely essential:

In our society we should question what had just happened, we should investigate it. We're one of the few countries in the world that having had an armed struggle for thirty years there is little or no fucking research into what happened, why it happened, what are the lessons to be drawn from it and how do we inform you people not to do this shit again. But I mean you know there simply isn't any and it is like people just want to shut it down, close it and move on without any research at all. The biggest most interesting factor for me was that in terms of the republican community and nationalism in Ireland I used to say to Irish government people and church people and in Ireland for two or three years in the mid-'90s that my biggest disappointment upon being released from prison was the failure of Irish nationalism to research and investigate the full effect of the armed struggle and publish to the people of Ireland its utter and complete failure, the damage it had done to the entire nationality, pursuit of nationhood and so on, how it had utterly and completely damaged it, the damage it did to relations between Irish people, Protestant and Catholic. And my worst fear was that the lessons that should be learned from it are just lost in the passage of time.[71]

Similarly, Mickey McMullan argues that republicans must critically analyse how they contributed to creating the circumstances in which violence emerged:

I think that circumstances ran ahead in the early seventies. One of the reasons why it ran ahead is because youth, immature youth contributed to propelling that conflict forward and into the situation that found [sic] particularly coming up to the hunger strikes. So I don't think that republicans are really involved in self-analysis. I think they are more outlooking. (...) The events of 1969 encouraged the youth of the time, and the enthusiasm of youth and innate rebelliousness of youth propelled the situation forward. I think there is a reluctance among many people to look at how republican youth contributed to the situation that we found ourselves up to 1994. And as it went on and on it became a clear case of them and us: They were trying to defeat us, we were trying to defeat them. We were not to be defeated, we had got off our knees and all of that there. So there is a vigour and enthusiasm in the early seventies which comes with youth, but the longer it went on and the more the people were suffering.[72]

This self-analysis, as McMullan calls it, generates conflicts of decision and a threat of cognitive dissonance that other former members of the IRA refuse to confront, avoiding, as one of them put it, difficult questions about whether people should have resorted to violence. Another former member recognised that a critical examination of past actions created 'guilt complexes' since it forced people to question what they had done and whether they should have done it. In such conditions, he advocated a subjective and elusive morality that he summed up in the following way: 'People were involved in a conflict and they believed that what they were doing was right, regardless of what the consequences of that there was.'[73] By contrast, other former members have chosen to question the received certainties about the past and the ideological reasons underlying IRA killings.

'For them to turn round and say it was all wrong, it's to totally undermine everything, it's to totally undermine a generation and a half of struggle. It was a total waste of time, I wasted my youth completely. It was easy for me to say that. One friend of mine went to jail for life when he was eighteen, came out when he was thirty-five, thirty-six. I'm ashamed of that because I know how I got into jail and I know that by that time, I would have been a couple of years older, and I know that I bear responsibility for it. His life was ruined. I bear responsibility for lots of other things that happened, and I look back on it now and I say to myself, "what was it all for?" The Provos, no wonder they're all torn, torn up inside, they can't come to terms with it.'[74]

'In Ireland it's: "look at what has happened to us during the years, look at the history of what the British have done to us". It's just victimhood. We are right and everybody else is wrong. And I think we have to stop, republicans in particular have to stop saying those things. Although we say we regret things that were done in the past we never say what things. It is a sort of general bland statement that is made. I think we have to be honest with ourselves. When I left the movement I went through what I think was the most serious period of conflict. I think I am emerging out of it but it caused me considerable grief, because, as I said, I faced a contradiction or a conflict in 1971 about who to join. (...) I went through a very intensive self-analysis from 1995 onwards. That involved a lot of anger, bitterness, resentment, every emotion under the sun involved. Because I had to look at personal involvement as well of things that I had been involved in and done. I don't think it is about salvaging guilt. I think it's about coming to terms with where you came from and where do you want to go. I think it takes time. Whether the majority of the republicans will engage in that or not, I don't know, I can't say. I think some of them already have. I think it's regretful that it hasn't been in the public domain. I think it's regretful that a lot of debates that are going on in republicanism have not been in the public domain. Because it disables people from seeing the extent of the debate or even the limit of the debate, depending on which way you look at it.

But yes I think there is a reluctance in the part of many republicans to engage in self-analysis of where they came from. I went to a conference last year organised by ex-prisoners, called "The Road Travelled", and they talked about everything but the road travelled. It was all about "the road yet to be travelled", reassertion or determination to continue with the struggle. And perhaps that is necessary within the context of provisional republican movement to keep people on board because you

still have like the Continuity and the Real IRA on the fringes just waiting to scoop up whatever elements are dissatisfied. But perhaps the day
will come when they will sit down and they will seriously genuinely
discuss the road travelled. Because when I look personally at the road
travelled, particularly in the context of the prison, and I have said this to
a friend of mine, although I was imprisoned by the British state for my
resistance against the British state, the treatment I received at the hands
of people who you should consider comrades was far worst than the
treatment meted out to me by the *screws* [prison officers] and so on and
so forth. Because again of my politics. Because I declared myself to be
a socialist and an adherent of James Connolly, which incredibly they
found to be communistic, but again that's ignorance. People didn't know
what that involved. So may be the day will come when they will engage
seriously in self-analysis.'[75]

The testimony of McMullan shows quite clearly how divergence from
groupthink in an organisation like the IRA causes serious problems for the
dissenting individual because of the very serious consequences of this; not
only the group's authority but also its cohesion is questioned, through the
challenge to the unanimity on which its rationalisation of reality is based. As
a result, the point can be reached where doubt is cast on whether being a
member 'was worth it', while also questioning the claim that there was
no alternative to the use of violence. Too many questions perhaps for an
organisation which claims to politicise and educate its members, provided
that this takes place within very strict limits that ensure obedience to
authority, since as an activist put it, 'if you think too hard when you are a
soldier, you confuse things'. In the words of Mickey McMullan:

During that period when I was engaged in self-analysis of where I came
from, there was a lot of anger and bitterness and everything else, and
during the course of a discussion I was having with some friends, one of
these friends said to me: 'The way you are sounding it is as though it
wasn't worth it.' And I didn't answer. I couldn't answer. And later on I
was thinking about it. I got angry that she actually asked that question.
Here was a woman, middle class, who had a career. In 1970 or 71, whenever, early seventies anyway, she went to London, pursued a career
there. I was over here fighting the struggle. She came back in the mid-
eighties, got involved in Sinn Féin. So worth in terms of suffering, my
suffering was up there and hers was down here. What is she comparing it
with? She has had a relatively easy life. She didn't go through torture,
imprisonment, faced death. Things like that there. She had the audacity
to ask me or rebuke me because I was suggesting it mightn't have been
worth it. People have asked me that many times and the way that I
answer it is: when you add up the suffering, the deaths, the killing, no.

For something less than what you had set out, when you go back to 1974 and what was on offer, if people had had the power to say 'let's work on this, let's see if we can move this along to a point', but circumstances dictated that that couldn't be the case. So when you do compare, no, I don't really believe it was worth it, no.[76]

As noted, the IRA has claimed to be an organisation that has promoted debate among its members and that has advocated the education of its prisoners. It has even highlighted the influence that the pedagogical methods of the Brazilian Paulo Freire had on them, as described by former IRA prisoner Laurence McKeown in his recollection of imprisonment.[77] However, McKeown himself provides examples that raise doubts as to whether Freire's model was correctly applied, since his recollection contains passages that clearly shows that any criticism of the republican leadership was seen as dangerous, and that discussions inside prison were seriously limited and reduced. As Mickey McMullan recalled, the organisation has always looked to control the debate, and therefore the true value of the educational processes to which some republicans have referred must be doubted. Another former prisoner who agreed with this authoritarian description of the IRA, describing it as 'the nature of the beast', summed up the serious deficiencies in the educational and politicisation processes that took place as follows: 'I remember that we used to get lectures about politics and what is republicanism and going through the "isms" of non-sectarianism and secularism and socialism and things like that. But we were always, we were talking among ourselves, you weren't getting outside opinions to challenge what you were saying, you might have played devil's advocate within your own group, but there is nothing as good as maybe having a unionist to sit down and say "no, you're wrong" and argue his or her position with you. Or some English person to tell you "no, you're wrong, this is what I believe" and then you have to have the conviction of your own beliefs to argue against them. So while we were political we hadn't got all the answers, we thought we had all the answers but as time went on we discovered we didn't.'[78]

Another member of the IRA described the idea of the republican movement as being open to debate as false, and defined the politicisation process undergone by its members as enormously deficient. In the opinion of this former prisoner, this politicisation was not a symptom of political maturity, and therefore he only discussed anything which diverged from the leadership's line 'with the volunteers who shared my point of view': 'You find that quite a lot of volunteers would shy away because they're very uncomfortable with any sort of criticism, because to a large extent they have never sat down and thought about it themselves, they're simply happy to follow like blind sheep, and I'm not being harsh on them, I'm not being derogatory, but they are simply willing to follow like blind sheep and when they come up against any sort of criticism, they become awkward because they have difficulty answering it.'[79] Throughout the conflict, those who have dared to speak out against the group's view have been marginalised time and again. For example, in 1978, Shane O'Doherty, after having been imprisoned for terrorist offences while an IRA member, published a letter stating that there was no justification for the use of violence. His new stance resulted in him being isolated by the republican movement and threatened by the IRA members who were in jail with him: 'The implication was that they would fucking kill me for this kind of activity.'[80]

These testimonies are a perfect example of how the questioning of group reinforcement and the collective identity causes conflicts which the IRA had to avoid to guarantee its survival, since its campaign of violence required a complete absence of criticism from its members. This point is well illustrated by the testimony of former IRA member Eamon Collins, who explains how his disenchantment with the group, on questioning its methods and effectiveness, did not lead to him immediately abandoning it: 'I felt as if I had no choice but to continue. I was impelled forward by the dynamics of the choice I had made some years before. It was as if I had boarded a fast train without brakes; I knew it was going to hit the crash barriers at some point, but I could not get off.'[81] Collins therefore avoided thinking about the doubts he was assailed with, and stayed on what he called 'the insane rush of the journey'. This need to avoid thinking about the doubts that may affect the cognitive and moral conscience of the group and its members can be seen in the words of another former IRA member, who recognised how 'deep down, you felt you were doing something wrong', a feeling that gave rise to the sort of personal reassurances that have been quoted above, and which he sums up in the following way: 'At the end of the day, I could have had a number of British soldiers [killed] on my conscience. Because I carried out the operations, I have to justify doing it, it doesn't mean to say it rests easy with me being forced to harm anyone or to take anyone's life, to me is just totally unnatural. It's just something that goes totally against my grain.'[82]

Such a revealing statement echoes those made by other activists regarding the need to justify their actions in order to confirm that their involvement in the IRA was really worth it, given the problems caused by the possible negative balance of their involvement. We should also recall how another volunteer quoted above insisted on differentiating his actions from those of a psychopath, emphasising that what he did was political in nature, otherwise it would have been immoral. Bearing in mind these factors, consider how Rice also indicated that the deaths of human beings 'would have weighed heavily' on his 'conscience', despite admitting that if he had been 'forced to' he would have killed.[83] Once again, the interpretation so common among republicans of the violence as a 'necessary evil' and the consequent justification thereof through various methods of moral disengagement can be seen. Such methods include what can be called the 'advantageous comparison'.[84] Like other activists, Rice compares his situation with that of

'British and American soldiers' who participated in the Gulf war. The use of such strategies eludes the responsibility of the individual in the commission of attacks causing loss of life, since the IRA is presented as being involved in an armed conflict which he describes as a war, thus rejecting any comparison with terrorist acts since drawing any such parallel would discredit its ideology and activities. For this reason, expressions such as 'the armed struggle' are preferred to those with less positive connotations. This type of language, which is linked to what some researchers have called 'fantasy war',[85] allows what for many is unpleasant and incomprehensible to be made respectable and comprehensible. As a former IRA member in favour of demystifying this concept put it: 'I don't believe for one minute that the IRA had a war. There was no war, it was a nasty little conflict where they shot this one, they shot that one. It's like an assassination campaign.'[86]

This particular 'fantasy war' contributes to the diffusion of responsibility that is also greater when individuals form part of a group. As Zimbardo has shown, individuals tend to change their sense of personal identity and responsibility when they become submerged within a group, and this allows them to carry out more extreme and aggressive acts.[87] The way in which IRA members see themselves as soldiers favours deindividuation so that, as a former activist confirms, above and beyond the personal 'problems of conscience' which he refers to, what prevails is obedience to authority and the need to carry out orders without challenging the correctness of a decision that in itself appears questionable, since to do so would create a substantial burden. As well as taking on the role of 'soldiers', IRA members also attribute roles to the victims of their violence, who are classified as either 'military targets' or 'civilian targets'. In this way, a certain dehumanisation is employed, aimed at legitimising the deaths of those who come within the former category, since they are seen in a generic way as a simple uniform and a symbol of the 'British presence'.

In a classic experiment, Stanley Milgram showed how people are capable of behaving in a cruel manner when authority over them is reinforced and how obeying orders is used to reduce the sense of individual responsibility.[88] Just like the participants in Milgram's famous experiment, IRA members claim to have had no choice other than the 'armed struggle', and they judge their violent acts on the basis of the feelings which they say they had when they committed them. 'I believe it went right against the grain of the vast majority of young men who went out and did it. I believe that anybody who relished in it were few and far between,' claimed former member Gerard Rice. 'I have human feelings, I do feel for them people' is how volunteer Bobby refers to those who he murdered. However, this apparent empathy does not mitigate the suffering of the victims of the violence, nor did it lead its perpetrators to stop what they were doing. In other words, cruelty is justified by an abstract idea to which individuals are subordinated. This type of behaviour has consequences clearly reflected in the strategy of the republican movement, a point which will be analysed later in the context of two important events in the history of the IRA and Sinn Féin, namely the 1981 hunger strikes and the peace process.

'We wanted to be IRA men who were heroes and patriots'

As noted, many members of the republican movement have tended to dissociate IRA actions from their effects, describing the use of violence as inevitable, an imposition that was beyond their control rather than a decision based on the use of their free will. It is, however, possible to interpret the use of violence in quite a different manner. Given that activists themselves recognise the enormous limitations and deficiencies of their politicisation prior to joining the IRA, questions must be asked about the way in which they reached the conviction that the use of violence was a useful and even essential means of obtaining their political objectives, as they often do in order to justify their decision to join the IRA instead of Sinn Féin. The following testimonies set out below show various interviewees' reasons for joining the IRA instead of the political wing of the republican movement:

'I wasn't interested in joining Sinn Féin. Certainly in my time in the republican movement it was a case of, if someone didn't qualify or wasn't good enough to be in the army they were steered into Sinn Féin.'[89]

'I have never been a member of Sinn Féin, I was member of the republican movement, the armed republican movement, not Sinn Féin. I never had much time for the whole Sinn Féin side of it. It was reactionary myself joining the republican movement, even though I always had political ideas in my head. But at that time I didn't see Sinn Féin as something I wanted to be a member of, they done a lot of talking and very little else and I felt that the time was for action, we had talked enough. I don't like that talking sort of side of it, I always felt it was always open to compromise.'[90]

It is interesting to compare the views of these two former activists, who joined the Provisional IRA at the beginning of the 1970s, with those of two other republicans who joined in the second half of the 1980s and at the beginning of the 1990s.

'Sinn Féin were not as strong as they are today. I felt Sinn Féin was just sort of in the background, I wanted to be to the forefront of the struggle, I felt that Sinn Féin's role was sort of behind the scenes. The politics behind the scenes just wasn't, I didn't feel that it was strong enough to put the Brits out. Once I had read up I came to the conclusion, like a lot of my friends, that the only way the British know is force. There's no politicking your way out of this situation with these people, the only thing they would know and understand is armed force, so that's the reason I joined the IRA.'[91]

'I think then still the army [the IRA] had more impact, it was more hands on, you could go out and do something and vent your anger at them. I never really thought of it at the time, joining Sinn Féin. I wouldn't be a very political person, so it was more the army, I could show more, I could stand up more, where in Sinn Féin I know I'm not very politically well spoken and I wouldn't have been able to have as much impact. (...) there was always that thing in your head, like, is it going to be effective, are you going to make a difference, but then there's only one way of finding that out: go in and try your best.'[92]

Despite the improvements to the party's organisational structure which had taken place in the two decades between the time the different activists had joined, the younger of the two quoted immediately above still argued that his decision was based on the belief that the IRA 'still had more impact' than Sinn Féin, which explained his preference for the use of violence to activism in a political party. The political option did therefore exist but it was rejected by this volunteer on the grounds that it did not guarantee the immediate satisfaction of the interests which he claimed to be pursuing, largely because of the limited popular support which it received. This is yet another example which shows how the argument that presents violence as the only viable means of attaining republican objectives does not adequately explain the real reasons for many young people becoming involved in IRA terrorism, as can be seen from the testimonies set out below. It is again necessary to examine this conviction about the effectiveness of terrorism, bearing in mind that factors such as youth, idealism, and pure emotions were very much present, making potential recruits more receptive to a series of values which favoured the use of violence over peaceful action. Consider the admission of one of these activists, who chose to join the IRA with 'the hope of it being effective' despite the fact that 'it was drawn out over the thirty years and it hadn't achieved it'.[93] This realistic admission casts some doubts on the belief that 'the IRA were a successful guerrilla army',[94] which was the reason given by other activists to justify their activism within the armed wing of the movement instead of the political one.

It is also very important to bear in mind that since the early 1970s the IRA campaign was not aimed at eliminating the grievances which at the end of the 1960s led to the initial demands for equal rights and a reform of the state, but focused instead on the 'national question'. This is a factor which Danny Morrison, a leading member for many years of both the IRA and Sinn Féin, used in 1992 to question the continuation of the armed campaign[95] and which other activists also agree with, as the following testimony shows:

The main focus was the national question. (...) Because when you take it, a lot of the people who were involved in the IRA maybe left school at fifteen or sixteen, what the fuck did they know about any other political philosophies and stuff? Who were their peers? Who was going to educate them? You had people coming up from the thirties, forties, fifties, sixties, who were great Catholics, great Nationalists but didn't know anything else. Weren't able to experience any other kind of cultures or influences of broader political situations. (...) Sinn Féin, it probably would have been a weak option, although in retrospect I think the people who were involved in Sinn Féin at that particular time were very brave because it is easy to be involved in any organisation if you are an anonymous face, you don't have the same if you are a public figure you are a marked figure, as well, like in terms of loyalists or whatever. More chance of being killed or set up.[96]

In a context such as that described by this activist, a much more critical analysis can be applied to the belief that violence was the only way of achieving the objectives which most of the nationalist community continued to pursue through the ballot box. While most nationalists had preferred the peaceful civil rights protests which, between the late 1960s and early 1970s, had succeeded in reducing the level of inequality between the two main communities in Northern Ireland, republicans had a different goal, namely what they called 'national rights'. From the republican perspective, civil rights would only be achieved after 'national rights' – the unification of the north and south of Ireland – were obtained, something which, they argued, could only be guaranteed by violence. Some former IRA members challenge this exaggeration about the effectiveness of violence in the following way:

The clearest possible answer is we didn't need an armed struggle to generate three or four members of parliament. The sad thing is that we had to put the armed struggle away to learn the very simple lesson that people would vote for Sinn Féin-type ideals in the absence of armed struggle, but during armed struggle they wouldn't. The other point is that never having tried any politics in 1969, 1970, 1971, 1972, 1973, never having tried a political movement how can they possibly justify that we needed all these killings, deaths, hunger strikes and multiple suffering on all sides to get four MPs elected! I mean, fuck! You can't justify that claim because we never tried the other route. It is not possible to justify the armed struggle when we've never tried the political struggle, where was there any evidence of a political struggle from the republican movement in the late sixties or early seventies? There wasn't any! We'd killed off Sinn Féin and we kicked them across the border, there were no Sinn Féiners.[97]

As mentioned earlier, while in prison in 1978, Shane O'Doherty published a letter in which he stated that there was no justification for the IRA's use of violence. In his opinion, the movement of which he had been a member had not explored other possible courses of action before having resorted to violence, nor had it properly assessed the costs and results that the use of violence would have, since the objective pursued was not 'worth' the suffering inflicted.[98] O'Doherty recalls how some Sinn Féin members were concerned about the republican militaristic approach: 'What is the point of all this bloody banging, shooting and bombing? Who is going to be exploiting this for political reasons? Where's the political arm going to be, the negotiating arm? And people mentioned like "negotiating" and everybody went "oh fuck, Michael Collins, fuck that, we're not going to negotiate we're going to win", you know. So in fact these guys were frozen out, and they ended up across the border in Donegal living in terrible conditions like sort of half on the run but never having done anything. And if you mentioned politics, if you talked politics in your IRA group they would sort of say "Ah, are you going fuckin' weak on the armed struggle? Have you not got the balls for the armed struggle? Sure politics is fuckin' going nowhere." We didn't want to be Sinn Féiners, we wanted to be IRA men, who were heroes and patriots, dead or alive.'[99]

Idealism was clearly a dominant force for O'Doherty and other young recruits, who preferred to be 'IRA men, who were heroes and patriots, dead or alive'. This idealism, which had a strong romantic and emotional content, affected the rationalisation process of a reality which, according to the republican viewpoint, meant that the use of violence was the only viable method. The testimonies of republicans themselves makes it clear that the problem was not the lack of alternatives, since these did exist, but rather that the movement did not want to use them. This point is evidenced by the split in the republican movement between the Official and Provisional IRA which occurred when the former opted to explore political alternatives, a decision that led them to call a ceasefire in 1972. Those who formed the Provisionals after the split in late-1969–early-1970 rejected the proposal to participate in the parliaments of London, Belfast and Dublin. Although Sinn Féin was a proscribed organisation until May 1974, the authorities took a flexible approach to it. Very often its members were not arrested and were allowed a fair amount of freedom to take part in public life, as is shown by the fact that a number of its candidates stood in successive elections. Detentions did, however, take place when express support for the IRA was given. For example, the Sinn Féin Vice President Maire Drumm was arrested following an incendiary speech in a demonstration held in the streets of Derry in July 1971, when she called on people to 'avenge' the deaths of those Catholics who had been killed in disturbances with the British army some days earlier.[100] As Gerry Adams has recognised, 'Sinn Féin was eclipsed by the IRA, and there was little appetite for political work of the more conventional kind'.[101] Within the movement differences of opinion existed about the need to take part in elections because of the legitimacy that this would confer on institutions to which both the IRA and Sinn Féin were opposed, even if this was done according to the traditional republican principle of abstentionism, whereby those candidates elected abstained from taking their seats. The opinion of Adams on this question is significant because it confirms that the political alternative did exist, but it was not chosen because of the movement's own incompetence. In his view, boycotting elections was 'short-sighted', but 'the reality was that, irrespective of elections' republicans 'were politically ill-equipped'.[102]

The deliberate submission of Sinn Féin to the IRA dictated by republican leaders was maintained throughout the 1970s despite the fact that in 1973 and subsequent years one of its leaders, Ruairi O'Bradaigh, considered the possibility of taking part in various elections in order to counteract the popularity of the SDLP in the nationalist community.[103] The Army Council, the most important IRA body, rejected this possibility and confirmed that 'Sinn Féin should come under Army organisers at all levels'.[104] In the second half of the 1970s, the isolation and weakness of republicans was such that its leaders advocated 'the construction of a new Irish Republican Army' that would have a cell-like structure, emphasising that its activists would have to 'control all sections of the movement'. Thus, although the 'radicalisation of Sinn Féin' was proposed on the basis of its participation in protest actions on social and economic issues, this process was totally controlled by the IRA leadership, and the supreme authority of the movement's armed wing was therefore consolidated. This led an IRA member to make the following assessment: 'the so-called struggle or revolution in Ireland happened arse about face. For many years, Sinn Féin was simply a mouthpiece of the IRA.'[105]

Unlike what happened following the IRA ceasefire declaration in 1994, therefore, in the 1970s the main republican faction – the Provisionals – dismissed the possibility of using exclusively political means to reform Northern Ireland, opting instead to try to destroy it. The reform process, which started at the end of the 1960s and gathered force during the first half of the 1970s, was complemented by a greater involvement of the British government through different political initiatives aimed at pacifying the region, a process which the Irish government was also involved in. This heightened the IRA's crisis of legitimacy. As former IRA member Anthony McIntyre has written, the organisation 'went into a serious decline' when the material needs which had nurtured its existence were satisfied between 1972 and 1974.[106] In the opinion of another volunteer, at that time 'apart from the British occupation, there is very little injustice there that's worth an armed struggle, and an armed struggle can't win on that basis'.[107] Despite this, republicans persisted with an extremist approach which continued to interpret violence as a basic instrument of its strategy. The contrast between the republican position in the two periods is summed up by another former IRA member interviewed by the author:

'I think people did begin to see change in the sense that the electoral systems were completely transformed, the allocation of housing, which had been a major issue of contention was passed to the hands of the Housing Executive and everybody in this country today will be fairly wholesome in their praise of the work of the Housing Executive. Many of the powers that were abused by local councils were removed. The whole gerrymandering thing of electoral boundaries and stuff was taken out of the control of local politicians and put into the hands of objective individuals and groups, and the whole issue of discrimination and employment was changing quite dramatically, young Catholics were moving into senior positions in various organisations, the whole growth of the voluntary sector in Northern Ireland, are all indications of quite serious attempts to reform. But I remember using the word reform in the early seventies and being looked at as if I was a crazy person. "Reform? You can't reform society, it has to be revolutionised." And I sit now and talk to people that denigrated me then and called me a fool, now being fully in support of the current peace process which is a process of reform.'[108]

'We were against class alliances. I mean, we considered Fianna Fáil and the SDLP to be the enemy also,'[109] stated another former IRA activist, with reference to the 1970s and 1980s, thus showing the contradictions of the republican strategy which chose to look for such alliances with constitutional nationalism in the 1990s which had previously been vehemently rejected. What, then, caused this change? As this book shows, idealism must be seen as being more important than the spurious claim that there was no alternative to the use of violence. Idealism, political immaturity and the absolutism that this led to, as well as the manipulation that existed in the republican movement, was used to attract young recruits and maintain their activism. The following testimonies reveal the mistake that was made in perpetuating the use of violence, justifying it as a response to external conditions that were quite separate from the republican movement, which prevented the development of a political current that was vital for the attainment of the objectives of the IRA and Sinn Féin.

'Armed struggle alone was never going to achieve it, and I think most people recognise that it hasn't achieved it in any country. Republicans, in the last thirty years, started off with their armed struggle without the political control over it, and a classic guerrilla war is supposed to be a war which is directed politically, not vice versa. It wasn't sufficient to win the struggle. In the early days, as a teenager, we thought this big romantic notion that we're going to drive the Brits out.'[110]

'When I remember the republican slogans of *Brits Out*, a slogan is only a slogan, you have to put some logic and some rationale to that slogan and I think I am now capable of doing that, twenty years ago I wasn't. *Brits Out* meant that was the solution. If the British Government just went, clearly it wouldn't have been a solution. Idealism, yeah, maybe to a certain extent, but naivety too.'[111]

This activist, like many others, concluded that the IRA had made a serious 'mistake' by ignoring for so long the 'primacy of politics' over violence.[112] The consequences of this mistake can be appreciated by examining the fanaticism that guided republicans, as is recognised by the former IRA activists who are quoted below.

'Because I had been involved, I can understand why people are involved. I can understand the heart and the passion, the desire that leads them into that. At one point, I would have went out and killed every policeman I could get my hands on. You get so tied up in the warfare that you lose humanity, you absolutely lose your sense of reality, compassion for people. And I was saying, I would rather see England getting bombed, than Ireland getting bombed and I would have said: "why should people here die, go over and bomb the football pitches in England, really, bring the message home to England". And I would have said things like that and at the same time, I would have thought I was a very nice, kind, considerate guy, but my whole vision was coloured and so influenced, there was absolutely nothing I wouldn't have did.'[113]

'When I left Long Kesh in 1976 I think maybe you could say that I was indoctrinated to such an extent that I believed the revolution was going on outside the gates of the prisons. Of course that was not the case. Because I was young and I was an idealist – you could say to some extent I was fanatical. And by this time I had become very heavily politicised. Idealism tends to border on fanaticism to some extent, and sometimes within a given situation it is hard to differentiate between one and the other. But fanatical in that I really did believe that we could achieve our objective which was the establishment of a thirty two county democratic socialist republic. And you are talking to someone who had never been in Dublin except for once in his life! Do you understand? Somebody who went into jail, shot at seventeen and then in jail at eighteen and came out at twenty. Do you understand? There is a degree of realism which isn't there in that the idealism is always to the fore and especially when you are being young and fanatic. The idealistic notion does leave you. The element of real politics enters into the thing and you start to look around you and say "Hold on, there are a million unionists here who share a part of this island", and then after a while we realised that the South don't really want to know us and the people down south ... the further the south you go, you may as well be in Cuba!'[114]

Although some republicans recognise that the fanaticism and idealism to which they refer started to be challenged by greater realism, the violence continued. The leaders of the IRA and Sinn Féin publicly justified the perpetuation of the terrorist campaign until 1994 on the grounds that it was the only available tactic. This was clearly not true, since the peace process was made possible quite simply because republicans chose options that they had previously rejected whenever they had been offered at different moments over the previous three decades. The following words of an activist illustrate this point: 'My aspiration is a united Ireland, but it has to be through the consent of the people, whereas before I would have said, "no, fuck them [the unionists], there has to be a united Ireland or nothing", like, you understand what I mean, you have to work with the situation.'[115]

Fanaticism, together with the ideological manipulation through factors typical of groupthink, decisively influenced republican strategy. It should be recalled that many of those interviewed for this book stated that they joined the republican movement largely as an emotional response without ideological reasons being particularly important for them. However, the extremist and absolutist principles summed up in the general expression of 'Brits out' were the ones which motivated activists to remain in the movement, after their initial 'gut' reaction had made them become members. It would be logical to expect that if the decision to use violence was taken on the basis of essentially emotional criteria, the correctness of such a decision should later be weighed up in order to confirm or modify the chosen course of action. This appears to have happened in the case of certain republicans during their imprisonment, as is shown by the following testimony of a former Official IRA activist: 'So when I went in the second time, I began to study. I had got married in the meantime, my wife was expecting a baby, there I was, going in jail, I was only what, twenty, I was facing another, best part of my twenties in jail. It was just a horrific time, it was a real nightmare time. And I remember this time saying to me, there was a great sign when, when we went up the steps into the A Wing, and I remember walking up the steps and we went into this cell and the cell was just a wee narrow nineteenth century cell and someone had wrote on the wall: "Mother Ireland, get off my fucking back!", you know, here's me: "that's just how I feel!"'[116]

It should come as no surprise that such reflections were more common in the Official IRA than in the Provisionals, since the latter group, like the INLA, went to greater lengths to maintain internal unity. Given the real possibility that IRA members would engage in similar reflections to those of the former Official IRA activist quoted above, the control mechanisms available to such a tight-knit group were used to prevent large numbers from questioning their activism, as will be seen in the following chapters. Besides, the situation which former young recruits faced after serving prison sentences was not at all favourable to the survival of a republican movement which was also witnessing how levels of popular support were falling. A republican activist illustrates this point, recalling the moment he left prison:

> The most painful thing for me was not to see the same degree of support. First of all people weren't coming to say to you 'I am leaving the key in my door if you have to come in through my door' – 'I am leaving you the key of my car if you need my car.' For example, people were not contributing to the supporting of the prisoners. Not everybody. There were people who [before] would have come out and supported you for one reason or another – maybe not for the same political ambitions as you had but because of their gut reaction to what was happening, and [now] they were saying 'hold on, things will have to change but we are going to change them in another way, I can't support this here, I can't endorse this here'.[117]

In these circumstances, the ideological manipulation of activists was particularly necessary, and the hunger strikes provided a powerful tool in this respect. As a prominent republican leader stated, 'I have no doubt that the deaths of hunger strikers encouraged young people to join the IRA, no doubt about it. They joined for an emotional reason, but they had to fight for ... you have to get them to fight for a principle reason (sic), not just emotionalism'.[118] These 'principles' were inculcated and protected through cast-iron discipline, which facilitated the perpetuation of violence motivated by the interests of the group leaders, despite the question marks that had been raised as to its true effectiveness. The questioning of the use of violence was clearly present from the early 1980s, as the following testimonies explain:

> 'The realisation that we weren't a national liberation army came long before 1986 when I came out of the jail. First of all the realisation was that we were a very small minority. It is a hard thing to admit that there, after all the deaths and all the suffering and all. I think myself you had to say "fuck, we have to be realistic here, unless we are realistic we are going to live in a utopia". In many ways that is what jail is, jail is a utopia in itself and generates a utopia mind set. But when you come out into the real world you can make different assessments with a greater degree of realism and you can see how everything is panning out on the ground. In that you can judge for yourself how people have moved on, they want work, their priorities are different from yours. Your priority had been this grand idea of a thirty two county democratic socialist republic of workers and small farmers – fuck! Small farmers! They are doing very well in the EEC, thank you. And we had opposed the EEC!'[119]

'Inside prison we were involved in all sorts of debate and looked at where the struggle was going to and I think there was a begrudging recognition, although it wasn't spoke too loudly, that we couldn't complete the final phase of the classic struggles where you actually went in and took over power, so people began to talk and discuss.'[120]

Former IRA member Robert McClenaghan also admits that by the mid-1980s he had reached the conclusion that from a moral and political point of view the armed struggle was not 'appropriate', since it was incapable of attaining its fundamental objectives: 'You had started to learn the lessons from the hunger strike period. I personally felt the mass movement of people is crucial but then the whole idea of building up an electoral base as well and then building up the party as a viable instrument for change, a viable vehicle. (…) the contradiction, who takes supremacy? Does the party control the army or does the army control the party? But in terms of republican politics the army has always controlled political events and the army has always controlled the party. What you needed was a reversal that the party would take control of the entire movement, and then if it was tactically useful to use armed struggle then you would use it. But equally if it was tactically incorrect or unnecessary then you would make that political decision to withhold.'[121]

He then goes on to recognise that the terrorist campaign prevented public support being obtained and electoral gains being made, while explaining the reasons that, despite this, the violence had to continue: 'I always felt it was always a bargaining weapon in terms of the negotiation. We now know, it is now a public record, that from the late eighties, Martin McGuinness was involved in serious negotiations with the British government about some sort of resolution. But the armed struggle was still carrying on.'[122] Thus, during the 1980s and 1990s the IRA continued to attract young recruits, and the motivation that they most referred to was their desire to use violence 'to get the Brits out'. However, the IRA leaders were aware that this would not happen through the use of violence. In short, those who killed and died for Ireland did not do so for the reasons officially given by the IRA. Ultimately, the IRA's absolutist ideology, fuelled by its fanatical internal atmosphere, had disastrous consequences, as is illustrated by the death of ten republican prisoners on hunger strike in 1981, an episode that will be examined in the next chapter.

4

HUNGER FOR POWER

'Where the hell did we go wrong?'

'I would be afraid to say that it was not worth it'

On 3 October 1981 the inmates of the Maze prison ended their hunger strike, which had cost the lives of ten IRA and INLA members. In a statement written by Richard O'Rawe, the Provisional IRA's Public Relations Officer (PRO), the inmates called off their protest with the following words: 'There were several reasons given by our comrades for going on hunger strike. One was because we had no choice and no other means of securing a principled solution to the four year protest. Another, and of fundamental importance, was to advance the Irish people's right to liberty.' In an earlier part of the statement the British government was blamed for the 'murder' of their ten comrades, while the authorities and politicians of the Republic of Ireland were accused of being 'accessories to the legalised murder' of these men. Blame was also laid at the door of the SDLP as well as the Catholic Church, which was harshly criticised for having 'pressurised' the inmates' families into calling off their strike and for failing to back up the republicans' demands, thereby adopting an 'extremely immoral stance'. The criticism of their 'hypocrisy' and lack of 'moral fibre' was completed with the following diagnosis: 'The logical conclusion of this analysis is that nationalist pacifism in the Northern Ireland contexts dooms the nationalist population to sub-serviency, perpetuates partition, and thwarts the quest for a just and lasting peace in Ireland.'[1]

Two decades later, the author of this statement took a different line on such a crucial event in the Troubles.[2] O'Rawe came to see that republicans themselves should also take a great share of the blame for the events culminating in the death of the ten hunger strikers. His analysis, especially important given his high-ranking position within the IRA during this decisive period, describes the hunger strike as a clear example of groupthink, whereby an atmosphere existed in which individual criticism of any decisions taken by the group's leaders had little chance of success. As a result, the wrong decisions were taken, decisions that caused the protest to drag on unnecessarily. Like other senior IRA members who took part in the hunger strike,

O'Rawe claims that all these deaths could have been avoided and, in stark contrast to his earlier position, admits that 'there was another way'.

The IRA statement also shows how republicans considered that they were driven by an unavoidable necessity to go on hunger strike, in the same way that they regarded themselves as 'forced' to engage in armed struggle. The statement also claimed a higher moral ground for the hunger strikers in as much as they had been capable of such 'selflessness' by giving their own lives for the good of the 'Irish people'. Gerry Adams emphasised this superiority in one of the commemorations of the twentieth anniversary of the strikes when he declared that republicans should feel 'blessed to even have known, even to be remotely associated with these men who brought our struggle to a moral threshold'.[3] In an interview with the author, Pat McGeown, who kept up his hunger strike for 42 days until his family intervened, reflected on this and other symptoms of groupthink such as the illusion of invulnerability. This feeling contributed to shoring up the conviction that the decisions taken during the hunger strikes were the right ones and the belief that the event strengthened republicans, as can be inferred from McGeown's words: 'This gives you a sort of a strength for you can say, "we can face anything", sort of the batteries are fully charged, "we can face anything". We are all fairly close in all ways, but the bond that holds us together is the fact that we are all totally of the belief that we were right. Once you have got that, it's not a case of convincing each other, it's a case that people would view me within the community here with certain amount of respect that sometimes it owes me because I don't see myself as any different, but I think that with all of us [who were on hunger strike], people recognise in a way, what I said earlier, that we sort of represent what [the struggle] is all about, and that bond means that we are all actually fairly close.'[4]

But for this very reason, as with the armed struggle, the qualms expressed by certain republicans about the hunger strike cast very unsettling doubts on the true significance of the decision to let ten men die. According to the republican mindset, the 'sacrifice' of the hunger strikes and of the armed struggle 'must have been worth it'. In other words, it was essential to be able to claim that 'these men had not died in vain'. According to a former IRA volunteer and brother of Patsy O'Hara, one of the hunger-strike casualties, republicans are 'in a situation where they can't say to their people the war was for nothing'.[5] This was borne out by another volunteer who claimed that it would be very difficult for him to say unequivocally that the IRA's campaign 'was not worth it': 'Purely on an emotional side, because when I think about it, when I think about of all the things I've been involved with and people I've been involved with and people who are dead now, I would be afraid to say that it was not worth it in case I was interpreted as desecrating the memory of people who are dead.'[6] In fact, and contrary to the official republican interpretation of the hunger strikes, this event confirms that, as the brother of one of the casualties recognised, the deaths were indeed 'in vain'.[7]

Republicans turned to hunger strike to claim the status of political prisoners after their 'Special Category Status' was ended in 1976. The start of this process, known as criminalisation, was rejected by republican prisoners, who began the so-called 'blanket protest' by refusing to wear the uniform given to them by the prison system, choosing instead to wrap themselves only in a blanket. Faced with the indifference of the authorities and public opinion, the protest was stepped up, the so-called 'dirty protest' beginning in 1978, when the inmates decided to smear their cell walls with their own excrement. In early 1980 republicans laid down five demands whereby they hoped to win recognition of their political status: the right to wear civilian clothes, the right to choose not to do prison work, free association with other prisoners, the right to receive weekly visits and parcels as well as other correspondence and the full restoration of the remission system, which had been abolished as a response to their protests. The lack of results prompted them to gear up their protest anew; in October of that year they opted for a hunger strike, called off in December in the republicans' belief that they had finally reached an agreement with the British government that met their demands. However, the hoped-for settlement came to nothing and in March 1981 the IRA member Bobby Sands started a new hunger strike that ended in his death; nine republican inmates followed suit. The strike was called off definitively in October of that year. Shortly afterwards the British government granted the original demands that had given rise to the protest.

Brendan Hughes, who in 1980 held the post of Officer Commanding (OC) of the IRA prisoners in the Maze prison and who, in the first hunger strike with six other men, kept up his fast for fifty-three days, accepted years later that the decision made was a miscalculation since they did not really know Margaret Thatcher's personality.[8] In his opinion the experience of the first error should have avoided a second hunger strike, which would finally take such a high toll: 'I believe it could have been [avoided], yeah. I've spoken about this before to people and I've always been advised by people like Jim Gibney, Danny Morrison and others that it would be too hurtful for the families of the dead hunger strikers to tell the truth. But that was the other attempt to bury the truth.'[9] As suggested by Hughes and O'Rawe, what republicans tried to cover up was the catastrophic error of judgement that led to the death of ten of their comrades. In his thought-provoking, case-based study of how groupthink might impinge negatively on a group's decision-making processes, Janis analyses several historical mistakes made by American political leaders. One of the examples used is the process that led to the disastrous Bay of Pigs invasion decision, prompting the American President to wonder: 'How could I have been so stupid?'[10] These sentiments were echoed by Richard O'Rawe about the hunger strike when he said: 'I couldn't comprehend how things had come to this. Where the hell did we go wrong?'[11]

Initially the Army Council, the IRA's ruling body of which Gerry Adams was a member, had expressed its reservations about calling the second hunger strike, fearing that it might distract attention away from the campaign of violence outside the prison. Brendan McFarlane, the new OC of the IRA, nicknamed 'Bik', and Richard O'Rawe, also seemed to be against a prolonged strike, both considering that the threshold of four deaths should not be passed. When replacements for the first four hunger strikers were called for in case the former should die, the Army Council sent communiqués to the prison suggesting that candidates should take their time before going ahead with their decision. O'Rawe, however, rejects the official republican line that portrays the Army Council as 'powerless' in the face of the prisoners' will to go ahead with the strike against the desires of the leaders of the movement. It should be borne in mind that at no time did the republican leadership give orders forbidding their men to go on hunger strike. This is a crucial point, since, as O'Rawe confirms, the orders would have been obeyed in the interest of group discipline. To have disobeyed the orders would have been tantamount to a 'mutiny' by the prisoners, something he regards as inconceivable.[12] Had the Army Council ordered the end of the strike, no IRA volunteer would have disobeyed such an order from the leadership of the organisation, since, as the IRA Green Book states, 'all recruits entering the Army declare that they shall obey all orders issued to them by their superior officers and by the Army Authority', stressing that 'you obey orders, whether you like them or not'.[13]

Therefore the leaders inside and outside the prison accepted the protest, harbouring the same fears about what the aftermath might be which O'Rawe described as a protracted hunger strike with little hope of a successful conclusion in which people died simply to show that they could not be defeated. Despite these contradictory stances, the hunger strike went ahead and potential replacements for the protesters were named in an attempt to put pressure on the British. As O'Rawe adds, the appearance of pressure was nevertheless based on the 'static position' that 'under no circumstances was Joe McDonnell [the fifth volunteer who was to go on hunger strike if one of the other four died] going to be allowed to die'.[14] The republican strategy was doomed to failure because in spite of all of the objections to a prolonged strike, McFarlane allowed for the possibility of a change of position in the light of 'changing circumstances', as revealed in a statement sent to the leaders outside.[15] There was, therefore, no 'static position'; a change in tactics was possible and, as events transpired, did in fact occur.

Bobby Sands died on 5 May 1981 and was immediately replaced by Joe McDonnell. A week later the second hunger striker died and was replaced by another volunteer, who in turn was replaced by Martin Hurson a few days later because of an ulcer disorder. After the third death on 21 May, a new volunteer, Kieran Doherty, joined the hunger strike. On this same day the fourth republican died, whereupon another replacement, Kevin Lynch, was brought in. All these men plus another two were to die in the following months despite the initial 'static position' of republicans, who had stressed that 'under no circumstances' could more than four men be allowed to die. The logic underpinning this situation was as tragic as it was ridiculous: republicans kept up the pretence that they were prepared to die to continue with their protest, in order to pressurise the British government into a U-turn, so the deaths came one after the other, betraying a determination that was as tenacious as it was unsuccessful. O'Rawe himself summed it up in the following way: 'I put myself in Margaret Thatcher's shoes; the only conclusion I arrived at was that, sooner or later, our protagonists' strength was bound to sap, and they would inevitably cave in to the constant pressure of endless deaths, coupled with dwindling support, and not a hint of a solution in sight.'[16] Even McFarlane agreed that the time would come when people would get used to the prisoners' deaths, just as they had grown accustomed to the violence outside when it had reached an 'acceptable' level.[17] Despite this, republicans kept up their protest, being swept along by a strategy doomed to failure, as O'Rawe described: 'The crucial question was that, if the British were to remain steadfast, would we be able to recognise that they were not for bending? In other words, at what point would we say enough is enough?'[18]

Trapped in a vicious circle, republicans agreed to 'step up' the process, bringing new men into the hunger strike, a decision that was once again approved by the Army Council. 'Can I have the Big Boy's [Gerry Adams'] attitude to 'scalation?' McFarlane had asked in late May before receiving a positive answer from his superiors.[19] Meanwhile secret negotiations between various parties went on in an attempt to stop the protest, which seemed less and less likely to achieve its initial goals. As O'Rawe explained, the 'battle of criminalisation had been won' after four republicans had died on hunger strike and the republicans had obtained excellent election results in both the north and the south.[20] Before his death, Bobby Sands had been elected as Member of Parliament in Westminster for the constituency of Fermanagh, South Tyrone, in a by-election held on 9 April 1981. Another two republican prisoners, Kieran Doherty and Paddy Agnew, were elected members *in absentia* of the Irish Parliament in the general elections of June that year. Doherty died in August after 73 days on hunger strike. One of the participants in the first hunger strike summarised the importance of such an achievement as follows: 'In many ways you could argue that we achieved political status with the election of Bobby Sands. In the eyes of Ireland, we had, in that constituency of Fermanagh and South Tyrone, a clear majority of the people that believed Bobby Sands was a political prisoner. That ultimately is the verdict of the people that were first and foremost our target constituency.'[21]

'If he goes on hunger strike, he's going to die'

In this context republicans made another mistake in rejecting a possible solution offered by *The Irish Commission for Justice and Peace* (ICJP), an organisation set up in 1968 by the Irish Bishops' Conference. One of the reasons for their rejecting this possible way out of the hunger strike was the republican demand for the negotiations with the British to be conducted directly with the IRA leaders outside – Gerry Adams and Danny Morrison – rather than through intermediaries. Although several relatives of the hunger strikers had shown their readiness to consider the proposals for reaching an agreement made by the clergy, this was rejected by the republican movement. Messages sent out of the prison by McFarlane warned of the danger involved in the work being carried out by various Catholic clergymen, including the priest Denis Faul, whom the republicans had dubbed 'the Menace' because of his constant criticism of the movement: 'I think we need to get those families on the right line of thought. Now it won't be easy, I know. I have boxed the hunger strikers to ensure they are 100 per cent sound on our position. That they leave no one in any doubt that we make the decisions and they get the points across to their families and bring them round.'[22] As O'Rawe now acknowledges, the demand for Adams and Morrison to be the negotiators was 'naïve', adding another stumbling block to the original five demands that had prompted the strike. This demand showed that the IRA leaders were in total control of the situation, and the volunteers were mere pawns in the game. Witness the fact, for example, that all the replacements had to be vetted first by the Army Council. The prisoners' subordinate role was also reflected in another message sent by McFarlane on 28 June to the leaders about the ICJP's different proposals:

> The alien elements (Church, SDLP and Haughey [Irish prime minister]) have already succeeded in undermining our position greatly. Families of hunger strikers appear ready to grab what comes as a feasible settlement. (...) if we choose to continue with the hunger strike we will be faced with a situation whereby Joe will die, followed by others and after X amount of deaths public opinion will hammer us into the ground, forcing us to end hunger strike with nothing to show but deaths that could have been avoided and a shattering defeat into the bargain ... if we can combat the undermining successfully and eliminate the prospect of a crushing defeat after further deaths then I feel we should at least maintain our position.[23]

This acknowledgement by the prisoners' representative is enormously significant, showing clearly the republicans' intransigence compared with the flexibility that the rest of the actors in the process seemed willing to show in the interests of finding a solution. Despite the negative consequences feared by McFarlane, republicans persisted in a suicidal strategy in which there was no sign at all of a contingency plan to 'combat successfully' that 'undermining' being suffered after the intervention of the 'alien elements' he alluded to. At the same time, popular support had dropped away alarmingly; republicans were unable to keep up their initial mobilisation capacity on the streets while they stepped up their campaign of violence. During the seven-month period that the IRA and INLA's hunger strikes lasted, they killed fifteen RUC policemen, eight British soldiers, seven members of the UDR regiment and fourteen civilians. This violence could only worsen the crisis, exacerbating the negative consequences for the hunger strikers, as is shown by the testimony of one of them: 'When I was on hunger strike my father came down and said to me "John, this is going to kill me and your mum", and he seen it in a very basic family way. He said "I understand what is happening but you have to remember one thing which is that what is happening outside is that UDR men, RUC men, British army are still being killed and blew up, there is still a campaign going on and so on and so on: how do you expect the British government to concede to these demands?"'[24]

The stubbornness shown by republicans was also reflected in a later message sent by McFarlane to Gerry Adams on 29 June: 'The question is, can we hope to move those people at all? They are insane – at least Maggie [Thatcher] is anyway. Joe [McDonnell] is a cert to die.'[25] A day later, following the British government's statement agreeing to consider proposals for changing the prison regime but stating that this could not take place while the authorities were being coerced, McFarlane considered the possibility of calling off the hunger strike. The reason for this *volte face* was his fear that the British gesture might be favourably received by the families and other high-profile participants in the process, thus damaging the prisoners' cause. Meanwhile the countdown continued for the men on hunger strike. In early July, the British government authorised the restoration of secret contacts with the republican movement through a member of the MI6 intelligence service nicknamed 'the Mountain Climber'. The British also authorised Danny Morrison, one of the IRA leaders, to visit McFarlane in prison. Two days later McFarlane sent O'Rawe a message containing the British government's proposals. In the latter's opinion, the proposals satisfied the republicans' demands and should be accepted.

According to O'Rawe, the only demand that seemed not to have been met was the right to mix freely with other prisoners, although he believed that this could be obtained afterwards, as in fact occurred once the hunger strikes were called off: 'Did these concessions go far enough? Was the glass half-empty or half-full? I thought it was three-quarters full. In fact, the British had gone further than I had considered possible: I felt it was almost too good to be true. I asked myself how the British government would sell this in Westminster. But that was hardly our problem: the proposals were there in black and white, direct from Thatcher's desk. I thought that the offer was sufficient for us to settle the dispute honourably. As I saw it, the offer from the Mountain Climber had reduced the gap between his bottom line and our maximum demands to the point that it wasn't then worth more comrades dying.'[26]

O'Rawe claims that McFarlane had initially agreed with him on the need to accept the Mountain Climber's proposals. However, this offer, in which the government also guaranteed its readiness to make a public announcement of the concessions it would make, was rejected by the IRA's Army Council as insufficient. In a second round of talks, which began on 19 July, the government made a new offer brokered by the Mountain Climber, which the Army Council again rejected. According to the dominant republican view of the hunger strike, the Army Council could not go against the volunteers' unswerving determination to continue with the strike until such time as all demands had been met. Nonetheless the revealing message sent by McFarlane on 22 July expressing the IRA's rejection of the latest British proposal showed that the decision was taken by republican leaders outside the jail. In this message McFarlane asked Gerry Adams to explain 'how far the British went',[27] which shows that neither McFarlane nor the prisoners were aware of all the details of the offer that might have saved their lives. As O'Rawe and Brendan Hughes confirmed to this author, the hunger strikers were never made aware of the concessions that the British were prepared to make before the Army Council rejected them. Hughes, a very respected figure within the republican movement, criticised how the leadership outside the prison made these decisions which resulted in the death of the IRA inmates: 'I accept in a situation like that there has to be secret talks, has to be secrecy of some sorts, but when you are talking about men's lives that are just dwindling away, they were entitled to the truth, the whole truth and nothing but the truth.'[28]

As regards the Mountain Climber's proposals, it is worth noting that, *after* they had been turned down by the IRA, McFarlane, who as we have seen was unaware of the details of the second offer, stated in a message to Adams that 'it would be wrong to capitulate',[29] even though in previous messages he had referred to the need to call off the hunger strike if after a while the British showed no signs of meeting all of the IRA's demands. The IRA continued to raise the stakes although it expressed gratitude for 'the Mountain Climber's "frankness"' when stating that the British could go no further.[30] In stark contrast to the republicans' bottom line set initially, they decided to go ahead even though there was no prospect of the British making further concessions. It should be emphasised that this decision to continue was taken at a time when six men had already lost their lives and the original limit of four deaths had been exceeded.

As O'Rawe admitted, after having tried to rationalise the wisdom that led the Army Council to reject the proposal, he could not avoid 'silently questioning the hitherto unquestioned hinterlands' of the leadership tactics.[31]

Note that the questioning of the authority's infallibility was done 'in silence'. This was one more sign of the groupthink pervading the upper echelons of the republican movement. This is clearly borne out by a message sent by McFarlane to Gerry Adams informing him of hunger striker Pat McGeown's doubts about the tactics handed down from the top. On 26 July McFarlane wrote: '... had a long yarn with Pat Beag [McGeown] this morning and impressed upon him the necessity of keeping firmly on the line. I explained that independent thought was sound, but once it began to stray from our well considered and accepted line then it became extremely dangerous. He accepted what I said alright. Also I stressed the need for all of us to have confidence in you lot.'[32] Thus, so-called 'independent thought' was considered to be acceptable only if kept within limits that guaranteed the volunteers' adherence to the party line. This attitude is typical of a movement within which orders from the top were obeyed as if 'we were sheep', as one of its former members put it.[33]

At the time McFarlane was writing these lines, six men had already lost their lives as a result of the hunger strike and others were likely to follow suit shortly. The volunteers' resolve was slipping, which was unsurprising given the ongoing tension and the pressure exerted by relatives and intermediaries. McFarlane explained this again to Gerry Adams in another message dated 28 July.[34] Other hunger strikers came to the same conclusion as McGeown and considered the need for a 'change of tactic'. McFarlane's reaction on this occasion once more betrays the thought and control mechanism being used: 'I told him straight that the decision was theirs – either we pursue course for five demands or we capitulate. No in-between solutions.'[35] As can be seen, the prisoners' leader posed the problem in absolute terms, likening any consideration of options other than the ones he had proposed to a capitulation. Significantly, the volunteer on hunger strike explained 'that he wasn't on about "half a loaf", but just a possible change in tactics' to secure their demands. McFarlane's response to this explanation was forthright. As he informed Adams, 'I said that we should keep firmly on our line and not deviate in the slightest, because to do so spelt danger.'[36]

The logical conclusion to be drawn from this is that the terms in which McFarlane addressed this wavering prisoner weighed heavily on the behaviour of these individuals who had been taught to see themselves as 'soldiers', which meant that they had to toe the line and generally accept that the version of their leaders amounted to 'the absolute truth',[37] as another activist put it. The fact that the hunger strikers were expected to think long and hard before airing any critical views is shown by McFarlane's response to some of the prisoners' suggestion that he, as their leader inside the prison, should perhaps 'take a back seat' and allow the prisoners to negotiate personally with British government representatives. As McFarlane stated in a letter to Gerry Adams: 'I explained the position about my presence being essential at any negotiations and that a break in the line now would hammer us for the future. I said that you lot were in the best position to advise and to read the situation and that you had agreed that my presence is a must at any talks.'[38]

For any individual who belongs to a group, the denial of approval is important since the desire to conform can become a factor which determines behaviour. At times fear of isolation might be a more powerful influence on conduct than making a mistake per se.[39] As several of the volunteers interviewed for this book stated in relation to the dictates handed down by their superiors, 'they would always obey orders even if they didn't agree with them'. Elisabeth Noelle-Neuman has highlighted a similar tendency in explaining the origins of the phenomenon she has termed 'the spiral of silence'. According to this theory, opinions receiving express support take on an appearance of greater strength compared with those that are silenced. An upward spiral may then set in whereby a given discourse or viewpoint is made to override all others that have not been expressed as forcefully. The latter views are then sidelined and those who hold them tend to be ostracised.[40] This type of psychological process clearly existed during the hunger strikes. Republicans were obviously more worried about receiving group approval than ensuring that the decisions taken were really the right ones which would lead to adequate solutions. Those volunteers who initially dissented from 'the party line' ended up opting for self-censorship after group pressure was brought to bear on them, so as to avoid any threat to the group's cohesion, thus safeguarding the IRA's leaders from any serious questioning of their leadership. The groupthink theory therefore helps to explain why the wrong course of action initially decided on was maintained, causing more deaths.

The analysis of this process also helps to refute the 'official version' of the republican movement which claimed that the outside leaders could not call off the hunger strike since such a decision was the sole responsibility of the hunger strikers themselves. This was a useful fiction that Gerry Adams also made use of when asked personally by Father Denis Faul to call off the strike. Adams, who as has already been pointed out was by now one of the IRA's leaders, told the priest that the Army Council could not go against the will of the hunger strikers. As noted earlier, however, the leaders outside the prison in fact had an iron grip over the protest. This is shown by the successive messages sent by McFarlane to Adams, some of which have already been noted in earlier pages, to which we can add another, in which the prison leader told his superior that it was not his intention to lay down the policy to be followed by the Army Council.[41] Witness also a message dated 9 August in which McFarlane told Adams that, given the INLA's lack of any more replacements, he intended to use his own, i.e. IRA members, 'unless you feel we shouldn't for some reason or other'.[42] It should be recalled that it was the Army Council that rejected the British proposals, against the will of McFarlane and O'Rawe, showing an inflexibility that would make it the target for criticism, even from one of the hunger strikers, Pat McGeown.[43]

Bear in mind here also how other hunger strikers had expressed their worries about the IRA's tactic in continuing the protest, fears which had been passed on to the leaders outside. All this casts doubt on the idea that the prisoners would oppose any order from the Army Council calling off the strike.

Authors like Taylor claim that 'had the IRA given the order to end the strike, which constitutionally it could have done, it was virtually certain that the order would not have been obeyed'.[44] He adds that the prisoners considered that 'to accept anything less than what their comrades had died for would be betrayal'.[45] Nonetheless, it was not the prisoners who decided whether or not the proposals were really a 'betrayal', for they were rejected by their leaders outside without most of the inmates even becoming aware of their contents. Likewise, an analysis of what was really offered to them shows clearly that they would not be accepting 'anything less' than the goals their comrades had died for. Not only had the British conceded 'the essence of the five demands', as O'Rawe puts it, but it was obvious that public opinion had been won over in the criminalisation battle. Given the way in which the republican movement operates and is organised, expecting the leaders of the Army Council to leave decisions affecting the whole IRA and Sinn Féin strategy up to the strikers, whose physical state had greatly declined, is implausible. Neither can it seriously be argued that those leaders outside who had imposed McFarlane's leadership of the prisoners as 'obligatory' could not have called off the protest if they had wanted to.

The hunger strikers' ignorance of the context in which their life or death was being decided is also revealed in Pat McGeown's criticism of the Army Council's intransigent decision to throw out Thatcher's proposals, as he expressed it to McFarlane: 'How can the Brits know what we want – I don't even know.'[46] Subsequent messages sent by McFarlane to Adams informing him of McGeown's constant doubts suggest that the latter was being affected by the so-called 'spiral of silence' described above. McFarlane wrote that McGeown had finally overcome 'his inner conflicts' after having 'opened up', something that must have 'caused him much pain'.[47] It is hardly surprising, then, that in a context where any stepping out of line created such 'pain', dissidents should opt to follow the official version. As McGeown's case shows, the dissuasion was coupled with the requirement expressed by a figure of authority like McFarlane that McGeown must not express his doubts, on the grounds that these could be 'highly damaging to the morale' of his comrades.[48] It should not be forgotten that McGeown himself had been on hunger strike for several weeks by this time. His words in a personal interview with the author also show the intense conflict generated by any non-conformist behaviour, because it meant breaking 'an enormously strong bond' forged between them: 'One of the things I have seen in the hunger strikers was this tremendous compassion for everyone else, almost sort of saying, "I have to die in order for yous to be free and I don't have a problem

with it." That was something that always struck me, that that was the motivation of the hunger striker, it wasn't sort of that "I am gonna die. If I can live
that's exactly what I want to do. But if I have to die for yous to be free that's
what I'll do." We knew that when it comes right down to it we could rely on
each other.'[49]

Decisions therefore emanated from the Army Council, whose leaders left
it up to the prisoners to decide whether to accept a *fait accompli* or to
challenge it, with the tremendous difficulties implied for volunteers whose
behaviour was conditioned by such a powerful group dynamic. It is hardly
surprising, then, that one of the prisoners should think that at a certain point
he no longer felt they would be dying for 'political status' but because they
couldn't let their comrades down: 'They hadn't let us down and now it was
our turn, one by one, to follow them.'[50] In this climate, the testimony of the
brother of one of the republicans who joined the strike on 17 August is a
clear indication of the dangers facing any prisoner within an organisation
like the IRA who dared to voice any disapproval: 'I remember one comrade
at the time when I was objecting to the hunger strike, called me disloyal to
my brother. And it was the closest I ever came to killing another republican.
And I said, what you don't understand is that I want my brother to live, I
don't want him to fucking die, if he goes on hunger strike he is going to die,
and anybody who goes on hunger strike is going to die because Maggie
Thatcher is not going to give in here.'[51]

Contrary to the republican movement's official version of events, O'Rawe
claims that the decision to call off the strike came from the IRA leaders
outside the prison rather than from the prisoners themselves. This is much
more likely in the light of the circumstances described so far. This is also
borne out by the final events running up to the end of the protest on 3
October. Only a few days earlier, on 29 September, after five prisoners had
dropped out of the strike following family pressure, Brendan Hughes and
Richard O'Rawe suggested to McFarlane that the strike should be called off.
McFarlane straightaway informed Adams that some comrades had asked
him to consider the end of the strike on the grounds that their difficulties
were 'insurmountable', whereupon the IRA leader in the prison stated that
he would only consider such a course of action 'when I believe we have no
chance of regaining the top position and pushing forward towards a feasible
solution'. McFarlane then fell back on an oft-repeated formula in his communications: 'We do face a critical few weeks, but I believe that we can
overcome the problem. However, if we cannot, then the reality of the situation would dictate an entire reappraisal.'[52] After the loss of ten lives and
with another six volunteers on hunger strike, McFarlane comes across as
completely blinkered in his thinking, continually claiming that they could
'overcome the problem', incapable of seeing that the only fruits to be
obtained from the continued application of such logic were further deaths of
his own comrades.

None of the versions of the hunger strike which claim that it was the prisoners rather than the Army Council that really called off the strike has been able to explain what could have happened in the space of a few days to produce such a turn around from the position expressed by McFarlane so forthrightly at the end of September. There is nothing in the existing literature on this point that shows the prisoners' desire to go against McFarlane's fierce determination as expressed in the statement in question, a statement which also left no room for doubt about his position of command in the prison. It seems, therefore, more plausible that the really decisive factor after 29 September was the intervention of the leaders outside the prison, who wielded maximum authority in the organisation's hierarchical structure. As O'Rawe explains, a communication from the Army Council was received ordering the strike to end, aware of the fact that the difficulties were indeed 'insurmountable'.[53]

The IRA's decision-making process during the hunger strike, as detailed here, represents a clear example of collective ineffectiveness. It also shows important motivating traits of the republican mentality, for, as some of the main participants acknowledge themselves, through their actions they were now pursuing different objectives from those originally envisaged. In other words, the point was reached where people were no longer dying to obtain the five demands, which had by that stage been written off as unachievable; they were simply dying because they were incapable of acting in any way other than that adopted by the group at the start. This dynamic is also shown by another episode in this tragic litany of errors. Years after the protest, Pat McGeown lamented 'not having been more honest' with Thomas McElwee, one of the men who died, when the latter expressed his doubts about the decision to go on with the hunger strike. McGeown in fact shared his comrade's belief that the hunger strike should be ended but he did not admit this to McElwee because he thought this would flout the orders given by his superior, McFarlane, who had already warned him: 'Don't make your opinions known.'[54] Another of the hunger strikers who died, Micky Devine, had confessed to McGeown his belief that the protest should be called off, as the latter explained when describing the consequences of the spiral of silence: 'He says, "After I die someone has to make the decision." I said "That's crazy because if you think now that the decision has to be taken, then why not take it now before you die", and he said, "No." What he didn't say but what it boiled down to was that he didn't want to be the one who took the decision. He didn't want to be the one who appeared to save his own life.'[55]

It should be stressed here that the Army Council was aware of the qualms of some volunteers about 'the official line', but refrained from expressly supporting their opinions to avoid giving them the impression that their doubts should be voiced. A hugely telling fact here is that Gerry Adams deliberately avoided asking McGeown about his stance in a meeting held with some of the prisoners on 29 July, even though the leader of the Army Council had been previously informed of McGeown's criticisms. Had Adams wished to call off the protest he would only have needed to ask McGeown to express his opinions in front of the other volunteers. This is suggested by McGeown's silent acceptance of McFarlane's orders after being warned that he was 'going to collapse the whole hunger strike' if he expressed his doubts in front of other volunteers.[56] The testimony of O'Rawe also shows that the intervention of the IRA leaders would not have been disobeyed; rather it would have completely transformed the tragic situation. He nonetheless admits that his 'own silence was reprehensible' since he should 'have been stronger' and called for an end to the strike sooner than he did.[57] As O'Rawe revealingly acknowledges, his lack of courage prevented him from overcoming his submission to such rigid discipline, thus helping to produce the disaster.[58]

The above analysis shows the importance of certain variables in the decision-making process during the hunger strike. This same approach can also be used to contrast the series of mistakes made at that time with what must, instead, be regarded as a correct decision: the 1994 decision to end the armed struggle. The overriding logic during the hunger strike was that the initial decision should be stuck to, the slightest deviation being represented as amounting to betrayal or disloyalty. Any disagreement was defined in terms that only reinforced intransigence, regardless of whether or not the initial decision showed itself to be the right one. Any rethinking of this decision was headed off by the blanket consideration that it was right when it was taken and must be right thereafter, even if the consequences seemed to indicate the contrary. As I will explain below, the armed struggle was maintained on this basis. If the blanket rejection of change which prevailed during the hunger strike had also been applied to the use of violence, the IRA would not have called its ceasefire in 1994 and Sinn Féin would not have accepted a peace process based on an agreement that not only failed to guarantee its fundamental objectives but even called for republicans to forego some of their historic demands. Conversely, if the republicans had adopted a flexible approach to the hunger strikes, the result would have been quite different. Instead, they opted for a rigid, absolutist approach and it was this attitude which, for years, prevented any rectification of the decision taken at the end of the 1960s to engage in armed struggle, despite its obvious inefficacy.

'I think there was another way'

'The hunger strikes was something that I deeply opposed from the outset. I knew they were going to end in death. I think there was another way. But sadly people were not in the position to dictate other ways.'[59] Mickey McMullan's opinion, shared by other members of the IRA, prompted him to define the prison protest that resulted in the death of ten activists as an 'enormous moral blow'.[60] The tragic consequences were not limited to the loss of life of the hunger strikers, as a former member recalls: 'We created another monster because a lot of new volunteers came in 1981 who were prepared to do another twenty years just because of the hunger strike.'[61] This 'monster' created by republicans would be used by the leaders of an organisation that had opted for the calculated combination of violent methods and political means. This dual tactic, involving an attempt to strengthen Sinn Féin's political position while maintaining IRA violence, was the mainstay of a strategy that became known as 'the Armalite and the ballot box', after Danny Morrison summed up the movement's objectives in this historic phrase at Sinn Féin's annual conference in 1981: 'Who here really believes we can win the war through the ballot box? But will anyone here object if, with a ballot paper in this hand and an Armalite in the other, we take power in Ireland?'[62]

As republicans themselves admit, IRA leaders tried to take full advantage of the hunger strikes applying this dual strategy. Thus, as the IRA campaign was stepped up, the prisoners' hunger strike was maintained in the belief that the suffering of republicans crudely exposed the British government's intransigence and helped to rally the nationalist community around such a dramatic issue. The feelings whipped up by the hunger strikes were likely to draw in nationalist voters that might be repelled by violence, as the following activist points out: 'When Thatcher refused to compromise at all and they died and died it marked a change in the ground force of nationalists even and not just republicans. And that is something that was locked into by Adams and the rest and thought "shit we could use this, we could harness this".'[63] Sinn Féin's publicity director at the time agreed that the hunger strikes provided 'intensive pressure and moral blackmail'.[64]

Armed struggle continued until 1994 despite this tactic being questioned within the republican movement itself. Once again, as with the hunger strikes, the influence of groupthink helps to explain the reasons for sticking with an unsuccessful tactic. But these decisions were motivated not only by psychological factors; politics also played a very important part.[65] The decision of the leaders of the republican movement to continue using violence was reached on the strength of particular interests. As Brown has pointed out, groups desperately seeking internal unity are especially liable to take bad decisions.[66] The IRA undoubtedly wished to wield a form of control that was based on group unity; hence the fact that they subordinated most of their decisions to this end. By doing so, however, they were not really making any progress towards the republican movement's main objective: the British withdrawal from Northern Ireland. The dual strategy of violence and politics was incapable of achieving its fundamental objective due to the tensions it produced, as Danny Morrison himself pointed out years after his 'Armalite and ballot box' speech at Sinn Féin's annual Congress in October 1981. It was at this event that some leaders proposed Sinn Féin's participation in elections on a regular basis before finally obtaining a supportive vote from the majority of delegates. In stating his intention of fighting on two fronts at once – contesting elections while supporting IRA violence – Morrison acknowledged that he was 'playing to the gallery', 'pandering' to those whose sole commitment was the armed struggle in order to reassure them that they 'could do the two things together'. It was however evident that they could not, since, as Morrison himself recognised, the support republicans could get was limited while violence remained in place.[67]

The conclusion to be drawn from this admission is that the strategy advocated by Morrison himself and adopted by the IRA was doomed to failure. Morrison refers to the limited support that would be obtained through the armed struggle, which meant that the dual strategy would be incapable of obtaining the grassroots backing in the north and south of Ireland that the republicans needed for meeting their political goals. This is shown clearly by Sinn Féin's election results in the north and south in the eighties. In the elections to the Northern Ireland Assembly, created in 1982, Sinn Féin won 10.1 per cent of the votes, increasing this share a year later in the elections to the British parliament, where Gerry Adams won a seat for the West Belfast constituency with 13.4 per cent of the vote. This growth rate was not sustained, however. A year later the republican vote in the election to the European parliament was 13.3 per cent, and in the 1985 local elections, the Sinn Féin vote dropped sharply to 11.8 per cent, falling even further two years later to 11.4 per cent in the British general elections. The slide continued and in the 1989 local elections the republicans obtained only 11.2 per cent of the vote. In this same year, the elections to the European parliament showed a further decline in the Sinn Féin vote to only 9.1 per cent. In 1992 Adams lost the West Belfast seat, Sinn Féin's vote falling to only 10 per cent.[68] In the Republic of Ireland the situation was even bleaker for republicans. In 1982 two elections to the Dublin parliament were held. In the first one, Sinn Féin won 1 per cent of the votes and disappeared from the second election. In the next elections, held in 1987, the republican vote amounted to 1.9 per cent, falling to 1.2 per cent two years later. In 1992 it rose slightly to 1.6 per cent and it increased again in 1997 to 2.6 per cent of the vote.[69]

By 1985 Gerry Adams considered that it was 'fairly obvious' that there were contradictions between the armed struggle and the electoral strategy.[70] The question, then, was what sense did it make to stick to a strategy introduced to win elections and support when it was being totally undermined by the violence that the IRA refused to give up? Why not renounce such an apparently ineffective tool? Morrison argued that they would have to live with that situation because 'it was only going to be armed struggle that created the political changes'.[71] Even if Morrison's version was accepted, his words show that republicans were not going to achieve the traditional objectives laid down in the demand of 'British withdrawal' and 'self-determination of the Irish people as a whole'. These claims were rejected by the rest of the participants in the conflict, not only the British and the unionists but also the so-called constitutional nationalists in both the north and south, who, unlike the IRA and Sinn Féin, thought that the unification of Ireland could be achieved only by peaceful means and only if the majority of the Northern Ireland population gave its consent. The pressure that republicans wished to exert through the IRA proved to be counterproductive, and lost them the vote of those nationalists who rejected violence. Republicans aimed to back up their violence by increased political activity, which would in turn have a positive knock-on effect on the terrorist campaign. Such political consolidation was not in fact forthcoming due to the contradictions highlighted by several republican leaders and summed up by another activist as follows: 'The step into politics was to win support for armed struggle, it wasn't to solely engage in armed struggle or solely engage in political struggle as such. I think that they faced numerous contradictions which were impossible to resolve. How do you win support, electoral support, when people were blowing your houses up, or doing something like Enniskillen and so on and so forth?'[72] This logic led to a sort of vicious circle such as the one described in the previous account of the hunger strikes; it also forced republicans to justify their actions and the resulting deaths, which they had to explain away as serving some purpose. Nonetheless, the attitude of Sinn Féin's leaders during the peace process confirmed the ineffectiveness of a campaign of violence they have now abandoned, aware that for a long time it had hindered further political advances, as the following example shows.

After the signing of the Good Friday Agreement in 1998, Sinn Féin was criticised by those republicans who condemned the acceptance of a document that, as was pointed out by Jim Gibney, member of the party's executive, 'from a rigid republican perspective should be torn up'.[73] Another prominent leader, Danny Morrison, summed up the reasons for this opinion in the following terms: 'Republicans sit in an assembly they never wanted. The British government never gave a declaration of intent to withdraw. There is still a heavy British army presence in some nationalist areas. The police have not been reformed. The equality and justice issues have yet to be resolved.'[74] Morrison also added other 'bitter pills that the peace process had required republicans to swallow': the amendment of Articles two and three of the Irish Constitution, which until then had contained the Republic of Ireland's territorial claim over the Six Counties making up Northern Ireland, Sinn Féin ending its traditional policy of abstentionism (refusing to take part in institutions related to the British administration) and acceptance of the consent principle, under which a united Ireland could come about only with the consent of a majority of its people.[75]

The arguments used by Martin McGuinness to defend the IRA against the accusations of a sell-out in accepting all these points, which flew in the face of traditional republican ideology, are highly significant. In his opinion, if republicans wished to reach a political agreement that better reflected their interests, they should work towards winning more votes for Sinn Féin candidates. There was indeed no other option, given that republicans' interests clashed with those of other actors: the unionist parties, the British government and constitutional nationalism as represented by the SDLP and the Irish government. McGuinness therefore warned that republican aspirations would be met in the future only if Sinn Féin increased its share of votes, both in the north and south of Ireland, ruling out a recourse to violence.[76] This radical change raises some questions. Given that the use of violence restricts the republicans' vote-winning capacity and since it is votes that determine the influence of any political formation and the degree to which its demands are satisfied, then why did republicans take so long to make such an admission? What was the point of a campaign of violence that was incapable of guaranteeing the main nationalist goals and could not even meet the other more general nationalist aspirations, given the lack of interest shown in them by the representatives of democratic Irish nationalism in the form of the SDLP and the Dublin government? The weakness of the IRA and Sinn Féin prevented them from 'republicanising' the peace process; in fact, the political process ushered in by the IRA's renunciation of violence really amounted to a means of 'de-republicanising' Sinn Féin.[77] The outcome of the peace process effectively raises questions about the IRA's decision to continue with violence throughout recent decades, although pursuing the armed struggle did serve to keep the group together and meant that the leadership was able to avoid the problem of openly discussing the inherent difficulties with this tactic.

This analysis suggests that Morrison's claim of the need for armed struggle as a way of putting pressure on the British government could be construed as part of the deliberate tactic of 'playing to the gallery' which he referred to after admitting the limitations of the terrorist campaign. An article written by him in January 1992 seems to have the same objective. Published in *An Phoblacht*, the article explained the IRA's refusal to accept a ceasefire in return for Sinn Féin being admitted into political talks, arguing that this did not constitute an 'incentive' for 'sacrificing' its 'key form of pressure'.[78] It should also be borne in mind that the IRA's alleged pressure on the British government was offset by loyalist terrorism, posing the credible threat that any concessions by the British government to republicans would provoke an intensification of this violence. However, years later Morrison himself argued the following in defence of the IRA's ceasefire to facilitate Sinn Féin's entrance into a peace process that had not met their aspirations: 'It takes great courage to be pragmatic when you have been fundamentalist for so long.'[79] This lack of political and personal courage is probably a decisive factor in understanding why republican leaders kept up the violence for so many years despite the inherent contradictions in such a strategy.

In contrast to the above, some republicans insist that the armed struggle was kept up in the belief that the dual strategy of violence and parliamentarianism would be successful. The IRA campaign would keep 'the pot boiling', while the hypothetical growth of Sinn Féin would legitimise the violence.[80] Those who take this view argue that the IRA aimed to become more professional in the interest of stepping up its pressure; the importation of the huge arsenal of arms from Libya in the mid-1980s was an important factor in improving the effectiveness of its terrorist campaign. Morrison himself tellingly challenged this view when he stated that: 'There was a time when I believed, naively, probably until 1984, that Sinn Féin could overtake the SDLP. Although I predicted that it could be done, I began to realise around about 1984 that it could not be done while the armed struggle continued. I believe that others in the leadership were of the same opinion.'[81] The date when this decisive admission was made is crucial, for, as the words of such a prominent republican figure reveal, it was accepted from this moment on that Sinn Féin had to put up with this situation as a sort of necessary evil, even though it was not at all beneficial to the party's interests. This serious contradiction stems from the close relationship between the political and the armed wing of a movement integrated by the IRA and Sinn Féin. Clearly the political party and the terrorist group were not independent entities. The alleged separation of both wings was a fiction that their members have often tried to maintain over the years, albeit unsuccessfully given that it has been proved beyond doubt that certain leaders, such as Adams and Martin McGuinness, were simultaneously members of the top executive body of both organisations. As Morrison himself admitted in 1992, 'The fortunes of Sinn Féin and the IRA are inextricably linked: they have the same cause and ultimate objectives and their memberships are drawn from the same pool of support. The decrease in the Sinn Féin vote has to be a cause of serious concern to the IRA. It is a situation out of which it cannot simply bomb its way. I am being necessarily alarmist because "indifference to setbacks" seems to be our middle name.'[82] The conclusion to be drawn from this is that since 1984 some of the top IRA leaders had continued to support the armed struggle despite being aware that this would not improve the negotiating position of Sinn Féin. As republican leaders had already admitted, this objective would call for a strengthening of the party's electoral position and this was at loggerheads with the continuing campaign of violence.

Despite this, Gerry Adams and Martin McGuinness continued to stress the need for armed struggle in declarations that were yet more examples of 'playing to the gallery' in the same way that Morrison had done it in an attempt to win the decisive vote in 1981. Thus, in the historic *Ard Fheis* (annual conference) of 1986, McGuinness used this tactic in an attempt to win the vote that would allow Sinn Féin to abandon its policy of abstentionism in the south, thus allowing the party to take its seats in the Irish parliament. To win over doubters who thought this tactic would weaken the IRA's position, the republican leader stressed in his speech: 'Our position is clear and it will never, never, never change. The war against British rule must continue until freedom is achieved.'[83] Days before the historic vote Adams had played 'the IRA card', arguing that those who withdrew their support for Sinn Féin if the party decided to abandon its abstentionism in the South of Ireland would also be withdrawing their support for the movement's armed struggle.[84] One month earlier representatives from all IRA units in Ireland had met up in what the organisation calls an 'IRA Convention' to decide their stance on this question. This convention approved the abandonment of abstentionism in the South, thus culminating in a subtle campaign orchestrated by Adams and McGuinness. Their guarantees that the IRA campaign would not be scaled down as a result of Sinn Féin's political activities were backed up by the news that four shipments of arms from Libya that had arrived since the summer of 1985 would help to intensify the operations of the 'army'.[85] One of the main leaders at that time claims that the promised rearmament of the IRA was used with 'cynicism' with the intention of defeating those who defied the faction led by Adams and McGuinness, thus conducting a sort of *coup d'état* that 'strengthened the most militant'.[86] Another prominent IRA member, Brendan Hughes, criticised the use that the leaders made of this question. At that time Hughes occupied a senior position in the General Headquarters (GHQ), the department in charge of organising IRA structures and running its campaign of violence. He explained how after the arrival of arms from Libya, Martin McGuinness himself authorised a series of operations that were to inaugurate 'a major push' by the IRA, just as the leaders had promised, to quell the doubts of those who mistrusted its intentions in promoting the abandonment of abstentionism:

I felt, and I said this at the time in 1986, when the weapons were coming in, the big weapons, and I toured Ireland and I got back to a meeting in Donegal, the meeting went on through the whole night and I believed that the army [the IRA] wasn't ready for this major push. We needed about another year of training, of recruiting before we could embark on this major push. And that's what it was supposed to be, a major push. We are talking about going into Crossmaglen and taking over billets, taking over army forts, that's the sort of thing we were talking about. And my recommendation was no, we're not ready for it, the army isn't ready for this, it isn't strong enough, it's not organised enough for them type of operations to go ahead.[87]

Hughes explains that, despite his recommendations, it was McGuinness himself who authorised this 'major push' which would spawn actions such as the one that took place in Loughgall. In May 1987, eight members of the

IRA lost their lives when they were ambushed by British soldiers of the Special Air Service (SAS) while attacking the Loughgall police station in County Armagh. The negative results that this operation had for the IRA confirmed Hughes's doubts: 'That's exactly the reason why I was saying we should not go ahead with these because they were not ready.'[88] This led him to suspect McGuinness's real intentions in giving his approval to such an offensive. It is worth noting that the mistaken decision to accept 'the major push' did not at all undermine the leaders' credibility. On the contrary, their defence of the armed struggle reinforced their credibility within the group, shielding the leaders from criticism despite the negative consequences that ensued from their decision, echoing the situation with the hunger strikes. Thus, by dint of what an important IRA member called the 'cynical use of the armed struggle'[89] by leaders such as Adams and McGuinness, the ending of abstentionism was achieved in 1986. They managed to do so maintaining the unity of the movement since those who disagreed found themselves in a weaker position.

The ending of abstentionism in the South meant that the revolution aimed at by republicans in the Irish Republic had failed. This forced them to acknowledge that most Irish people considered their state institutions to be legitimate, a fact that called into serious question the IRA's *raison d'être*. It no longer made any sense whatsoever, therefore, for the IRA to claim to be the 'legal representative of the Irish people' with the intention of justifying and legitimising its violence. This was the subtext of McGuinness's message when he pointed out that after sixty five years of struggle republicans should accept that they had failed to convince the majority of the Irish people that the republican movement was relevant to them.[90] The logical conclusion to be drawn from this admission was the need to adopt a similar attitude in the North, including the ending of violence, since republicans had also failed to convince most people from the Six Counties that their project had any relevance for them. This could be deduced from another telling admission made by Gerry Adams in 1983, when he acknowledged that people in Northern Ireland could not achieve 'Irish independence' on their own. In his view, the republican aim required a solid Sinn Féin presence in the South which was clearly lacking.[91] Another former IRA member summed up as follows the inherent contradictions in this attitude:

What I felt was a contradiction as well, how do you recognise one partition parliament and refuse to recognise the other? You are giving a notion of credibility to a section of the Irish people in a partitionist section of Ireland and you are not giving that equal credibility to people living in the rest of the island of Ireland, that is the North, the Six Counties. So I felt that it was inevitable that with the dropping of abstentionism and the recognition of one partition parliament, logically you had to recognise other partitionist parliaments.[92]

Despite the above-mentioned inconsistencies, IRA leaders did not consider it to be the appropriate moment to risk threatening group unity by any sudden ending of the armed struggle. They considered it better to continue down this line even when it was obvious that, at best, it was not advancing the republican cause and, at worst, it was proving counterproductive. Another activist described the IRA leadership's position on this question in the following way: 'People were coming along on the backs of the IRA. People were being told "let the politicals do what they want and it won't affect the IRA. Stay with the fighting men." I knew it was going to affect the IRA. You can't ride two horses in different directions or the same horse in different directions. If you bring the system down from within you crash yourself under the weight of it if you are within.'[93] Taking a similar line, Ruairi O'Bradaigh, who opposed the abandonment of abstentionism and left the party to form Republican Sinn Féin, compared Adams's attitude with that of Michael Collins, the historic republican leader who in 1921 was accused of betraying republican ideals by signing a treaty with the English which did not guarantee the hoped-for republic. Like Collins, Adams 'surrounded himself with these people and used them as a leverage, and they were the conscience of the movement – they were more republican than anyone else and yet they were the ones who worked internally on the movement to accept the Treaty of surrender and who intimidated the elected deputies and all that type of thing. The Adams leadership had the same modus operandi – that they were more republican than anyone else, that they were the conscience of the movement and they then were best situated to betray the movement when the time came. In 1983 they got control and by 1986 they were going into the Dublin parliament but they wouldn't go to Stormont or Westminster. The inevitability of gradualness bit by bit by bit, they do it – advance three steps, retire two and then come along again – and so on and so on and see what the traffic will bear. Meanwhile they were continuing the war, which if they had all this in mind, continuing the war would not have been justified.'[94]

'Some people said what they thought and were ostracised'

The republican strategy seemed to be guided by this 'cynical use of the armed struggle' to which the previously quoted IRA activists referred, as confirmed by other militants' descriptions of the leaders' manipulation of the terrorist campaign. In the process that culminated in the abandonment of abstentionism, the voices raised against the contradictions of this dual strategy of violence and politics were skilfully quelled by members of the leadership. Ivor Bell, who in the early eighties had been appointed Chief of Staff of the IRA, expressed his concern about the possibility that IRA operations, especially in Belfast, had been cut back to avoid damaging Sinn Féin's vote in the British general elections of 1983 and the European elections of 1984.[95] Between 1984 and 1985 Bell tried to muster support for calling an extraordinary IRA 'convention' in which he intended to limit Sinn Féin's electoral strategy, which, in his opinion, was inhibiting the terrorist campaign. Adams' leadership nipped this rebellion in the bud, submitting the dissidents headed by Bell to what the group called a 'court martial', which ordered his expulsion from the IRA on the grounds of betrayal.[96] Eddie Carmichael, 'commander' of the Belfast Brigade, was another of the expelled members, as was Dan McCann. The latter was subsequently readmitted into the organisation and died soon afterwards when he was shot by British SAS soldiers in Gibraltar while preparing a terrorist attack. Another activist explained the type of methods used by the IRA to head off any dissidence:

> When I was in prison in 1984, the first hints of some sort of dissent, some reports in papers about hawks and doves appeared. And I knew the Belfast Brigade OC, Eddie Carmichael – you had reports in the paper that Eddie had threatened Adams, reference that he suspected Adams was leading to exactly where we are now. And he had threatened Adams. But inside … , the persons that were inside jail were saying this is a figment of some reporter's imagination, this isn't true, don't believe it and we were getting papers in and pages taken out of them by the staff, not by the *screws* [prison officers] but by the IRA in jail, for fear that we would start thinking. (…) If you were not open to their sort of opinion, following the leadership, then you were pushed out completely. (…) [Dan McCann] was on the same side as Eddie Carmichael was. Dan himself was under severe pressure from people. He was being back-stabbed and vilified because he was recognised as a hawk, he was one of the ones that was rocking the boat. I remember at his funeral, a man saying to me, that had he died the year previous there wouldn't have been enough people at the funeral to lift the coffin. Yet when he was killed there were thousands at his funeral. It shows you how things change, you know. They were going through this process of making sure … anybody that answered back, anybody that questioned things – it was noted, and at appropriate times they were pushed aside, gradually pushed out. So it ended up what you had in Belfast was an apolitical rampant [sic], people who just wouldn't question anything. Do as they were told and that was it.[97]

Brendan Hughes admits that he accepted the IRA's smear campaigns carried out against anyone who questioned the commitment of leaders such as Adams and McGuinness to the armed struggle: 'I've been trying to do it for some time to get Ivor to give his version of events at that period. There were so many lies told about Ivor. I was in prison when Ivor was court-martialled and sentenced to death. And I was informed, because myself,

Ivor and Gerry [Adams] were very close and I was informed by the leadership, by Gerry, that Ivor had went off the rails and stepped outside the army line. Now, that was something that you never [*should have*] done, so I was one of the people that was briefed. Again, George Orwell: Ivor was a good boy yesterday, he was a bad boy today: good pig, bad pig, good horse, bad horse. And I done it, and I done it. But, I think it's important because Ivor has been a main vein in this whole struggle and he is so concerned about his own safety, because remember the sentence of death is still hanging over his head, him and his wife.'[98]

Former IRA activist Tommy Gorman believes that the organisation used the same tactics with Eddie Carmichael, extending him 'an offer he couldn't refuse: to leave or get shot dead'.[99] The 1986 split was accompanied with threats from the IRA leadership towards the members of the new splinter group led by Ruairi O'Bradaigh, Republican Sinn Féin, forbidding them from setting up a military alternative to the Provisional IRA and thus snuffing out dissidence.[100] Hughes' testimony is particularly revealing of the methods used by the IRA to marginalise dissent, methods which he had accepted without reservations. He expressly criticises Adams and McGuinness for expelling Ivor Bell, destroying his credibility within the IRA through 'lies' simply because he had predicted that the movement was advancing towards 'constitutionalism', as was in fact borne out by the new situation ushered in by the peace process:[101]

When I got out of prison I was informed that I was not to have a conversation with Ivor, I was not allowed to talk to him, he was disowned, he was a person unacceptable and I was ordered not to speak to him. Because he was dismissed with ignominy from the IRA and he had been sent to Coventry and no-one was to have any dealings with him whatsoever and I went along with that for some time. Conspiring to bring down the leadership led by Gerry. That was the reason given. That Ivor was conspiring along with others to bring down the leadership. Dan McCann was one of the people as well dismissed at that time, he was eventually killed in Gibraltar. He was allowed back in after he went and gave his apologies and so forth, that he was mistaken. Dan was a good IRA man. He just wanted to operate and he got sent to Gibraltar and died there. I mean that was another period at that time that the British had so much intelligence coming in, they just took them three out. They were the three people, if they had been alive today I don't know if they would have gone along with this situation, I don't believe so. Most of the people who wouldn't have gone along, either, as I say, were killed, resigned or broke away into another organisation. And it obviously suited the leadership of this particular period for people like that to go.[102]

The testimonies given confirm the existence of tactics also used during the hunger strike which were mentioned above. Thus, the activists were subjected to considerable group pressure, which led them to self-censorship, and also generated a psychological knock-on effect that pre-empted any open questioning of the leaders' decisions even when doubts were harboured about them. The submission was almost total and uncritical, strengthening those opinions that were explicitly supported since they were endowed with an apparent superiority over those where the lid was kept on within the group. Group cohesion was thus guaranteed in the face of potentially divisive issues such as the continuation of the hunger strikes and the terrorist campaign. The words of Brendan Hughes explaining why he continued to obey the instructions of his superiors even while recognising the validity of the arguments of his comrades who were accused of betrayal and threatened with death are revealing. As he now admits, he knew from the 1980s onwards that IRA operations were at certain moments curbed so as not to damage Sinn Féin's electoral chances, which was precisely the opposite of what Martin McGuinness was so forthrightly declaring at the time.[103] As Hughes put it:

> What you've got to remember here as well is that deep sense of loyalty. Me sitting here now, I would never have done that at that period or even shortly after that period or even right up until the ceasefire was called. There was that great loyalty there, even though I was mistrustful of a lot of people and I disagreed with a whole lot of things. That sense of loyalty was still there and I think it is important not to underestimate that, that sense of loyalty that was there and is still there. Where people are so afraid or so loyal that they will not even say to you when they find something was wrong, they will not say it because the old cliché 'Stay within the army lines, because to step outside the army line will give ammunition to the enemy', and that's very important because it's very true. The anti-British thing is there in that anybody who speaks out against the leadership is seen to be anti-republican. And I am absolutely not anti-republican.[104]

The effectiveness of the above mentioned control mechanisms, which served to draw the sting from the criticisms of the leaders' strategies and tactics, is confirmed by another former IRA member who argues that people who spoke their mind 'would have got ostracised' and things would have 'started to go wrong for them'.[105] This activist goes on to explain how attempts were made to isolate those who questioned certain IRA actions: 'They were made to feel like "have you lost it?". They made it really difficult for you. Or maybe an operation they were going to cancel and somebody would say "Jesus, I don't think that is right, he is not as bad, as so and so and all": "Just do what you are told", you know.'[106] Other activists confirm that although doubts were raised about certain targets, the attacks still went ahead since

orders had to be accepted to maintain discipline. A senior figure like Danny
Morrison accepts that the IRA depended on the 'exploitation' of this loyalty
based on the principle of 'do this and don't query it'.[107] This blind obedience
could be seen as a consequence of the deficient process of politicisation of
many IRA members, a logical result of the procedure for joining the group,
as analysed in previous chapters. As a former member put it, 'a lot of IRA
people have very closed minds' and share the view that 'the IRA is right
even when they are wrong'.[108] Another one summed it up as follows: 'The
IRA is not an intellectual society. That's not to speak nastily or pejoratively
of them. The fact is that you're talking about a group of people who are
largely working class folk who are not naturally inclined towards the world
of academia, they're not life's wordsmiths. You're not talking about second
year political students in Queen's University or anything like that who were
given over to debate.'[109]

Under such circumstances, the need to avoid open criticism or questioning
tends to be regarded as normal. Once the group dynamic has been broken,
criticism is articulated more openly, albeit not without consequences, as the
following activists show:

> 'I've no problem with being used. I think everyone that joins an
> organisation, especially a military organisation, any soldier is going to
> be used, that's quite acceptable. It's the abuse. It's when it moves from
> being used to being abused, and being told lies and abused in that sort of
> way for other people to bring about their political objective. Because
> when you join the IRA or whatever organisation you offer yourself to
> be used but the main line that they were pushing to try and stop the
> abuse was to try and ensure that the people you are working with are
> politically educated in that they know what they are doing and have an
> understanding of what they are doing. What is abuse is when you bring
> in a load of robots, right, and just send them out to do operations or
> whatever – that's abuse and that's what has been happening.'[110]

> 'Within the movement the secrecy which I suppose was needed
> through the military campaign has transferred into the political cam-
> paign and you have to remain silent and say nothing but follow the
> leaders blind and we find that very difficult to do because we feel the
> leaders are going in the wrong direction. And the fact that we have
> spoken out, the whole campaign of vilification, ostracisation and general
> demonisation has been waged against myself and others. I mean people
> I have known for thirty years will walk past me on the street, grown men
> walk past me on the street like they are children. What we fear is that
> people here are so petty, that petty minded, they would be petty minded
> enough to get us shot.'[111]

In 1999 Eamon Collins was beaten and stabbed to death by IRA members, showing the fears of this republican to be very well-founded. Collins was an IRA member in the 1970s and 1980s; convinced of the uselessness of the armed struggle, he dropped out and then became one if its fiercest critics.[112] It has already been shown that the leadership in the past did not put up with any questioning of their determination to use the armed struggle. Curiously enough, the methods they used to stifle criticism differed little from those used in the peace process, when leaders also chose to discredit those who dared to question their final decision to give up the armed struggle, just as those expelled a few years earlier had predicted. In this context, the IRA resorted to very similar tactics of sidelining and intimidation, as will now be seen.

In 1973 Marian Price went on hunger strike after being convicted for her involvement in car bombings in London. The IRA unit sent to London to carry out this mission included Gerry Kelly, today a senior member of Sinn Féin who accepts the Good Friday Agreement signed in 1998. This political compromise was denounced by Price as a 'sell out' on the grounds that 'the Provisionals have surrendered'.[113] She considered it 'pathetic' that Kelly and other republican leaders now condemned the actions of former comrades who split off from the group to set up the Real IRA in opposition to the peace process. She therefore criticised the term 'micro group' used by these leaders to belittle the campaign of the Real IRA due to its lack of grassroots support: 'When Gerry Kelly went to London with me he'd no mandate, what's changed?'[114] Such criticism led to several IRA members visiting Price at home to inform her that her 'views were not acceptable' and that she should 'shut up' or face the consequences.[115] Several Real IRA members were personally threatened by their former comrades in the Provisional IRA after the bombing in the Northern Ireland town of Omagh, which resulted in twenty-nine deaths. Paddy Fox, imprisoned in the past for his activism within the Provisional IRA, was kidnapped and beaten by IRA members after criticising the participation of the IRA and Sinn Féin in the peace process. After the Omagh massacre there was a backlash against the Real IRA which was exploited by the Provisionals in order to deal with those critical of their so-called 'peace strategy'. Such threats were backed up in October 2000 by the murder of Joseph O'Connor, member of the Real IRA. The authors of the crime, committed in broad daylight in Ballymurphy, a republican area of west Belfast, were identified as members of the Provisional IRA. In a post-murder statement published in the main nationalist paper of Northern Ireland, two former prisoners of the organisation, Anthony McIntyre and Tommy Gorman, condemned the murder of O'Connor and blamed the Provisional IRA for it. They were then subjected to a campaign of intimidation in which their houses were surrounded by pickets led by local Sinn Féin members, demanding that they leave the community. Gerry Adams himself helped to smear the reputation of these republicans by accusing them of being 'fellow travellers' of the Real IRA.[116] He did so despite the fact that

Gorman and McIntyre had repeatedly expressed their rejection of any form of violence, underlining 'unambiguously' that there were no circumstances under which Real IRA violence could be justified.[117] The public declaration made by both also concluded with the crystal clear statement that 'republicanism should never again use guns in pursuit of its ideals'. Paradoxically, such a clear rejection of the armed struggle was nowhere to be found in the declarations of Sinn Féin leaders at the time. In fact, it was not until July 2005 that the IRA announced the end of its campaign.

The treatment given to McIntyre and Gorman by the local paper *Andersonstown News* bore a certain resemblance to the smear campaign directed against other critical voices within the republican community. The newspaper described Gorman as a 'maverick' who was 'no stranger to controversy', accusing him of making an 'inflammatory statement' that had unleashed 'deep anger' in the community, making its members feel 'vulnerable'.[118] Thus the danger to this community was not considered to be the fact that someone could be shot down in broad daylight in what Gerry Adams described as a 'republican stronghold', but rather the condemnation of this murder by someone written off as a 'dissident'. The use of this term is significant due to its connotations, as Marian Price pointed out: 'Volunteer Joe O'Connor was clear in his opposition to British rule; he did not dissent from republican principles or ideals [...] I know they like to term people like myself dissenters, but we haven't dissented from any republican principles, they are the people who have strayed from republicanism. I believe today the same things that I believed in the early 1970s when Gerry [Adams] was a comrade of mine. So he is the one that has changed, not me.'[119]

Price was quite right to say that the so-called dissidents had not in fact dissented from the principles of traditional republicanism, which defended the armed struggle against the British for as long as they remained in Ireland. Adams himself had asserted as much years earlier: 'Armed struggle is a necessary form of resistance. Armed struggle becomes unnecessary only when the British presence has been removed ... if at any time Sinn Féin decide to disown the armed struggle they won't have me as a member.'[120] The Provisionals' condemnation of the violence perpetrated by 'dissidents' therefore runs counter to the previous positions of the group led by Adams.[121] In this doublethink situation the group leaders strove to impose their 'regime of truth'. Their 'official version' did not tally with objective reality; instead a sham reality was constructed which fulfilled the same function. In other words, 'dissidents' are not really those who have ceased to adhere to the fundamentalism of traditional republican ideology – the Provisional IRA – but rather those who follow such immutable ideas – the Real IRA. Dissidence is thus defined in terms of the size and power of the group rather than any underlying ideology. Domination is therefore exerted by means of the same group dynamic which was analysed when looking at the hunger strikes and their aftermath.

Former IRA member Mickey McMullan pointed to the inconsistency and 'hypocrisy' of the republican leadership for failing to face up to the contradiction of murdering people and then condemning those who were only doing what they themselves had been doing for years on end: 'What legitimises armed struggle of the Irish people is the continued presence of Britain in Ireland. That's the raison d'être of the Provisionals' armed struggle against the British state for twenty odd years.' Hence this republican's criticism: 'That hypocrisy and refusal to face up to that contradiction, that angers me. That's why it's nothing about Ireland. It's got fuck all to do with Ireland. It has got to do with power and people dictating, fascism, it angers me deeply that I was part of it at one time.'[122]

In recent years, when former IRA activists have raised doubts about the Provisionals' strategy, they have been strongly criticised in an attempt to mask the leadership's difficulties in explaining away the changes in direction with a semblance of consistency. Efforts were then made to silence those who questioned the usefulness of the armed struggle, otherwise the errors of the group leaders would be brought to the fore. Republican dissidence thus ends up as a victim of one of the movement's fundamental principles over the years: the fomenting of group cohesion by breaking down its members' sense of individuality. Declan Moen's comments on this principle with respect to the prison protest, when the inmates were deprived of their political status, make interesting reading since they come from a former IRA prisoner. He points out how the authorities tried to undermine the republicans' sense of group identity by means of a policy of individualisation, such as the attempt to assign a number to each one for identification purposes.[123] Group membership was not recognised by the authorities, who ignored the organisation's hierarchy. In Moen's opinion, this criminalisation process also tried to foster a sense of guilt or shame among the prisoners, hence they were labelled 'terrorists' or 'criminals'. He points out, however, that republicans' resistance to these tactics was sufficiently strong, given the intensity of 'the subordination of individuality to group identity', which was favoured by a 'collective mentality' based on the 'confidence obtained from having large numbers of like-minded people in the same environment'.[124]

The factors that this former prisoner highlights as important in the republican struggle are precisely those that favoured the manipulation and imposition of policies described in previous pages. We have seen how republican leaders exploited group-reinforcement mechanisms to break down any sense of individuality. This same process often emerges in their narratives, characterised by the reproduction of a 'party line' previously imposed on them by the leaders. The result is paradoxical: on the one hand, republicans can safely claim to have been non-conformist with the system, as is shown by their subversion both inside and outside prison, while on the other hand they were indeed 'conformist' vis-à-vis the group they belonged and submitted to. As Moen himself points out, republicans see the subordination of the individual to the group as something to be proud of. Nonetheless, this phenomenon has created a community in which any criticism or thought-out analysis concerning the party line is barely tolerated. According to this logic it is not the individual who thinks; this task is reserved for those who lead the movement. Republicans saw the subordination of the individual to the group as an efficient means of resisting the state's attempts to criminalise their cause, extolling what they define as their 'military discipline' through-out the conflict. Some of those who accepted this subjection, however, changed their opinion and came to see themselves, in the words of Brendan Hughes, as having been 'abused', as it became clearer that this subordination, which is guaranteed by 'cohesive' and 'strategic' thinking,[125] is a double-edged sword that can also be used against those who question the effective-ness of armed struggle. A former member illustrated this point by calling attention to the 'counterproductive' effect of the murder of unionists for the republican cause, even though the decision to go for these targets was not challenged for a long time: 'Sometimes you have to turn round and say "look, that's fucking wrong" and if you are not able to do that there in an environment or in a movement there's something wrong.'[126] The following example is also revealing.

A year after the signing of the Good Friday Agreement, the *Andersonstown News* published a series of letters to the editor in response to ex-IRA member Tommy Gorman's criticism of Sinn Féin's strategy. Gorman had proposed the opening of 'a process of self-analysis' for republicans to debate 'what was all the death and destruction about'. At the same time, distancing himself from republican *dissidents* still maintaining the armed struggle, Gorman made it clear that his was 'not a call to arms, by any means', stressing that 'armed conflict is not an option'.[127] Another former prisoner who was also interviewed for this book declared himself 'offended' by Gorman asking an open question that he deemed as 'insulting': 'Was it all for nothing?'[128] This question effectively challenged the prevailing groupthink, as did another of Gorman's articles entitled 'Was it in vain?'[129] Sinn Féin's acceptance of the peace process showed that the goalposts had now been moved, and this opened up the terrible possibility that the violence and suffering caused by the IRA's armed struggle had indeed been 'in vain'. As another letter published in *An Phoblacht* pointed out, the justification for the war had disappeared because the IRA's objectives had been watered down, as was proven by the participation of republicans in a peace process that annulled their traditional claims for the immediate withdrawal of British troops from Ireland and the reunification of the north and south of the island, which would now only come about with the consent of the majority of the Northern Irish population.[130] Gorman summed it up in the following terms: 'They are leaving it up to demographic changes to make a change. I mean why at the start didn't they say "right, everybody don't use the pill, don't use contra-ceptives, don't become involved in abortion". A *baby boom* would be less painful than a car bomb or any amount of car bombs. They would have been more effective if it was about out breeding the other ones.'[131]

If the IRA had kept up the armed struggle for years with a different objective from the declared goal of forcing the unification of Ireland, which could not in fact be achieved by this tactic, then, as Gorman suggested, the conclusion could indeed be reached that the violence and suffering had been in vain. The nature of this debate resulted in those who put forward such a provocative argument being discredited. Some of its supporters therefore decided to remain anonymous, believing that 'freedom of speech in some republican circles is a figment of imagination',[132] or that 'people are asking questions and not getting answers' since they were 'becoming tired of being fed the same old rhetoric by the republican leadership' although 'many are just too afraid to talk out because of the repercussions that might ensue'.[133] Another former IRA member, Anthony McIntyre, also entered the debate supporting Gorman's argument, which earned him insults and the accusation of being manipulated by unionist and British interests by presenting 'republicanism as a fractured, defective machine whose moving parts are starting to fall off'.[134] The voices of dissent raised by these former IRA prisoners appeared to be more explosive than the violent actions of the dissidents of the Real IRA, in that they threatened to disrupt the republican unity built up through a process of deindividuation over years. A movement proud to admit that its survival depended on all of its members strictly adhering to the party line had no choice but to sideline and discredit the dissidents. This fundamental IRA and Sinn Féin policy was able to justify internal repression on the grounds that it maintained the movement's unity and internal order.

The effectiveness with which this internal dissidence was stamped out shows the power of what could be called the leadership elite within the movement; the importance of their role can therefore hardly be exaggerated. Tom Hartley, a Sinn Féin member for many years who was considered as one of Gerry Adams's right-hand men, asserts that Catholics like him are 'hierarchical'. In his opinion, Adams could take part in secret talks safe in the knowledge that his party would support him even without knowing what was at stake, for the republican leader acted 'like an archbishop', and his authority was respected by all the other leaders and members of Sinn Féin.[135] This republican believed that Irish Protestants would never operate in the same way, because they were, in the words of Hartley, 'democrats to their arse, if you allow me the expression'.[136] The activists interviewed admit in general that the peace process was conducted exclusively by the republican leadership without the grassroots members being aware of what was going on, something that most accepted uncomplainingly. Harry McGuire summed up this feeling by pointing out that 'leaderships are there to lead', while also declining to question the decisions taken by them: 'Time will judge the effectiveness of it but I think it is good leadership. I think bad leadership is that you sit on your hands and you don't lead. They will be judged by history.'[137] A former Provisional IRA activist gave an example that bears out Hartley's comments:

> The awful thing about it is that there are a number of Provisional supporters who would attempt to argue with you about The Good Friday Agreement and they haven't even read the thing. I had one and he said to me 'oh, we got 90 per cent by war, we're going to get the other 10 per cent through politics'. And I said to him, 'What was the 90 per cent that you got through war?' I said, 'Was that to get into Stormont?' He says 'oh now, now, don't you start' or something, this is the great war cry, you know. 'By the way,' I said 'have you read the Agreement?' 'No, but', I said 'No, but what?' 'No, but Gerry says.' So, you know, what Gerry says is gospel, he's become the Pope of the Provisionals, he's totally infallible, you know, and that is very sad, it is a sad reflection on what is left of the Provisional movement. And I don't say that with any joy because I was a member of the Provisional movement.[138]

The leadership cult within the republican movement is similar in many respects to that existing in other groups. There is a fundamental difference, however, in that the IRA is a violent, secret, undemocratic organisation that, like other terrorist groups, paradoxically resorts to democratic arguments to justify its existence, in its case by claiming to be the rightful representative of the Irish people.[139] With the benefit of hindsight, some of those who formed part of the IRA now appreciate the illogical nature of this way of thinking, which demanded that the activists be 'robots', as several of them indicated, to be able 'to blindly follow the leaders' and 'keep quiet and say nothing'. Tommy McKearney gave the following description of the profoundly undemocratic nature of the IRA leadership and thus of the organisation per se: 'Seven men juntas not only deny the people their right to be consulted as the governing authority in a democracy. Militarists by their very nature are bound to stymie the development of the cause they claim to serve.'[140] Brenda Murphy, another of the IRA activists interviewed, also acknowledged this important structural shortcoming in an organisation that purports to be a movement of national liberation. She admits that they were incapable of obtaining the support of the majority in Northern Ireland and that the IRA was 'an undemocratic movement', although she accounts for her actions on the grounds that 'the ends justified the means'; hence the fact that 'we wouldn't give a damn if the whole of the Six Counties said "no, you can't do this". We would have went ahead and done it because we felt justified to do it, so it was anti-democratic.'[141] As another former member of the organisation put it, 'Their attitude was "we have the right, we're going to carry on, we have the moral right to carry on the struggle, and fuck the people", that was the attitude.'[142]

The following examples show the authoritarianism that has always characterised the internal functioning of the IRA. It is crucial to assess this variable,
often overlooked, in order to fully understand the republican movement.
Several IRA members have confirmed that in June 1973, Patrick Crawford,
one of the IRA prisoners in the Maze prison, was killed by his own comrades
on the orders of republican leaders outside the prison.[143] It was a common
practice, during incarceration, for the IRA leaders inside the prison to read
the letters received and sent by the inmates. This was no different from the
situation existing outside the prison: those inmates who broke the group's
code of conduct were ostracised and stigmatised as though they were
informers. Several interviewees confirmed that sometimes IRA members
themselves would torture their fellow prisoners in the Maze, some of whom
cut their veins in an attempt to escape such abuse.

From the start of the conflict, the IRA had traditionally ordered its
members to refuse to recognise the courts' authority if arrested and tried,
otherwise they would be accepting the legitimacy of the state that was
bringing them to trial. They were also denied the possibility of declaring
themselves guilty of minor offences in return for reduced sentences. In the
mid-1970s, however, the IRA gradually began to change its tactics for pragmatic reasons, given the need to avoid the imprisonment of its members, so
that by the late 1970s and early 1980s nearly all republicans were now
recognising the courts in which they were being tried. The IRA's change of
tactics on this issue provides an important lesson, since the volunteers who
had previously broken the rule of not recognising the authority of the courts
had been ostracised and stigmatised, even though time would eventually
show that this radical stance was impractical and ineffective. Brendan Holland was one of those volunteers who broke this rule. When released from
prison in 1977, he left the IRA because of the 'movement's authoritarian
nature':

> Revolutionary organisations become more and more authoritarian as
> the conflict deepens. I said to myself why should I rejoin, end up being
> shot dead or doing life, and for what? This is what I increasingly said
> to myself – for what? Because the struggle was increasingly, purely a
> military struggle, dictated by the [IRA] army council and the British.
> The mass movement from the early seventies had declined. The demo-
> graphic impulse from the people had declined. The IRA were taking
> more and more control. Politically I just didn't agree with it, but yet at
> the same time I felt guilty about not being back in. There was comrade-
> ship involved. I was ambivalent about it but decided not to.[144]

The republican movement had striven to build up an image of prison life
that stressed camaraderie and group unity. As volunteer Albert pointed out,
however, this 'sanitised version' does not tell the 'true story'. In fact, the

same behaviour happened inside and outside the jail, as he confirms: 'I had serious problems with the forms of organisation that the movement applied in the prison. It was a very harsh, it was a very severe and oppressive form of collective [system], it didn't leave much room for the individual, so, I mean, there were some of the things that was minor, some was major, but I always found myself that, on most things I always found myself opposed to the sort of leadership line, sometimes justifiably so and sometimes not. I mean, sometimes I was maybe responsible for maybe criticising when it wasn't required. But the same mechanisms they used in the jail, to marginalise people, they use out here. They're identical.'[145]

This same activist then criticised the movement's attempts to give an airbrushed version of events that simply makes no mention of the authoritarian and degrading practices suffered by those who had broken the rules laid down by the leaders. He does so by referring to the hunger strikes which have been used as the subject matter for a play and a film, both written by one of the participants, Laurence McKeown, who is also the author of a book on the prison experiences of the republican movement.[146] As regards these writings, volunteer Albert, who has spent over a decade of his life in prison and is therefore well aware of its functioning, stated that: 'It's all an attempt to present a very sanitised view of republican history according to those acceptable to the movement at any given point in time. Is a very acceptable history of the Blocks, and a very sanitised history which leaves out an awful lot in relation to the various tensions and the various conflicts that existed within the prison. The movement has always had very effective mechanisms for dealing with dissenters or critics within its ranks.'[147]

He also interprets these works as part of 'the battle over the legitimacy of the republican position' in history which, 'isn't over', an expression used by another member of the organisation who still holds an important post within it.[148] From the republican perspective, therefore, the past must be presented in such a way that the conflicts that could emerge following a rigorous examination are defused. As the first part of this chapter has shown, the IRA could have avoided the death of their comrades on hunger strike. This is not an interpretation that the IRA would be keen to publicise, as a movement in which often republicans equate the death of the hunger strikers with that of the 1916 leaders. These should be borne in mind when reading the following paragraphs about the events related below, in order to gain a better understanding of the republican mentality and the repressive motivation which has had such a powerful effect on it.

John Nixon, a participant in the first hunger strike, kept up his fast for fifty-three days. In 1998 he received threats from the IRA when he considered standing as an independent candidate for the council elections in Armagh. Although he admits that his decision was 'very parochial', he argues that the threats he received shows what the IRA could be capable of if the group had more power: 'This was seen and interpreted as a direct threat to the political hegemony, the power building basis of the Provisionals. They wanted to manipulate all things local and I was seen as a threat because of my republican background, and therefore I was seen as a direct threat in the whole electoral fight. I had entered the political arena, and they didn't like this a bit. They said to me if I stood I would never stand again. Which meant that they would blow my legs off. Only some time before it a fella called Andrew Kearney had been murdered in flats over in Belfast [by the IRA]. He was shot in the two legs.'[149] This activist, who was on the point of losing his life in the 1980 hunger strike, finds it ironic how 'the heroes of the past' are not 'the heroes of the present' if the movement so decides.

When discussing the authoritarian nature of the republican movement, it should be remembered that the leaders of this organisation were the same as those who had denied for years that the IRA had got rid of the bodies of over ten people whom they had killed in the 1970s. It was not until 1999, after pressure exerted on Gerry Adams by the United States government, that the group would finally admit its responsibility for these crimes, thereby also showing that they had been lying beforehand. Such diverse examples show how rigid discipline was used to maintain the leaders' hegemony. This not only provides us with an important insight into the nature of the people who accepted and ordered the implementation of such a *modus operandi*, it also confirms that repression was systematic. The backing that a terrorist group obtains is largely the result of its skill in harnessing its power sources to maximise its influence and authority.[150] To this end, the IRA also tried to extend its network of control into the communities by taking on an extreme vigilante role. By assuming the role of the Northern Ireland police, republicans tried to reinforce their legitimacy as an anti-system force, imposing an arbitrary and cruel system of 'justice' ranging from beatings, kneecappings, shootings in ankles, hands and elbows to other types of punishments such as expulsion from the community, whereby those individuals accused by the IRA of carrying out activities defined by the group as 'antisocial' were sent into exile and forbidden to return.[151]

In order to preserve the groupthink that was needed to guarantee the maintenance of internal power, republican leaders implemented disciplinary measures in pursuit of an intention that has been summed up as follows by one of the IRA members interviewed for this study: 'They hate to be challenged or they hate to be questioned, so sometimes you can antagonise them by asking why, what, or what for.'[152] It was precisely the absence of answers to the questions 'why or what for' that caused many to leave the organisation, after which they were subjected to the usual smear campaign and intimidation. In the mid-1980s a group of IRA prisoners asked to be transferred from the Maze to another prison. They had questioned the party line in terms of the abandonment of abstentionism, the effectiveness of the armed struggle and the need to continue with it, and they now feared that if they stayed in the Maze they would be physically attacked by their comrades.

Tommy McKearney, one of the prisoners who left the IRA for this reason, claimed that his criticism was distorted and presented as a hostile challenge to group loyalty. This was borne out when an IRA-authorised statement circulated in the prison describing the 'dissidents' as 'counter-revolutionaries' and 'people offering assistance to the enemy'.[153] As the IRA leaders stressed, they were not prepared to put up with their authority within the prison being undermined,[154] hence the deliberate hostility towards anyone who broke ranks. McKearney had suggested that the Adams and McGuinness leadership was geared towards 'parliamentary reformism', while he also criticised the stance of those who walked out after the policy of abstentionism was abandoned. In his opinion neither militarism nor abstentionism were capable of achieving a democratic republican movement which at that time was still 'elitist', 'voluntarist' and 'lacking broad popular support'.[155] From his point of view, the abandonment of abstentionism showed the IRA's inability to attract mass grassroots support while carrying out acts of violence. These actions were also incapable of influencing the will of the British government in that they did not manage to 'deny them control of the territory'. Under these conditions, his conclusions shook the very foundations of the principle of the armed struggle in republican thought: 'The question is: Can the British Government be forced to withdraw from Ireland as a result of public pressure, or influenced by acts of physical force? Maybe the question should be, can the British Government afford to be forced? No matter, in either case the answer is no.'[156]

5

LOSERS

'We had gone as far as we could with armed struggle'

'Armed struggle has not been effective'

In the mid-1980s, the IRA leadership vilified Tommy McKearney for arguing that the IRA's armed struggle had been ineffective. Ironically, broadly the same arguments used at that time by McKearney are put forward by today's republican leaders to justify the peace process, as the following testimony shows:

> If for thirty years or so you're conducting an armed struggle and it hasn't achieved your goals, well then either you're going to have to escalate it to a level whereby the achievement of your goals becomes closer or you reassess it, and I think that is what's happened. The armed struggle was in progress from say 1970 until 1994 and throughout that period, there were always attempts being made to escalate it, to get more people involved, to instigate more attacks, that was always happening. By 1990, maybe before that, I think it was becoming clear that Irish republicanism was incapable of raising it even more. My own opinion is that the IRA could have continued the armed struggle at the same level for another hundred years, but then you have to ask yourself, will that achieve anything just by sustaining an armed struggle? It's not enough. If you're involved in armed struggle, it's not enough to sustain it just to keep the war going. The war has to, there has to be some progress, there has to be the prospect of victory and I think by 1980 that didn't exist and the IRA had attempted to escalate it, to raise it even more and weren't able to do so.[1]

Like other activists, in the mid-1980s McKearney had warned that there was no prospect of victory. Yet despite the fact that there was no real confidence in the republican movement's objectives being satisfied through violence, terrorism continued. The reasons given by some activists in order to explain why this happened also points to the existence of a conflict between the interests of the movement as a whole and those of its leaders. In short, for

138

the latter, group unity, which had become of more importance than the organisation's traditional objectives, justified continuing with a tactic – the use of violence – even when this very tactic hindered the attainment of republican aims. The response given by one of the interviewees when asked about the need to examine the mistakes made by the IRA is revealing:

> From my own point of view, the changes that happened within republic-anism didn't happen soon enough. For instance, the decision to partici-pate in the Dublin parliament in 1986, I would have been in favour of that happening long before that. But again I'm not, I'm not sure of the usefulness of that exercise, you know, there are a lot of things, a lot of developments within republicanism over this past thirty years I would have preferred them to have happened earlier, but I'm conscious of the fact that it's a large organisation and that unity is a cornerstone of republican strength and it's not enough for someone to have a great idea, the bulk of the republican movement has to first of all come round to that idea for it to take a life.[2]

The desire to maintain group unity may explain the decision not to end the terrorist campaign, even when this had clearly proved itself to be ineffective. However, the fact that such a serious decision was taken in order to prevent internal divisions in the movement inevitably raises important questions. As one interviewee pointed out: 'If our leadership at a particular point in time decided that at some future point the armed struggle should be run down or should be completely done away with, then there is a moral issue when you continue to send people out to die and people out to kill knowing that your long term view is something different.'[3] In such a dangerous scenario, the IRA's need to rationalise past events can be seen once again, as highlighted by Danny Morrison's testimony:

> I actually thought the armed struggle would probably intensify more than it did, in the late eighties, early nineties. And what I saw was a campaign that was just on a plateau and I was in Crumlin Road jail seeing lots of people coming back in again for the second and third time. And I began to wonder, I could see that the IRA could still get new recruits, could still fight on and on and on, and I was just concerned that it was going to go on forever. As being one of these, you know, 'look at us, we have fought non-stop for forty years', instead of 'here, this is what we've produced from an armed struggle'. It's a flawed political situation, but we've continued to advance our aims and objectives in another way and we have still managed to secure our community; we've made it feel comfortable.[4]

However, as pointed out in the previous chapter, in 1984 this same leader was already aware of the ineffectiveness of the dual strategy of violence and electoral politics. The inherent tensions in such a strategy, undermine the credibility of Morrison's explanation put forward in order to portray the 1994 IRA's ceasefire as the best outcome after the escalation of violence which he allegedly expected between the late 1980s and early 1990s failed to materialise. Therefore, former IRA members see Morrison's assessment, which in general terms coincides with the republican movement's official explanation for ending the violence, as a *post hoc* rationalisation of events, which studiously avoids the need to face up to the mistakes of the past. One former activist, Brendan Hughes, described such a version of events put forward by certain leaders as 'a big lie': 'Because that justifies what was happening in '86 and '87, that it was only realised in 1991 when it was actually realised long before that, or some people accepted and realised that. And if people accepted and realised that at the leadership level, then it's immoral to send people out to die. That's why it's had to have been brought forward to 1991. (…) I was sending people out to die in 1986 and this was going on. And people will say that I have been on a campaign since then that was totally immoral. And to a certain extent that's true. I do think it was totally immoral to send people out to die when the intent was there to run down the war. That's not what the people were being told in 1986, they were being told that the war was getting stepped up. And for someone like Danny [Morrison] to justify that, he is certainly not the type of leader that I would want to lead me.'[5]

The *post hoc* rationalisation of the continued use of violence at a time when its effectiveness was called into question serves to protect the IRA from criticism: 'I think armed struggle has not been effective for them one bit. Cause they went political. They've done what they said they wouldn't do. They fucking done it. So why did all those people, innocent civilians and IRA people die, cause they've just went and done what they said they would never do. You tell me, how was it effective? They got wearing their own clothes in prison, wow! fuck me! Enough people died so they could wear their shirts and jeans, didn't they? That's my argument to them. They could have been there years ago. The SDLP has been pushing for fucking years. It was up to Sinn Féin to say: "Right, we'll go into government" and I think they could have done it years ago, absolutely.'[6]

As a result, with regard to the republican argument that the armed struggle was the only effective means of political action given the indifference of the British to the demands of non-violent SDLP nationalism, the same interviewee points out: 'When did they listen to the violence? The British government has only listened to them since they have gone in politically and started to do things, the government has given things in return. I think that could have happened years ago as well. If they were doing the armed struggle now, the watch towers would still be up, the soldiers would be on the ground, the whole fucking heap, believe me, they would be getting their fucking arses kicked by now. They went into politics because they had to go into fucking politics. Remember they were riding two horses, the gun and the ballot box for many years. What won? The ballot box. It fucking won, not the gun, the ballot box.'[7] It is therefore not surprising that another interviewee should emphasise that 'certainly the SDLP has a stronger argument than Sinn Féin do. The SDLP have a much stronger argument in saying that had everybody followed the path they took all these things would have happened much sooner. Their thing is that it was the war that stopped the reforms and made it more difficult for the unionists to have a bit of compromise and all this.'[8]

The rationalisation of the armed struggle employed by IRA and Sinn Féin leaders is similar to the mechanism of legitimation used in relation to the hunger strikes. This makes it all the more important to analyse critically such arguments, exposing the flaws in the reasoning and the risks for the republican movement of allowing such an alternative explanation to take root and flourish. Like other activists, John Nixon claims that following the hunger strikes it was clear that the armed struggle did not have the support of most of the Irish people. To illustrate this point, he compares the huge numbers who attended Bobby Sands' funeral with the relatively disappointing turnout for that of Michael Devine, the last man to die in the hunger strikes: 'It was a realisation at that time that the armed struggle, that the way that we chose to pursue our aims had to be questioned and queried big time.'[9] This contrasts with the perspective of veteran republican Jim Gibney when remembering the deaths of his former comrades twenty years on: 'Those who died on hunger-strike not only set a new moral frame or context from which everything else derived, they propelled the struggle forward into a new arena: they strengthened the struggle at a time when it was under extreme pressure. (…) When the year was over, it was obvious to the leadership of Sinn Féin that an electoral strategy was needed. The prisoners gave the leadership the courage to open up this front. That also meant that a party had to be built. (…) We learnt that you can't stand outside the institutions of State, which the people legitimately recognise, and expect to grow as a party or secure political influence. (…) That year we learnt that the struggle was truly national, and the Twenty-Six Counties was not a tag-on to what was going on in the Six Counties.'[10]

By stressing the political value of what happened, Gibney strives to find some logical justification for the deaths of the hunger strikers. However, such an interpretation is mainly another example of the movement's policy of *post hoc* rationalisation. This is confirmed by another of the hunger strikers, Brendan Hughes: 'It's total nonsense. The hunger strike both inside and outside of the prison was literally dying off. Demoralisation had set in in the inside and in the outside, the hunger strike fizzled out, fizzled out because the stomach had been knocked out of people both inside and outside the prison. To justify any political gains from that, again I think is disgraceful. Ten men died to bring about a couple of demands within the prison and it didn't work. What worked was physical action in the prison, physical action, destroying the prison and making the prison unworkable and that's what worked and that could have worked before ten men died.'[11]

The need to open this 'new front' referred to by Gibney was already clear to those leaders who began to take control of the movement after the disastrous 1975 ceasefire, and even before this watershed year. As far back as the early seventies, prominent republican Kevin Mallon had warned of the need to 'fill' the 'political vacuum' by strengthening the 'political wing' since, in his opinion, 'if military action is an end in itself, then you've defeated your own purpose'.[12] As the republican newspaper *An Phoblacht* noted, as early as 1970 republican leaders were in favour of extending and strengthening the political wing of the movement beyond the six counties of Northern Ireland.[13] In the mid-1970s, the weakness and marginalisation of the organisation, together with its lack of economic and human resources (the latter as a result of the constant arrests of its members), were such that Billy McKee and Seamus Twomey, two of the IRA's leaders, even considered ending the campaign in 1976.[14] Two other leaders, Martin McGuinness and Ivor Bell, also took the view that the IRA was 'close to defeat'.[15] The restructuring of the movement's organisation in the second half of the 1970s was in response to this delicate situation. It should also be noted that the split at the end of the 1960s between Officials and Provisionals was due to the latter's refusal to complement the campaign of violence with a greater involvement in politics. From the second half of the 1970s onwards, however, the Provisionals gradually came to accept the ideas which they had rejected when they broke away from the Officials.

It was at this time that Gerry Adams wrote: 'We need to expand our struggle onto a Thirty-Two County basis. We are fighting for National Freedom but one major drawback appears to be that we are restricting ourselves a great deal to the North. I don't necessarily mean military action because I accept that we cannot properly fight a war on two fronts, that is, against two well equipped and aggressive war machines, but we can, and we must, capitalise and build on the situation which exists in the Free State. If the people involved in the armed struggle within the Northern war zone are not to be let down at the end of the day. Republicans living in the Twenty-Six Counties must get themselves involved in arousing the national consciousness of our people in that part of our country.'[16] In 1979, in the traditional annual commemoration of Bodenstown, Gerry Adams advocated something similar, stating that the republican movement's objectives could not be achieved 'solely by military means'.[17] Prior to this, in the symbolic Bodenstown commemoration in 1977, Jimmy Drumm, another senior republican, had made similar suggestions when he stated that, contrary to the IRA's exaggerated claims, the British were not about to leave Ireland. Drumm recognised that violence in itself was not enough to achieve victory and that republicans' isolation on the question of the armed struggle was 'dangerous'.

As a result, he advocated 'forging strong links between the republican movement' and the rest of 'the working class in the Twenty-Six Counties' in order to create 'an irrepressible mass movement'.[18] As Henry Patterson has pointed out, these ideas were not new, having been put forward by Cathal Goulding and other leading lights in the Official IRA, yet they had been derided by the Provisionals at the time.[19]

It was Gerry Adams who wrote Drumm's historic speech and ordered him to read it in what some activists now call a 'public act of humiliation'. In 1974, Drumm was arrested by IRA members, including Brendan Hughes, who at that time held one of the top positions in the Belfast organisation. Hughes had got wind of the fact that Drumm had made contact with the British behind the backs of Belfast's republican leaders. However, these contacts had the seal of approval of the leaders in the South, and led to the 1975 ceasefire. After the calamitous failure of this ceasefire, which, in the opinion of Martin McGuinness, left the IRA in its weakest position in its recent history,[20] the leaders in the North forced out the southerners and took control of the movement. Drumm's speech has to be understood in this context, which a former IRA volunteer described as Adams 'humiliating him for the purpose of saying to the previous leadership "we are marking your cards here, you people have been wrong, and one of your people who negotiated the '75 ceasefire is making this point now that the strategy was disastrous and our earlier strategy was disastrous."'[21]

The way in which republicans claim that they have applied another of the lessons to be learnt from the hunger strikes shows how group unity prevailed over everything else. Although there may be a certain logic in such an approach, as we have seen it led to the wrong policies being maintained until it was felt that a sufficient number of activists would accept a rectification without this causing the IRA leadership serious problems. According to Gibney, republicans 'learnt that you can't stand outside the institutions of state, which the people legitimately recognise, and expect to grow as a party or secure political influence'. If this was really the case, the most logical thing for the movement to have done would have been to take immediate steps to achieve this end, above all by giving up the traditional republican policy of abstentionism which, nevertheless, did not happen until 1986. Gibney himself would later admit that 'abstentionism was a millstone round Sinn Féin's neck' and that by sticking to this principle 'there were opportunities lost in the previous seventeen or sixteen years before 1986'.[22] Adams showed extreme caution with regard to this issue declaring, on becoming President of Sinn Féin in 1983, that the latter was an abstentionist party and that he did not intend to ask for changes on this matter.[23] Nevertheless, Adams left the door open to such a U-turn when suggesting that the question of abstentionism would have to be considered once it was taken on board that most voters in the South accepted the legitimacy of the institutions of the Irish state. This calculated ambiguity allowed him to prepare the ground for his

victory, three years later, in the decisive vote on the abandonment of abstentionism, using the methods described above. Once again, it can be seen that,
in the republican movement, any decision making which involved important
changes was judged to be appropriate according to the criteria established
by its leaders, their survival at the top of a united organisation being a para-
mount factor. The result was an unnecessary prolongation of the conflict
without bringing the IRA's stated objectives any closer. Merely continuing
to exist was the most important thing, since as Sean MacStiofain, the IRA's
chief of staff between 1970 and 1972, warned, 'if a revolutionary movement
is not active, it dies'.[24]

'People died. The question is, did they need to die?'

When the ceasefire broke down, two volunteers lost their lives and the
reason they lost their lives it was for a stronger negotiation position. It
was a stronger negotiating position in terms of what the British and the
unionists wanted and everybody else wanted. It wasn't in terms of
obtaining a British withdrawal and a united Ireland. So those two
volunteers in my mind did not die for Ireland. They died for a partitioned
Ireland. So when you look at it in those terms, no, I don't think it was
worth it. In much the same way I don't think the armed struggle was
worth it over a period of twenty odd years. In terms of human sacrifice
and suffering. So that's what that left, that's a ruthlessness that you are
dealing with. I don't have that, I think that's wrong.[25]

This was the way in which a former IRA member criticised the organisation's
policy with respect to the use of violence which its own leaders appeared to
view as an ineffective means of achieving the ends declared. This was confirmed by the fact that following the 1994 ceasefire declaration, the break-
down of the truce in 1996 was not the beginning of a new campaign of
violence aimed at abandoning the peace process. Instead, the objective
was quite different. Despite breaking its ceasefire, the IRA immediately
approached the British government through an intermediary and in secret
conversations set out the context in which it would restore the ceasefire,
offering concessions which went beyond those previously considered in the
lead up to the 1994 ceasefire.[26] There is therefore no doubt that, as the activist
in question pointed out, IRA actions had nothing to do with the objective of
a united Ireland, were not part of a war of liberation, and they were wholly
inconsistent with the dynamic of the peace process, since 'you cannot bomb
the same people with whom you are trying to seek agreement'.[27] This situation led some republicans to ask themselves how long the IRA and Sinn
Féin kept up the pretence of fighting for a victory which they knew they
would never achieve. As the following examples show, the first half of the
1980s has been identified as a key period.

'That is the whole cynical part of it. At the one time, McGuinness and other people were speaking with MI5 and other secret British organisations. At the same time there was a struggle of some sort going on – people were getting sent out to plant bombs or bring about ambushes on British army or RUC. That half war-half peace situation is always a bit hairy. But again, there was very little honesty or openness. I understand there is need for secrecy on some things but it would have been a lot more honourable I feel if they had called it off then. In '84, '85 because a lot of us realised that we had gone as far as we could with armed struggle, and after that violence became more gratuitous, violence for violence sake. It wasn't achieving anything.'[28]

'I think it was becoming clear by the mid-eighties that certainly the first demand of sovereignty wasn't going to be achieved by the continuation of the armed struggle. It was time, I thought, time to maybe rethink it.'[29]

Mickey McMullan states that he is '99 per cent' sure that from the 1980s onwards the republican leadership was aware that the armed struggle was ineffective. Between 1989 and 1990, at the request of the Army Council, he took part in discussions with a small number of prisoners about the possibility of a ceasefire: 'The debate was already going on in the outside. We were banging our heads against a brick wall. We were not getting anywhere [with the armed struggle]. If you go back to the seventies it was the same, the newest weapon, it was going to be the great saviour, it used to be the armalite, and then it was the rocket launcher, and then what do you call it, the Russian job, the RPG, and then it was the semtex, and then it was the M60, and then the anti aircraft, anti air, surface to air missile. All these innovations and weapons and so on and so forth. And then it was the big bombs in London. But at the end of the day you were running round and round in circles. It wasn't breaking the will of the British, no matter what you were throwing at them, they were standing firm. And, yes, the question arose: why were they here? They were here because of the unionists. Because at the end of the day they just couldn't abandon them. They were their people and they couldn't abandon them.'[30]

As McMullan recalls, this debate had started outside the prison and was restricted to 'leadership people within the jail': 'About 1990 it intensified in the Blocks where it was agreed to have a controlled debate and that the conclusions of that debate would be passed to the Army Council on the outside. That happened in 1992.'[31] The conclusion reached following this 'controlled' debate was that the IRA had to call a ceasefire. McMullan recalls that the IRA was not in a position to demand anything in return for such a historic abandonment, since 'continuing the war was futile'.[32] Another volunteer illustrates this feeling of futility which characterised the IRA's campaign: 'In 1988 I was in jail over there in the United States, I was held there for nine years under an extradition warrant, and there was a news-paper came in and it was about this soldier, he was a part-time soldier and he was shot at the border, and he was a farmer, he was a part-time soldier, farmer, and I kind of read it and I looked at it and I said to myself, "what did this achieve?" And it wasn't like a moral thing. I just looked at it and I says, "this is not achieving anything, it's just another dead soldier". And in this instance, it was another dead farmer, just a farmer out doing his field, he was a part-time soldier, and I said to myself, "something has to be done".'[33]

This 'controlled debate' to which McMullan refers began at the urging of the leadership outside the prison. As was seen in the last chapter, the way in which the republican movement operates suggests that the final decision about an issue which was crucial to the organisation was never going to be taken by prisoners, but only by leaders. As a prominent figure like Danny Morrison noted in a letter to Gerry Adams dated 17 October 1991, 'a debate is a major mistake if it's in the absence of the leadership having made up its own mind'.[34] It would not, then, come as a surprise to learn that between 1991 and 1992 the IRA leadership could have decided to call a halt to the terrorist campaign, although this may not have been officially announced until the summer of 1994.

'People died, the question is, did they need to die?'[35] Tommy Gorman's words, which question the continuation of the IRA's campaign from the 1980s onwards, could, as was noted above, equally apply to the tragic episode of the hunger strikes. In a similar way, the need for republicans to justify such deaths can be seen. Thus, prolonging the violence long after its ineffectiveness had been recognised was rationalised as a means of extract-ing concessions in exchange for calling a halt to the violence. This is clear from the testimony of one of the activists, when answering the question that other volunteers have asked about the objectives of the IRA's actions and the reasons for the deaths that ensued during the period that runs from the moment that it was accepted internally that the armed struggle was ineffective until the final announcement of the ceasefire: 'They worked around the situation where they could call it off. Unfortunately it's not like a switch where you could just switch it off. (...) It's not a nice clear cut thing where you say "OK, stop", or else, I mean, you just surrender, you just throw up the white flag and say "OK, here we are, we're packing it in". If you think OK, we can't get anywhere, the armed struggle is going nowhere, now, what can we do? Do we just keep on going? No. That's not an answer, that's not an option. Do we just stop? That's not an option either. OK, let's try and create conditions that enable us to stop and progress at the same time. So they did, they were working towards those conditions and when those conditions were there, they called it off, they stopped it.'[36]

Another former IRA member, Margaret McKearney, also saw a certain utilitarianism in the way that republicans handled the pre-ceasefire period, although she does not accept that this justified maintaining such an approach for years. In her opinion, if the IRA had called a ceasefire in the second half of the 1980s, its leaders would not have survived politically: 'It could have been done but it couldn't have been done and sold as a victory. Also the people weren't demoralised enough. The way I'd look at it is that if they called a halt in 1986 you wouldn't have McGuinness sitting in Stormont in 2001, he would have faded. It had to have been honourably stopped in '86, '87 as a defeat, whereas it stopped in '94 as victory, as a perceived victory, not a victory, stopped in '94 as a perceived victory, it could be sold in '94. They knew that if they stopped in 1986 that that was it, they'd go back to the Bogside, they'd go back into Andersonstown and they'd do what they had to do in the forties, had to do in the fifties, hold the candle of faith and hand it to another generation.'[37]

Gorman agrees in describing the republican campaign in which he took part as a failure, disagreeing with another former activist who argues that the ending of the armed struggle could not have happened earlier since it would have been interpreted as a 'surrender': 'No, that is not surrender, it is just saying that we have failed, that we are not going to carry on here with violence for violence sake. We realise that any more violence at this point in time would be counter productive and would end up with more people dying on the streets for no reason. So let's reassess where we have come and let's reassess what we should do in the future.'[38]

These testimonies reflect that there was a degree of rationalisation in the way the IRA assessed the possibility of giving up the armed struggle and how this had to be handled. Nevertheless, this rationalisation process, which necessarily involved weighing up the various pros and cons involved in a given course of action, begs the following question: was it really necessary and proportionate to continue using violence in order to try and strengthen the position of Sinn Féin in a hypothetical negotiation which it was known was not going to satisfy the group's main aspirations? As many of the interviewees recognise, armed struggle went on not because it helped to bring the attainment of republican objectives nearer but because in its absence, and given the weakness of Sinn Féin, the political insignificance of the movement would have been exposed. The limited results that IRA coercion could have for Sinn Féin in the polarised context of Northern Ireland were seen in the previous chapter. This essentially confirmed that the effectiveness of IRA violence was largely restricted to maintaining power and hegemony in republican circles, a view shared by Marian Price:

Why didn't they accept defeat with honour? If they had come to the position that they were defeated there is no shame in admitting defeat. The shame comes when you are defeated and you refuse to tell your grassroots that you're defeated, you try to sell defeat as some sort of victory. When the first ceasefire was called they had people going up and down that road with tricolours, up and down the Falls Road, screaming, celebrating, they told the people that there was some sort of victory there, in actual sense what they'd done was they had surrendered and they tried to sell it to the public as some sort of victory. That is hypocrisy, it is also cowardice because if they were defeated they should have had enough in them to put their hands up and say 'we fought the best we could, we did all we could, we couldn't do it, the war is over, the good guys lost'. They tried to pretend that they had won something when they had won nothing, and they have been pretending ever since. They pretend that walking into Stormont is some sort of achievement. Anybody could have gone out and electioneered and got voted into Stormont in the 1960s. There didn't have to be a war for it.[39]

By contrast, other former activists refuse to recognise the failure of the armed struggle, despite justifying the ending of violence on the grounds that this had ceased to be effective: 'From a very moral point of view, you do not continue an armed struggle just for the sake of it. If you think you cannot achieve anything by continuing an armed struggle, you don't do it.'[40] This idea once again raises doubts about the precise moment when the IRA admitted that it was not achieving its objectives through the armed struggle since, according to the republican discourse, 'for anyone to even think about armed struggle they would have to be very clear that it would be counter productive and it would be immoral unless there was some point of success; it is like the just war theory'.[41] As will be confirmed below, the IRA lacked this expectation of success many years before it finally decided to end its campaign and, therefore, applying the republican movement's own logic, the only conclusion that can be reached is that the violence was immoral. Likewise, continuing with the armed struggle under the pretext that in this way political concessions would also be obtained must also be called into question, as a former IRA member puts it when pointing to the immorality of the group's actions: 'If you are an organisation that is prepared to make a political gain on the back of taking away the lives of civilians, then if you are prepared to do that when you have no power, what are you prepared to do when you have a lot of power to maintain that power? Shit! Would we kill lots of people to stay there?'[42]

'If your armed activities are inflicting more suffering and hardship than they are alleviating then you have to seriously question the activities that you are involved in.'[43] This was how a senior activist justified the need for a ceasefire in 1994. Once again, applying the republican movement's own logic, a ceasefire should have been called much earlier. As previously noted, the 1980s was seen by some activists as a key period, a point confirmed by a former IRA prisoner who claimed to have discussed the possibility of a ceasefire in the Maze prison in 1988. In the summer of that year, Martin Lynch, the IRA's Officer in Command inside the prison, held intense conversations with Anthony McIntyre and Mickey McMullan about the path to be taken after it was admitted to them that certain leaders within the Army Council were in favour of calling a ceasefire.[44] Once again, it can be seen how by 1988 part of the IRA leadership, Gerry Adams and Martin McGuinness, according to some interviewees, had already stopped thinking about a possible victory through the use of violence. Having reached this conclusion, the logical consequence would have been to stop the violence or to leave the IRA if the group failed to take such a decision. Yet these individuals not only continued as leaders of the IRA but also used their privileged position of power to isolate and eliminate those republicans who feared that the leadership was making the terrorist campaign contingent on the political strategy of Sinn Féin, which they felt would ultimately lead to the violence being abandoned. The facts show that the Provisionals persisted in a strategy that had the same defects which they now attribute to those splinter groups who still advocate the use of violence. For example, it has been common to criticise those IRA dissidents who opposed the Good Friday Agreement on the grounds that their actions were not 'going to lead to the British out of Ireland or a united Ireland', their bombs being, therefore, 'futile'.[45] Applying this same logic, the Provisional IRA's terrorist campaign should also be seen as 'futile', since, as its leaders recognised, it was not capable of achieving these same republican objectives. Nevertheless, the leaders of the Provisional IRA continued using violence, thus clearly preventing it from achieving its political objectives.

On various occasions in 1990–91, the IRA used what have been called 'human bombs'. In a perverse version of suicide terrorism, the terrorist group obliged civilians to drive vehicles loaded with explosives into military targets while the families of the drivers were held hostage. This tactic was approved by the IRA leadership of which both Gerry Adams and Martin McGuinness were members. Although in 1984 Adams warned that 'there are varying degrees of tolerance within the nationalist electorate for aspects of the armed struggle' which obliged the IRA to be more selective in its use of violence,[46] and despite the fact that in 1989 he spelled out to volunteers their 'massive responsibility' since they could 'advance or retard the struggle' through their operations,[47] the republican leader authorised actions that, without any doubt, damaged the republican movement's aspirations. The public outrage and disgust at the use of human bombs was something that republicans should have expected, as Adams' comments confirm. There was also a wave of criticism for other IRA public relations disasters, which underlined the fact that it was impossible to wage a 'clean campaign' where there were no civilian victims or attacks which caused tremendous political and social damage for republicans. All of this pointed towards what various activists have called the IRA leadership's 'cynical use of the armed struggle'. Such a conclusion helps to understand what was the true scope of what republicans have called 'armed propaganda', a point which will be analysed in the next chapter.

'You are in the business of victory or death'

In contrast to the frank admission of defeat made by certain activists, the official republican explanation for the ending of the campaign of terror attempts to avoid the sense of failure as well as the cognitive dissonance which would emerge from any assessment of the ineffective and counter-productive nature of violence. The republican movement has therefore chosen to claim that the peace process arose out of the military stalemate between the IRA and British security forces, which, given the mutual recognition of the impossibility of victory, had chosen a negotiated non-violent solution. A former member of the IRA sums it up in the following way: 'I think most people would agree there was an element of a stalemate in the war. The war had reached a point where there was what they called almost an acceptable level of violence. Both sides could live with what was happening, but nobody was going forward, the British were not winning and couldn't win it, the IRA at the same time, they weren't winning, but nobody was losing either. Nobody was weak enough to lose and nobody was strong enough to win, so there had to be a some sort of alternative tactic tried, so the ceasefires, the talks process and all the rest were the alternative.'[48]

Even British government sources have given some credit to this interpretation. Peter Brooke, former Northern Ireland Secretary of State, declared in 1989 that it was difficult to envisage the military defeat of the IRA although security forces could contain republican terrorism.[49] As an IRA activist explained, this interpretation 'gave both sides a way out'.[50] Nonetheless it is possible to question the accuracy of that alleged 'stalemate'. As Brooke explained to this author, at the time he made this statement the British had privileged information which confirmed that senior leaders of the IRA and Sinn Féin accepted that the British government 'were never going to give in to force'.[51] Thanks to its intelligence services, the British authorities were aware that within the IRA the effectiveness of the armed struggle was being questioned. This was backed up by Sean O'Callaghan, a former IRA member turned informer, who claimed that between 1984 and 1985 Gerry Adams confessed to him that he had entered into secret talks with the British government, something which MI5 confirmed to him in 1986. O'Callaghan says that the British secret service saw a certain flexibility in Adams' posture which made them believe that it might be possible to do a deal with him.[52] In this same year, Adams sent, through an intermediary, a letter to Tom King, then Northern Ireland's Secretary of State. Although the letter did not show any marked change in Adams' position,[53] some sources claim that other secret communications revealed a willingness to call a ceasefire.[54] It is in this context, then, that the words of Brooke must be understood. Aware of the fact that the IRA leadership had accepted that its terrorist tactics had failed, Brooke tried to give the republicans a possible way out that would not be seen by the latter as a defeat. This idea of a 'stalemate' seems, however, to be at odds with the facts. A former IRA member put it this way: 'Militarily republicans were basically defeated, but the deal was that the way out of it was [a] conflict resolution situation, that sort of language started to come into play, it was never heard of before until the early 90s, this sort of language started to come into play and the purpose of it was a huge public relations exercise.'[55] In the words of another interviewee, once republicans had 'accepted a certain road, people were more than happy to give them a helping hand'.[56] This was confirmed by another former IRA member:

> I don't agree that we had reached a stalemate. The IRA had to win this war. The British government only had to prevent the IRA from winning the war. So in a sense there wasn't a stalemate. The ceasefires can be viewed as a victory for the British government. The fact that the IRA wasn't able to achieve its demands through armed struggle, and I do also believe that the attitude of the Brits through the years of the peace process has been based on the fact that certainly from a British government point of view they see the ceasefires having been called from a position of weakness rather than a position of strength. In overall terms, I think that the British government feel that they had the situation under control. It's interesting that people lend credence to this stalemate theory and it's interesting that it's trotted out so often in the media. It's as if your enemy is allowing you to save face. In a sense it wasn't a military defeat because the IRA at the point of ceasefire was still intact, it was still armed, but effectively it didn't seem to be going anywhere and it was sustaining very heavy losses.[57]

By insisting that the IRA has not been defeated, what the republicans are trying to do is implicitly detach themselves from the political nature which they have tried to ascribe to their actions throughout their history. Danny Morrison, a prominent Sinn Féin figure for a long time, explained years before the ceasefire that the IRA would 'not inflict a military defeat on the British', although Irish republicans were seeking 'a political defeat of the British' that both he and the leadership believed possible.[58] According to this rationale, the 'military stalemate' that republicans conveniently refer to in order to argue that their decision to give up violence does not stem from the IRA's failure is completely irrelevant. This is so because, as can be seen from Morrison's quote above, it was the political rather than the military dimension which was of greater importance for their aspirations. In response to those who argue that the IRA has not been defeated militarily, the obvious answer is that the terrorist group has suffered a clear political defeat, since it has failed to attain any of its main objectives. On the republican movement's own terms, then, where the success of military action was judged in terms of the political end result, it is hard to agree with those who claim that there was ·

no military defeat. In short, because the IRA failed to attain its political aims, military action must also be seen to have failed.

The relationship between military and political factors was made clear by Adams when, as early as 1979, he stated that the IRA and Sinn Féin's main objective was the full reestablishment of the republic demanded in 1916, warning that attaining this goal would require the use of both political and military action, while also predicting 'the defeat of the British'.[59] Prior to this, Ruairi O'Bradaigh had already recognised the impossibility of achieving a military victory, stating in 1971 that he could not imagine the IRA 'pushing the British into the sea' although the organisation could force them around the 'conference table'.[60] The correlation between the political and the military victory is therefore clear, since it seems logical to deduct that the former, which would take place at the negotiating table described by O'Bradaigh, could only be obtained if republicans had previously shown themselves to hold the upper hand militarily. Perhaps for this reason, years earlier Danny Morrison was also very clear when he explained the IRA's objectives and what failure to achieve them would mean: 'It's a question of surrendering or being successful. And it isn't a question of stopping. And also, because something hasn't been achieved after twenty years it does not render invalid the prospect of success.'[61] The scenario which he described in absolute terms meant that stopping the violence without having first achieved the stated objectives would amount to a defeat. This is exactly what has happened. Years later, a letter written from prison by Morrison in 1991 reflects how this black-and-white approach had been replaced by a more realistic, flexible stance, one in which defeat is defined in a slightly different way: 'We can fight on forever and can't be defeated. But, of course, that isn't the same as winning or showing something for all the sacrifices.'[62] The consequences of the republican change in position were summed up by O'Bradaigh when he rejected the need to show flexibility as a response to the alleged 'military stalemate'.

> When you say flexible, what you are saying is that republicans should abandon republicanism and go into constitutionalism and begin to bargain about Ireland's rights, and history has shown us where that type of thing ends up. Once you are in the business of revolution, you are in the business of victory or death. If you don't succeed you go to the wall and you don't cry about it. That is the business you are in. If you were in another type of business, which is constitutional – well that is the give and take, and all that type of thing, negotiation of Ireland's rights. That is a different ball game altogether and any attempt to combine those two can be quite disastrous because the revolutionary movement is built up on revolutionary principles and people are encouraged to adopt certain attitudes.[63]

The contrast between the opinions of these well-known republicans shows that the current approach of O'Bradaigh is absolutely no different from that adopted by Morrison in the past. In short, if the IRA leadership were to apply the reasoning used by Morrison years earlier and which O'Bradaigh still maintains, the IRA ceasefire and the peace process would have to be seen as a defeat rather than the result of a 'stalemate'. This point is worth stressing since it calls into question once again the decision to continue with the campaign of violence despite the doubts that had arisen as to their effectiveness. It is also possible to argue that in accordance with the logic now used by republicans to justify their revisionist approach, the ceasefire could and should have been called much earlier, since the 'military stale-mate', which in their own words was the reason for the 1994 ceasefire, had existed for decades. As early as 1975 O'Bradaigh had declared that nobody could win the war in Northern Ireland,[64] anticipating the 'stalemate' between 'the main forces in the conflict – the liberation forces and the occupation forces –' that Gerry Adams also acknowledged in 1988.[65] Having admitted that the IRA was unable to alter the balance of power, it did not make sense for Adams and Sinn Féin to demand, in the same year, that the solution to the conflict would only happen when republicans' demands were satisfied – self-determination for the Irish people as a whole and British disengagement from Ireland – despite the opposition of Northern Ireland's unionists.[66] By contrast, throughout the peace process Morrison showed a realism which had been lacking during the previous decades: 'Exactly, if republicans were strong, wouldn't they have got a united Ireland? The fact is the IRA didn't drive the British army into the sea, and they're sort of like surprised? Oh, hold on, we didn't win? No, we didn't militarily win. Wake up!'[67] It is there-fore clear that although the republican leadership were well aware of the limitations of the armed campaign as far back as the 1970s and 1980s, they did not extract the most rational conclusion from that.

The strategic contradictions of IRA violence meant that the terrorist cam-paign was seen by its leaders as a means of putting pressure on the British, as summarised by the following testimonies of O'Bradaigh and Morrison:

> 'At all times the question of outright victory in the sense of physical victory and holding territory and all that kind of thing never happens. It is the case of preventing them ruling. It is a question of continuing and seeing which side is able to wear down the other.'[68]
>
> 'I know that it will become so costly for them that they will not want to stay here. ... It isn't a question of driving the British army into the sea. It's a question of breaking the political will of the British government to remain. And that's why ten years ago [in 1977] the IRA stated the theory of the long war.'[69]

This exhaustion, which is referred to as the driving force behind the 'long war' aimed at wearing down the British which the republicans claimed to have adopted at the end of the 1970s, totally failed to break the British will. Apart from the strategic weakness of scaling down a campaign of violence to the point where its aspirations were reduced to wearing down the enemy given the restrictions inherent in the armed struggle, there was another factor which was often overlooked by republicans: unionist opposition. On this point we should recall the words of one of the activists interviewed: 'It wasn't breaking the will of the British, no matter what you were throwing at them, they were standing firm. And, yes, the question arose: why were they here? They were here because of the unionists. Because at the end of the day they just couldn't abandon them. They were their people and they couldn't abandon them.'[70] Not even an escalation by the IRA, which certain sectors believed to be feasible, appeared to offer the possibility of breaking the deadlock in which republicans recognised that there had been for years. Certain republican leaders had suggested stepping up IRA violence, the idea being to launch an offensive based on the successful North Vietnamese Tet campaign of March 1968 which led the USA to reconsider its position in Vietnam. The hope was that an escalation of violence would lead British public opinion to call for the withdrawal of troops from Northern Ireland and a radical change of policy in the region. Plans by republicans included objectives that required the control of considerable areas of Northern Ireland in order to provoke a violent reaction from the British or their withdrawal given the resulting damage, on the assumption that in benefiting from the surprise factor this would guarantee the success of an offensive that would have to be relatively short. This highly ambitious plan failed partly because the British security forces and intelligence services were able to infiltrate the IRA,[71] but also because it was extremely unlikely to have succeeded anyway, given the conditions in which it would have been put into practice. This has been recognised by various former members:

'There was another ongoing tactical debate within the IRA about the merits of a larger column of men, that instead of having the usual IRA party in my time would have been three to five men. Now that then transferred into those who were saying that the IRA should operate not maybe so often, but in larger units of maybe twenty five to thirty men which would allow them to attack or engage larger units of the British army, do substantial damage and safely make their getaway, make their retreat. But then that throws up all its own problems, the risks are well documented by now, but the risks to bringing together a substantial proportion of your strength. Then there is the question of how to arm your strength because if you have that many men, you need weapons adequate to the party and all my time in the IRA, the IRA had a never-ending problem with sourcing arms, sufficient arms and of sufficient quality.

There's a big difference between the quality of arms which will intimidate neighbours, it's one thing to create distress on the street, in a civilian society, but quality of arms vis-à-vis a regular army from the NATO forces such as the British army or others that you could mention the difference between the type of rifle that will intimidate your neighbours and the type of rifle that's capable of contesting the ground with the NATO forces, which the British were, still are.'[72]

'There was never, ever going to be a military victory. The British Government is nowhere near extended in terms of its commitment in respect of troops and armaments and security personnel to the Six Counties, nowhere near extended. It is probably one of the most sophisticated fighting governments in the world, so to even think that you were going to face down and defeat a British Government was lunacy. (...) Look at the number of people who filled the jails and the number of people who died. The war in Ireland wasn't about new weapons or greater supplies or anything else, the war in Ireland was so multi-faceted that [to] adopt that sort of view, took you down the road of just pure militarism, it led you nowhere. I mean it is a fairly well accepted fact that a small group of people could carry out and continue an armed campaign if they had a limitless supply of materials and financial resources. But what does that prove? What does it do? It does nothing. So all of the bogus arguments about the shipments from Libya and the Sam 7 missiles and all the rest, that is exactly what they are, they are bogus arguments. I mean if the IRA had Sam 7s sure they would have been able to take down more helicopters. Would that have made a qualitative difference in the British Government's view of what they should do in Ireland? I don't think so. I mean, do the British Government give a great deal of concern for what happens to their squaddies? Maybe they do, but I don't think so. So if the success rate of the IRA went up from thirteen or fourteen a year to thirty or forty, would that make the British Government more reluctant to want to pull out, to reform a constitutional set up, etc., etc., etc.? I just don't believe it. I don't believe the British Government were so concerned about the welfare of their troops that that would become an overriding factor.'[73]

'The tactic of the car bombing was too indiscriminate'

The possibility of escalating the campaign of terror advocated by some republicans was faced with a number of problems. Not only did the IRA have to exercise a degree of self-control if it wanted to avoid prejudicing Sinn Féin's electoral aspirations, but, in addition, it was faced with logistical and operational restrictions which explained the decision reached in the 1970s to reduce the level of violence. Likewise, if the IRA really wanted to overcome the military stagnation which it alleged existed, it would have needed to intensify its campaign to such an extent that this would have serious counter-productive effects in relation to its initial aims. As early as 1978, a report prepared by the British Army predicted that the IRA would not increase its level of activity for fear of a vigorous response from the security forces that would seriously damage it. The report predicted that republican leaders would avoid attacks that could expose a large number of their activists, and rather than intense activity, they would opt for a campaign of wearing down the British forces, with terrorist acts being chosen on the basis of their propaganda value.[74] As a former member of the IRA pointed out, the document prepared by Brigadier James Glover in the second half of the 1970s reflected the fact that republicans were already admitting their incapacity to carry out an offensive such as that which some republicans claim to have advocated at a later stage: 'If you are not going to have all out war, what else is there? Because then, General Glover had announced that we were in a stalemate. It was a recognition that the IRA could never defeat the British state. So you had that stalemate in the early eighties. How do you get out of the stalemate? You have to break it somewhere, so you either break it with all out war or you go the other way.'[75]

After 1972, the year in which the largest number of fatalities occurred at any time during the three decades of the conflict, the level of violence dropped noticeably as the limitations of the terrorist strategy gradually but clearly emerged.[76] Despite this, in May 1972 the headline on the front page of *Republican News* proclaimed 'How the war is being won'.[77] The article claimed that the main reason for this victory was the new tactics being used, such as the car-bomb. However, praise for the apparent military effectiveness of the IRA seemed to be in contradiction with the more realistic analysis of republicans acknowledging that 'the IRA does not have the support of the majority of the population of the Six Counties, this being an additional problem'.[78] The recognition that the IRA had been confined to 'the Catholic ghetto areas', together with other restrictions such as those outlined above, condemned to failure the escalation of the armed struggle hoped for by some members. Throughout the 1980s, the number of fatalities among the security forces fell, yet at the same time the number of civilian victims rose. The statistics show that during the three decades of the conflict, republican terrorism claimed the lives of about one thousand members of the security forces as well as seven hundred civilians, as well as more than two hundred members of different terrorist organisations, including the IRA itself. One former IRA member explained in the following way the failure which these figures reveal:

What the IRA tried to do was to kill soldiers who were occupying their streets and that the bodies going back to England would create a mood like the troops out movement in America. And that's what the IRA was trying to do, trying to create a troops out movement, trying to get the

English people, the British people to realise that they weren't winning this war. But the IRA just never managed to crack that nut. Never managed to achieve that point. Some people would argue, 'oh, you were just around the corner from achieving it'. But were we? I don't think so.[79]

Another republican active in the Derry area sees now in a much more critical light the use of car bombs which, years before, the IRA had described as particularly useful: 'I think that militarily the dangers of car bombs, they were just too difficult to ensure that there were no civilian casualties and I think there was (a) the declared aim of the car bombing was unachievable and (b) the tactic of the car bombing was too indiscriminate, there was too many problems associated with it, it was too difficult to control and therefore you ended up with civilian casualties which no one wanted, which was (a) a tragedy for the people who were killed and (b) it was a political disaster for the aims of the struggle.'[80]

Even in an area such as South Armagh, where IRA activities have always been seen as particularly important, the true scale of its operations show the need for caution when assessing the impact of violence. For example, as a result of the twenty-four attacks carried out by the IRA's snipers in this area between March 1990 and March 1997, nine members of the security forces lost their lives, a figure which was hardly likely to deal a serious psychological or military blow to the British army, as some authors have wrongly claimed.[81] This can be deduced by comparing the level of deaths throughout this 7-year period with the much higher figures of thirty-three deaths of British soldiers between 21 March and 30 April 2003 during the military operation in Iraq which ended in the overthrow of Saddam Hussein.[82] This type of trend led a British minister for Northern Ireland to downplay the IRA's effectiveness by comparing the limited troop losses which republicans had inflicted with peacetime casualties caused by accidents to soldiers stationed in Germany.[83] Therefore republican expectations of success for their terrorist campaign should be assessed with more realism, as is clear from the following testimonies of former IRA members:

'If they [the IRA] could have intensified the war they would have intensified it. I can understand the republicans who say that it is a sell out and we should have intensified, but see just from my time from when I was operating in this district, it was hard to fuckin' move. I would say for every twenty jobs we went out on only one came off, the other nineteen times you had the whole problem of getting your gear out of dumps, getting houses, taking houses over for jumping off from and having all your sort of backup people you would need and not being able to move either because there's civilians in the way or the Brits didn't come in or there was something. There was always something. I would say about one in twenty we were able to move on, the rest you were pulling off from without doing anything. So I think if we could have intensified it, we'd have intensified but the practicalities were [that] we couldn't. What more were you going to do that you weren't doing, because up until the ceasefires came there was no order from the IRA that you weren't allowed to kill British soldiers or RUC. If anything they would shout at us at meetings, you know when you have a meeting they would shout at you about "How did that go wrong? How did that go wrong? That fucker should be dead? Get out and do it. That is what your job is to do." There was no holding you back.'[84]

'Whenever they say "Oh, the IRA should have intensified the war", that's exactly what the IRA did do, but the IRA wasn't going to foolishly intensify the war and risk scores of volunteers' lives. In 1987, the IRA lost eight volunteers at Loughgall, they lost three in Gibraltar in 1988, they lost several men in Coalisland attacking the barracks there. So the IRA had to be very frugal and careful and protective of its volunteers, in order to ensure the war would last. It's easy having an uprising and being defeated. What's that going to prove? (...) They used RPG7s, they used 12.7 (12.7 × 107 mm DShK) machine guns, but it maybe turned out to be the semtex which was the best weapon of the lot in military terms, not necessarily obviously in human terms but in military terms. I think that the IRA realised that even though they had all this weaponry which could sustain them in a long war, that the British Government, whose personnel was changing every four years, apart from Thatcher was there for 11 years. But basically they could absorb all this. When the IRA volunteer was continually on the run, you know planning, getting killed or going to jail, the other side could absorb it. And it was only occasionally that the IRA fired mortars into 10 Downing Street, or did the Brighton bomb earlier, or carried out a large attack that was in the news for a few days, or fired mortars at Heathrow Airport and then they did the big one at Bishop's Gate in Canary Wharf, and big bombs in Manchester. Even though the IRA was capable of doing those bombs and maybe not sustain the campaign because they have to keep changing all the time once the British intelligence was on top of particular operations, it appreciated, it could fight on forever without necessarily winning. (...) Imagine if the IRA had thrown all of its resources, or much of its resources into an intensification which lasted for two years, and which left a thousand people dead and a thousand people in jail, and you still didn't manage to change the British Government and then you say: okay, now we have to cease fire. The British Government would turn round and say, "fuck you, what are you going to cease? What are you going to negotiate with? You've got fuck all, take yourself off! Your prisoners will stay in jail until we say so." That could have been the other scenario, a desperate one, and that's what's called defeat.'[85]

The reasoning of these former activists reveals the ineffectiveness of IRA violence, since the group has been incapable of breaking out of this 'military stalemate' which republicans have referred to since the 1970s. The previous opinions also show the futility of the armed struggle if we take into account the limited achievements of the republicans in negotiations before or after the ceasefire which, as a respected republican like Danny Morrison has admitted, obliged the IRA and Sinn Féin to swallow a lot of 'bitter pills'. These reflections question his own justification as to why the IRA had not stopped the violence earlier which, as was noted above, was based on the following belief: 'I actually thought the armed struggle would probably intensify more than it did in the late eighties, early nineties, and what I saw was a campaign that was just on a plateau.'[86] Yet the problems referred to by Morrison in earlier paragraphs cast doubt on the viability of the hoped-for escalation of the armed struggle between the late 1980s and early 1990s. This is an important observation since it contradicts the official version disseminated by the republican movement in order to defend the continued use of violence until 1994 despite its ineffectiveness. Some IRA members have interpreted these contradictions as demonstrating that republican leaders opted for 'a cynical use of the armed struggle' in order to ensure their survival within and their control over the organisation. In the same way that the promises made as regards maintaining the armed struggle during the first half of the 1980s strengthened the position of leaders like Adams and McGuinness at a critical juncture, these individuals' commitment to an offensive that was bound to fail guaranteed their hegemony within the IRA. In addition, it allowed them to justify their historic strategic U-turn in embarking on the peace process as a reasonable and necessary choice given the sterility of an apparent escalation in violence.

The internal distribution among IRA units of a document written by the group's leadership after the 1994 ceasefire seems to have had the same objective. In this document, which recognised that republicans lacked sufficient strength to achieve their main objectives alone, the acronym TUAS was continually used without any explanation being given as to what it actually stood for. When the report was leaked to the press a year later, the initials were interpreted as meaning Totally Unarmed Strategy, implying that the IRA had completely given up the armed struggle. However, those IRA activists among whom the text was first circulated are adamant that TUAS actually stood for 'Tactical Use of the Armed Struggle'. Unlike the former interpretation, this second version fitted the initials of the acronym word for word, implying that activists received the news of the ceasefire with the guarantee that this did not mean a definitive abandoning of the armed struggle, but only a tactical truce that could be interrupted if this was considered appropriate.[87] A member of the organisation judged the reasons for the frequent and calculated ambiguity with respect to the armed struggle in this way: 'Gerry Adams has managed to do something that no republican leader has ever done. He has brought the republican movement down a road of political compromise with the British state without causing any serious split. So whilst people may criticise his cynical use of armed struggle, there is also an argument that says that because he was so careful in his management of this, he has avoided the sort of historical problems that republicans have when these things happen.'[88]

Nevertheless, the TUAS document acknowledged that the very weakness of the republican movement required the violence to be stopped, admitting, by implication, that a hypothetical future return to arms would be incapable of overcoming the obstacles which had made it necessary to call a ceasefire in the first place. The possibility of going back to a tactic which had proved to be incapable of achieving the republican movement's objectives was therefore left open. However, it can be observed how the need for a peace process based on the search for an agreement with the other actors involved in the conflict, above all the unionists, gained ground within the republican movement. This became the basic premise of the IRA's decision to call a ceasefire in 1994, as well as its subsequent backing for the Good Friday Agreement. The decisive admission in the 1980s that the peace process should be based on the search for an agreement with the unionist community which was, at the same time, being violently attacked clearly demonstrates the IRA's flawed reasoning. At the same time, the republican movement's moral justification for the violence on the grounds that it was fighting a just war fell apart, as one interviewee pointed out: 'That raises for me though a very serious moral issue, and to go back to what I said earlier that in order for a war to be justified and justifiable, I think one of the key elements has to be a reasonable chance of success. If you're now saying to me that the reason why many republican activists continued with armed struggle and didn't call a ceasefire earlier was because there might have been a split within the republican movement, and that's a very spurious reason for the continuation of armed struggle, there is no morality in that. If you accept that the stated aim of your armed struggle is unlikely to succeed then you should stop, there should be no other criteria.'[89]

In addition to these question marks, the testimonies set out below clearly show the limitations and ineffectiveness of the IRA's terrorist campaign, and highlight the serious deficiencies in the republican strategic analysis.

'For a period of time there was very strong armed struggle, but that armed struggle could not be sustained, the armed struggle of the '71, '72, '73 period couldn't be sustained as people began to be shot, be lifted, weapons were caught, as escape routes were cordoned off either into the South or into different areas, as you put up all the security paraphernalia etc., it became much more difficult to operate militarily within the Six

Counties, very difficult to operate in England as well. As Britain increasingly found ways to combat the IRA, it became more and more difficult for the IRA to make major inroads, and have major victories against the British. The amount of effort, the amount of money the British were using, the way in which they started to cut off finance to the republican movement as well, you know ... They started to try and cut off finance to the republican movement, the way they cut off publicity to the republican movement through their censorship policies, the way in which they forced people to stop supporting the republican movement because people began to realise that this struggle is going to go on for years and years and years. (...) As people began to realise the war was going to take a long, long time, it became more difficult to sustain it, even to sustain your own energy within the war, and you're talking about the most committed people. You were depending on your most committed people as opposed to just the popular upsurge because most people are prepared to do something for a short space of time that's going to be self-sacrificing but they're not going to spend their whole lives, dedicate their whole lives to some self-sacrifice, the vast majority of people. You were getting your most dedicated people that were doing it, and a lot of these people were getting picked off and all this type of stuff. So I think the point I'm trying to make is that it became increasingly difficult to, for example, kill members of the British army, it just became very difficult to kill them, I think. Because they had the body armour, because they were in tanks, because they had all this surveillance equipment, because they had all these detection equipment, they could detect bombs and they could detect signals and all that type of stuff and it became increasingly difficult for republicans to fight the war. (...) I think that if republicans had been able to intensify the struggle, you know, for a prolonged period of time, they would have done it, I think that they just weren't capable of sustaining it.'[90]

'Operationally as well but I mean, there's also the demoralisation of your own communities and people, and you were always very aware of you having to operate within a context of your own communities and you begin to think that "How much are we impacting on bringing it down on the heads of our own people?" And the England campaigns couldn't be sustained all the time. There was a load of things that came about to say, "Let's really look at what we're at here."'[91]

'You don't fight a war believing you are going to lose. What sustains you is the fundamentalist conviction that it can be done; it can be achieved. At some stage, whenever you start to doubt that, you have to change your analysis.'[92]

'Violence was counterproductive'

The declarations of the activists cited above show that fundamentalism was a dominant part of the republican psyche, something which must be borne in mind when assessing whether or not the IRA's actions were rational. As M.L.R. Smith has noted, republicans have insisted on presenting themselves as entirely rational actors, while at the same time they have avoided essential questions of the 'real world', which their strategies required them to answer.[93] The result has been a deficient rationalisation process strongly influenced by fundamentalism, as the group members themselves admit, which has led to decisive strategic errors such as those previously stated. Another decisive mistake has been their flawed analysis of the true interests of the British government and the unionists. Although the IRA possessed the capacity to keep the armed struggle going, this was not really a show of strength; as one activist put it, 'the Brits are never going to stop me and some other guys getting weapons and taking a crack at a soldier, but you're pissing against the wind'.[94] The IRA's violence was therefore reduced to a sort of 'ritualism'[95] that was insufficient to achieve the republican movement's objectives which, since they were not supported by the remaining actors, could only have been attained by imposing a considerably superior force. The persistence with the armed struggle confirmed that the republican interpretation of the conflict ignored the vital importance of the internal situation and the total opposition to their plans shown by the majority of the population in Northern Ireland in general and the unionist community in particular. As Bishop Cahal Daly, one of the fiercest and most consistent critics of IRA violence over the years, put it, 'the real "British presence" in this country is 900,000 people who live here, who belong here and who would still be a British presence in Ireland if the British administration and army were to withdraw next week'.[96] It is enormously significant that many activists now share this view, having previously rejected it for many years, as the following testimonies highlight:

'We were very, yeah, very clear-cut, everything was black and white, united Ireland or nothing. Loyalists, unionists weren't considered at all.'[97]

'[When somebody said] "these people are unionists", [we would reply] "no, no, no, they're Irish and that's it". We would kind of fucking dismiss them like little children. We used to say to them, "our war is against Britain, not you". I think we realised that they were saying, "yeah, but we're the British too, we're British, we've a British identity", so I think that's made us change a wee bit.'[98]

'The biggest revolution within republicanism has been the recognition that there are a group of people on this island who consider themselves to be British and that we have to somehow contend with them, not in a contentious way, but have to reach an agreement with them. The simplistic notion that we had of driving the Brits out, that that was the end of the story, and everything would be very happy after that, I think the realisation by republicanism that it was not as simplistic as that has been the biggest revolution within republicanism over the last hundred years, two hundred years, because we always saw it as being the problem of getting the Brits out of Ireland and therefore everything else would fall into place. We are acknowledging that we have a group of people here whose allegiance is to Britain, we would prefer that it wasn't to Britain but nevertheless that's how it is.'[99]

'What's become very obvious after thirty years is that the IRA isn't capable of bombing one million unionists into a united Ireland. So whatever the outcome between the conflict between the IRA and the British government, you still have to deal with one hundred, or one million unionists who are very determined not to go down that road. I've spoken to many volunteers who have always felt that the IRA was much too soft on unionists and loyalists, that there should have been a more direct and sustained attack on their communities as an attempt to weaken their resolve. And if you look at situations like that historically throughout the world you find that that doesn't happen, it usually strengthens the resolve of the person being attacked to resist. (...) The movement's sort of view of unionism has always been very naïve, you know, this idea that they're, that they're, you know, sort of, that they're Irish men who don't know they're fucking Irish men. (...) I think we always knew we couldn't move them, even through violence, so therefore we believed that the thing to do was to put enough pressure on the British government to say to the unionists, "listen, it's just costing us too much to be here in terms of resources, economic wealth, manpower, you better sort this fucking thing out with these people or we're pulling the plug". That's a very simplistic approach but I think that for a long time our approach was very simplistic.'[100]

As well as acknowledging that the republican view of unionism was wrong,[101] these activists admit that the IRA's terrorist campaign strengthened the British identity among the Protestant community as a sort of defence mechanism against the aggression suffered. The consequences of this radical shift in the republican mentality are devastating, as the veteran activist John Kelly points out. In his opinion, once this 'hard reality' replaced the simplistic analysis that had previously been at the heart of the republican strategy, the conclusion was that armed struggle was futile.[102] The use of violence was therefore counter-productive, not just at present, when republicans have changed their way of thinking about the unionist community, but also throughout a conflict fundamentally shaped by an internal dimension, namely the antagonism with unionism, which has traditionally been overlooked by republicans. This is confirmed by the opinion that members of the republican movement now express in relation to the effects of their violence. By way of example, Jim Gibney explains how, quite logically, the unionists identified with the security forces, perceiving terrorism as an attack on both their government and their community, which clearly reveals the IRA's mistake in believing that 'until the British military presence in Ireland was smashed the Protestants could not be won over to the national struggle':[103]

> I think that if you're talking about hurting the unionist community, the IRA probably hurt them more by killing RUC men and women, UDR men and women, members of the Crown forces who were also members of the unionist community. Also the bombing campaign of the IRA, it was largely against towns where there was Protestant business people. So, of course, it goes without saying that a campaign of that nature leaves a legacy behind, a legacy wherein there is deep pain and hurt on the unionist side. We'd be fools not to recognise it.[104]

Similarly, another former IRA prisoner recognised the mistake of those who advocated murdering more unionist politicians: 'What if you had killed Paisley, for talk's sake? What good would that have done in terms of, it would have just kind of reinforced that fundamentalist DUP [Democratic Unionist Party] mandate that they have.'[105] Further, Jim Gibney now takes a radically different view than that of the republican mouthpiece *An Phoblacht* when in November 1981 it claimed that the 'execution' of the unionist politician Robert Bradford 'should knock about two or three years off the British occupation of Ireland':[106] 'We're specifically talking about unionists here, elected representatives, they have a special role in society, they are the public faces of the unionist community. If some of those politicians are killed, then that community is going to feel it much more than, say, if a member of the Crown forces was killed who came out of that community, so in my opinion, whatever the IRA did in the past, it would be disastrous for anybody to think that they could advance a republican agenda by shooting elected representatives of the unionist community. It would not advance one inch the objective of a united and independent Ireland, in fact, it would set it back, it would reinforce the divisions that are there, it would create a mentality wherein the unionist people would retreat even further away from the notion of talking to republicans or engaging with republicans, so for me, it's not only politically the wrong thing to do, it would be morally the wrong thing to do as well, especially if, on the one hand, you're trying to say to the unionist community, "we believe a united Ireland is in your interests", you know, "but then we're going to kill those people you elect because we think we can advance a united Ireland by doing so". It doesn't make sense.'[107]

As these opinions reveal, republicans made key strategic mistakes and IRA violence created a chasm in Northern Irish society which exacerbated distrust between the two communities. The following testimonies illustrate the negative effects of the IRA's violence, lending support to the view that the armed struggle has to be seen as a sectarian campaign.

'Quite a lot of the Provisionals would tell you today that the unionists are British, you know, and they maintain that Britishness with their flags, they maintain it with their culture, and therefore, when you say, "Brits out", what do you really mean? Do you mean "Prods out" as well? And very largely the Protestant community interpreted "Brits out" as "Prods out" and they responded to that, that's why I'm saying that the outcome of the politics of the Provisionals was sectarian, however well intentioned they might have thought they were, the actual outcome of their activities was to create and enhance sectarianism. (. . .) You can't ignore the fact that busloads of Protestant workers were blown up by the Provisionals deliberately, you can't ignore the fact that you were going into houses on the Shankill estate and killing people, going into the Shankill, shooting people dead, and then turning round and saying, "I didn't kill him because he was a Prod, I killed him because he was a member of the security forces", the community didn't see it in that light, they were saying, "this is an attack on us, this is targeting our community". Similarly when they blew the Shankill up with the Shankill bomb, they said they were attacking the UDA, the Shankill community said, "no, you've torn the heart out of our community", and the result of that bomb is still apparent today with the sectarianism.'[108]

'I lived in the Markets and there was an awful lot of bombs that left the Markets for the city centre of Belfast. People in the Markets loved to see that town going up. But by the mid-1990s the droves of the nationalist population, most of the workers in the city centre were from the Nationalist community – they were the people who were losing jobs when Belfast was blown up. They were the people who we were relying on for support for the armed struggle. I mean it would be silly … I remember I was talking to this guy one time and he said that the economic bombings should be stopped on the basis that …, I mean, you never heard of the RAF bombing London during the Second World War, he said that Belfast is a nationalist city, it would be silly and counter productive to put our own people out of work. (. . .) If you look at what the Continuity IRA in particular is doing. The Continuity IRA blew up a hotel in a nationalist area packed full of nationalists at a wedding during Drumcree. Now the IRA on the other hand went and put a bomb in the middle of Portadown and blew Portadown up. They just never claimed it, but everybody knew it was the IRA that done it.'[109]

The interviewee was talking about a car bomb which exploded on 14 July 1999 at the Killyhevlin Hotel in Enniskillen. A republican splinter group called the Continuity IRA claimed responsibility for this attack. At the same time this activist refers to another terrorist attack, this one perpetrated on 22 May 1993, when the Provisional IRA blew-up a van full of explosives in the centre of the mainly Protestant town of Portadown, injuring six people and causing significant losses.

The armed struggle is considered by many former IRA members to be intrinsically sectarian, something that they believe also reveals the flaws in the alleged political motivation with which the group has justified its actions. It must be recalled that the objective of traditional republican ideology is the unity of Catholics and Protestants – all of whom are considered to be members of the Irish nation – in order to create an egalitarian society. However, as some of the activists interviewed put it, 'you are not going to get the support of Protestants if you kill them'. Seamus Lynch, who was one of the main leaders of the Official IRA in Belfast at the beginning of the 1970s, stresses this point in various anecdotes extracted from his experience in prison during that period. Lynch recalls having had a conversation during this time with Gerry Adams, who at that time was already an influential member of the Provisional IRA. Adams criticised the Official IRA's position and the politicisation carried out by its leaders in an attempt to bring together the different communities. For Adams the unity of the Catholic and Protestant working classes which was meant to form the basis of republican demands had a different meaning, as can be seen from his words in that meeting: 'He said to me, "you know, we can just wreck this working-class unity that you talk about, overnight", he says, "with six well placed car bombs". I says, "what do you mean, Gerry, explain that to me?" He says, "well, when you get out of here, if you organise the workers together and the people to come together, we put a car bomb in six Protestant working-class areas, that's all your unity up in the air". I says, "Gerry, tell me, what does this united Ireland mean to you, how much does it mean to you? Like, that disgusts me, even the thought of that." He says, "I'm prepared to wade up to my knees in Protestant blood to get a united Ireland." I just said, "fuck off! End of debate."'[110] This attitude is mirrored by that of other republican prisoners, as Lynch confirms when recalling how other inmates cheered while watching on television the news of an IRA car bomb which exploded without warning on 11 December 1971 in the Protestant Shankill Road of Belfast killing two adults and two children.[111]

In these circumstances, the use of violence also had negative consequences for one of its declared objectives: the defence of the Catholic community. In Chapter 2 it was seen how the Provisional IRA has, throughout the conflict, claimed as its own the task of defending the nationalist minority and how it has explained its coming into being as a response to the need to defend the Catholic population. However, the ineffectiveness of the IRA in this regard is clear, as some former members are prepared to admit, revealing the mistake of those who believed that 'the primary function of the IRA in Northern Ireland has always been community defence and protection of the

Catholic minority from state and loyalist attacks, and the national liberation struggle is secondary to that'.[112] 'I wasn't defending the community, I was proactively attacking the British state,' stressed one of the interviewees expressing a view shared by other republicans, who ensured that, in practice, defence was not one of the group's main tasks given its inability to guarantee it. Faced with loyalist terrorism throughout the 1970s, the IRA was less reticent about carrying out numerous revenge attacks whose effects clearly prejudiced its cause, as is clear from the comments of a former IRA member: 'Oh, yeah, they were sectarian, especially in Belfast. I've a cousin who was shot dead, a Protestant, but she was a blood relative, a young girl, 18, was executed by the IRA because a few days before, a young 18-year-old Catholic was shot dead by the loyalists, so they immediately retaliated. And that's when the war became madness, became crazy and it went totally in the face of their republican ideology.'[113] This spiral of violence was typical of this era, as the following example shows. On 5 April 1975, five Protestants died when the IRA placed a bomb in a bar in Belfast's Shankill Road. Only hours before, the UVF, a loyalist terrorist group, had murdered a Catholic in a pub in the north of the city. In this context, the failure of armed struggle can once again be seen, as a former republican prisoner notes: 'I came to the conclusion that, for example, my activities in shooting soldiers and policemen didn't contribute to republican ideology, what it did was give justification to the UVF and the UDA to retaliate or react against my community.'[114]

Nevertheless, the need to defend its own community has been one of the reasons repeatedly given by the IRA throughout the peace process for refusing to comply with the British and Irish governments' demand that it give up its arms. Thus, one of the republicans interviewed stated: 'If the IRA was to turn around and decommission tomorrow you would find a huge backlash from people within nationalist communities who feel that that's their line of defence.'[115] Two weeks after making this comment, the IRA announced that for the first time in its history it would proceed to decommission part of its arsenal. There was no reaction along the lines predicted by this republican. In view of the IRA and Sinn Féin's attempts to reformulate the debate about disarmament by making it an issue of self-defence, some of the group's volunteers expressed the need to debunk this myth that the IRA played the role of defender of the nationalist community. Statistics show clearly that the Provisional IRA has been the main perpetrator of violence throughout the conflict, being responsible for half of all fatalities,[116] including a considerable number of Catholic civilians. It is therefore impossible to argue that 'the IRA's guns defend people living under the threat of death'.[117] Instead, it would be more appropriate to state that their violence made it more likely that the nationalist community would be a victim of loyalist terrorism, as experience demonstrates.[118]

For years the republican movement insisted that there was no link between IRA violence and loyalist terrorism, although recently many republicans have changed their position somewhat. Throughout the peace process there has been a notable reduction in the level of violence, although the terrorist groups are still operating, particularly on the unionist side, Catholics having been murdered and attacked on a number of occasions. A press release published in February 2003 stated that, according to the statistics of the Northern Irish police, in the last three years an attack with home-made pipe bombs had taken place every two days.[119] The Sinn Féin press service and the weekly *An Phoblacht* constantly publicise loyalist aggressions. For example, in May 2002 they denounced the fact that about one hundred people had been forced out of their homes when the Catholic enclave in Short Strand, east Belfast, was besieged; in the same month, they reported that the UDA had organised a campaign of sectarian attacks against Catholic communities in Belfast, and, on these and other occasions, they have alerted nationalists to stay on their guard.[120] If analysed from a republican perspective one would expect the IRA to be fully involved in defending the nationalist community in such situations. The explanation for the IRA's inaction given by one of the republicans interviewed demonstrates what would happen if it did respond, clearly exposing the futility of retaliation when it was used in the past: 'At this point in time I think it is amoral. I think if we get back into that situation you are leading the spiral, the spiral will lead us inevitably back to a bigger conflict. I think it has to be resisted at all costs. Also I think it plays into the hands of the people who are actually doing it. I think the people who are actually doing it want that type of response, I think they want people to retaliate so that they can then use that as some sort of spurious justification for what they are doing because memories are very short. Within a few weeks who started it will not matter. When everybody else is getting killed on the streets it will not matter who started it.'[121]

168

6

WINNERS?

'This is a propaganda war'

'The IRA were doing their own people harm too'

As we have seen, the republican movement was aware that it did not have sufficient strength to attain its goals through the use of violence per se. Instead, the continuation of terrorism was also justified for propaganda reasons on the grounds that the media coverage obtained made it effective. As various authors have pointed out, 'in the pursuit of recognition and attention, a major, sometimes only, aim of terrorist action is media coverage'.[1] In this way, wide media coverage of attacks reaffirmed the group's sense of power leading republicans to perceive IRA violence as a simple 'means of communication' through which it was possible to send a 'violent, loud, persistent and adamant message'.[2] The IRA campaign became a mere expression of protest consisting of terrorist actions that were defined as effective by those who perpetrated them, although the apparent perception of power that such attacks helped to create masked their real weaknesses. It is rarely the case that as a result of the attention paid to terrorist activities the grievances used by terrorist groups to rationalise their conduct disappear. Republicans themselves have also recognised that while violence may be translated into spectacular images and media attention, normally this did not have anything like the decisive effect needed to bring them close to attaining their stated goals.

An Phoblacht/Republican News has been the hub of the republican movement's propaganda efforts, as is shown, for example, by the first page of the edition of 9 January 1992, when, under the heading 'The centre cannot hold' and next to a photograph of the damage caused by an IRA bomb, the following could be read: 'For the eighth time in just six weeks IRA Volunteers in Belfast have succeeded in penetrating massively increased security around Belfast's city centre to ferry a huge van bomb into the heart of one of the most closely guarded sectors of the occupied Six-County area. The message which rang out loud and clear with the bomb's deafening detonation was that in spite of every British effort the ingenuity of a people determined to be free will never be exhausted.'[3] The same edition celebrated this and other explosions in Belfast, a pattern often repeated.[4] However, the consequences of this type of operation were not as positive as the republican propaganda machine wished for, as a former activist explains: 'At one stage they started blowing up all the government buildings and all things like that there and then it got to the stage that they didn't care they were blowing up Catholic shops, all to just get media out of it and that shouldn't have been the way. They should have just kept it to the way it started off, government buildings and places like that – maybe even Protestant buildings to keep them out of the area and bring Catholic businesses in, but then I think they got a wee bit lazy there and just for to get media on them started hitting Catholic businesses. No, it shouldn't have been the way of it because they were doing their own people harm too.'[5]

Other republicans shared this viewpoint, describing the bombings in the centre of Belfast, which *An Phoblacht/Republican News* was so full of praise for, as 'counterproductive'. In marked contrast with the views of these activists, the belief that the use of violence was an effective and vital part of the republican strategy was also reflected in the following *An Phoblacht/ Republican News* headline: 'London bombs put Ireland onto election agenda'.[6] Yet the same newspaper contained a much more realistic article which fully accepted that the attitude of the British electorate towards Northern Ireland was one of 'apathy and contempt'. In contrast to the frequently triumphalist republican rhetoric, the armed campaign had, as the article noted, been unable to make the Irish question a main issue in the main British political parties' election manifestos,[7] thus implicitly acknowledging the ineffectiveness of IRA violence.

Unlike in previous eras, IRA violence from the end of the 1960s onwards did not divide British political parties, reflecting a consensus which to a large extent also existed in the media. As Smith has observed in his study of IRA strategy, republicans looked 'both intellectually and physically vulnerable' without being able to 'field solid evidence for the effectiveness of their strategy'.[8] Despite this, violence has dominated republican strategy because of its perceived propaganda value. As Gerry Adams put it, 'the tactic of armed struggle is of primary importance because it provides a vital cutting edge. Without it, the issue of Ireland would not even be an issue. So, in effect, the armed struggle becomes armed propaganda.'[9] Other IRA members also define the group's campaign as 'armed propaganda' understanding their violence as a means of influencing public opinion. Therefore, terrorism became 'theatre',[10] the media being an integral part of the violent strategy which would convey to different audiences the message sent by the perpetrators. Authors like Wilkinson, Tugwell and Crelinsten warn about the manipulation and exploitation of this 'co-existence' by terrorists, arguing that groups like the IRA try to use the media to project a sense of invulnerability in an attempt to demoralise the government of the state under threat. This depends, of course, on the message being plausible, which makes it necessary to use mechanisms of self-justification and guilt transfer in order to achieve dissuasion. Further, those who try to subvert the system try to mobilise the support of the masses. However, terrorists also aim to obtain support through fear, stressing that opposition to their objectives will come at a price.[11] The intensity of the relationship between the media and violence, which is defined by some authors as 'symbiotic',[12] can also be understood if it is accepted that terrorism is significant in political terms for what it represents, and not just for what it actually achieves. Lomasky has pointed out that 'the terrorism that plays itself out in newspapers and on television screens to rapt audiences around the world, is to be understood as activity that is primarily expressive in character rather than outcome-oriented' since that kind of violence mainly expresses 'virulent and unregulated opposition to the preconditions of successful civility'.[13] Applying this definition, the media is a vital part of a strategy based on political violence, a point confirmed by Wardlaw, who maintains that terrorists try to stage manage the form and the moment in which they carry out their 'spectacular' attacks in order to obtain maximum public impact.[14]

However, having established the connection between violence and the media, care must be taken not to distort the nature of this relationship. In this regard, contrary to what certain academics claim, the mere media coverage of terrorist actions does not in itself inevitably promote the cause in question or improve the image of the group concerned.[15] Walter Laqueur, for example, argues that terrorists and journalists share the belief that those who make headlines have achieved some power and a political gain.[16] However, the reporting of the Irish conflict and the violence perpetrated have very often lacked in-depth analysis, with no explanation given for the motives behind terrorism and the general context in which it has taken place.[17] This phenomenon is very common in other areas affected by terrorist activities.[18] Therefore merely recognising the existence of an organisation like the IRA by reporting on its activities is not the same as legitimising it. In short, what the perpetrators of violence really want is 'good publicity', something that is not automatically achieved just by appearing in the media.

This reductionist approach, whereby obtaining media coverage is treated as irrefutable proof of the effectiveness of violence as part of a political strategy, has been common among republicans. Bowyer Bell took a similar line when defining IRA operations in England as effective because 'the war was brought home to Britain'. This author also described the IRA campaign as 'attractive to the media' since it provided 'hard news with good film to be sent by satellite feed to New York or Bonn' which had the effect of 'raising the visibility of the struggle, encouraging the faithful and horrifying many but to useful purpose'.[19] Yet at the same time Bowyer Bell recognises that the IRA campaign 'grew increasingly irrelevant after 20 years of violence'.[20] Thus, when the IRA's terrorism is analysed within a wider strategic framework than the immediate context in which it took place it is clear that its alleged effectiveness is illusory in the long term. It should not be forgotten that the IRA's ultimate objective was to undermine the will of the British government. Short-term considerations were not an especially important part of the group's strategy, a point illustrated by a former IRA member who admits that politically their actions had very little influence on events:

> At all times the military campaign has to be kept going because the goal of a united Ireland, the goal of a British declaration of intent [to withdraw] is linked to it by stating that we will never stop this war until such times as the British give a declaration on intent to withdraw. So that is the field of play, and within the field of play people can kick the ball this way and that way, get a good operation one day and a bad operation the other. At certain times the IRA would change tactics, they would concentrate on civilian contractors, they would bomb England, they would do a variety of things but it was never seemingly with any short term political objective. The IRA would argue that the politics of the IRA, the military campaign of the IRA was military politics, it was just a form of continuously applying pressure. But it was applying pressure to the central state apparatus as opposed to the decision making processes on a day-to-day basis. It wasn't about negotiating at that level, it was about applying maximum pressure as they seen it to the British State. Whereas in more broad based political campaigns you could argue 'right, we will kill a soldier today because we want Ballymurphy cleaned up or we want torture stopped – we will kill one tomorrow because we don't like the British digging up playgrounds in South Armagh'. It didn't really operate that way in my view.[21]

The IRA's 'armed propaganda' had fundamental shortcomings which affected the evolution and the outcome of the group's terrorist campaign. This weakness was identified by activist Tommy McKearney in the mid-1980s, voicing a criticism of the use of violence which, as has been seen in previous chapters, the leadership saw as dangerous despite the fact that IRA leaders would ultimately use similar arguments in order to stop the terrorist campaign. McKearney summed up the inherent problem in the use of violence as follows: 'The basis of the problem lies in a misconception that force can be used to change or undermine the will of the opposition, that by carrying out a sufficient number of operations at a certain level, the opposition will become unwilling to pay the price in political unpopularity. Inextricably connected to this method of thinking is the ever present need for propaganda. (...) In turn, what is the strategy underlying the campaign of force? It quite obviously is not designed to deny the opposition territorial control. If it were, no energy would be wasted on irrelevant targets. It patently isn't designed to support the authority of an alternative administration: there isn't one. (...) It is a strategy based on a theory crudely summed up in the often repeated phrase of "send them home in boxes and they'll scream to bring their troops home". The logic being that public opinion in Britain will force their leaders to organise for withdrawal. The target, therefore, is British "public opinion" more than actual British armed might.'[22] Under those circumstances, McKearney put forward the following course of action: 'I started to question the value or the efficacy of the campaign in the middle eighties. That's when I was saying that this is a propaganda war and I started to say that if you're to make the war effective we have to have clear objectives and it has to be a greater input and it has to be a vast escalation. Short of that it's not worth losing our own lives and taking the lives of others.'[23]

As seen in the previous chapter, such a 'vast escalation' was not a viable option, casting doubts over the expectations of success. Therefore, the abandonment of the use of violence seemed the most reasonable way forward. Hence the glaring inconsistency in the IRA continuing to employ a tactic whose very nature prevented the group from achieving the ends it sought. This strategic failure was covered up by claiming that the IRA's attacks came within what its leaders called 'the long war'. In choosing such tactics and terminology, they were skilfully able to avoid the criticisms that the usefulness of violence could give rise to, since each action was understood as part of a process whose end was not fixed. In this way, a sort of 'life insurance' was created for the leadership, as one member stated: 'It never comes to a time where people can say, "you were wrong", because they simply say, "it's not over yet, it's not over yet". So it's a very clever thing.'[24] The nature of the attacks carried out by the IRA supported this analysis, as can be seen from McKearney's interpretation of one IRA action which the group called a notable success but which he labelled 'a fairly ineffective operation'.[25] In May 1974 some forty IRA members attacked a base belonging to the UDR, a British army regiment, in the Northern Irish town of Clogher: 'The only casualty on the night was a female member of the UDR shot, she was running for cover. She was at several hundred yards, the IRA didn't even know that night that they had hit anybody, they just machine-gunned the centre and mortar-bombed it. (...) The IRA estimated that it had been a successful operation on the basis that although they would have preferred to have killed a male member of the army, at least they had inflicted a casualty on the army, they had bombed the building, they had gained considerable propaganda and all men and weapons returned safe. So as far as the IRA was concerned, it was a success. I think that a more knowledgeable guerrilla army would have said that they just dissipated resources.'[26]

This state of affairs was not restricted to terrorist actions within Northern Ireland, as illustrated by an article in which a republican sympathiser recognised that the IRA campaign in Great Britain lacked 'any clear focus', mainly consisting of attacks on targets with 'no military significance and no discernible relationship with Ireland'. The result was not that British people were 'more sympathetic to the Irish liberation struggle', but 'just less bothered about it'.[27] In this context, unlike at the beginning of the 1970s, the IRA appeared to take more care to avoid civilian injuries, having interpreted that this was what the so-called 'armed propaganda' required. This is reflected by a former activist when referring to 'Bloody Friday', on 21 July 1972, when twenty IRA bombs exploded in the heart of Belfast without any prior warning, killing nine and injuring hundreds. In her opinion: 'It was terrible that day. It was scary, but again they got a lot of publicity. I know it was bad publicity I suppose, yeah, all those people being killed. But again I think it was still letting them know: "right, we are here, we can do damage, are you listening to us?"'[28] Nevertheless, as another former IRA member describes, the effect of the publicity given to terrorist acts frequently means that its end results are deceptive. In 1973, Shane O'Doherty sent a number of letter bombs to prominent personalities, such as Reginald Maudling, British Home Secretary at the time of 'Bloody Sunday' in Derry, when fourteen unarmed civilians were shot dead by the British army. None of the 'targets' of this letter bomb campaign were killed, although others, such as those who handled the envelopes, did suffer injuries including amputations. The victims included a secretary, a security guard, a policeman in the bomb disposal unit and various post office employees. One of the letters reached the official residence of the British Prime Minister at 10 Downing Street, although it did not actually explode. Although O'Doherty indicates that through these actions the IRA obtained a great deal of publicity, the effectiveness of this strategy must be doubted when analysed in a wider context:

> Nothing else apart from publicity and disruption, but also showing a certain daredevilness that others could emulate and showing the volunteers to come after you, 'you can do this. We can reach London.' (...) Fifty bombs would explode in Northern Ireland but not get any news in the British papers. But one letter bomb going into 10 Downing Street hit all the British newspapers' front pages, highlighted the issues, made the British public aware there was a problem across the water. There's no question, as I said earlier, that violence concentrates the minds of governments wonderfully. There is no question that violence grabs all the publicity. I mean, one person, Timothy McVeigh, who has an issue with the Federal government over Waco, certainly commanded the world's attention for, how many years? Since the bombing. But you know, he killed one hundred and sixty eight innocent men, women and children to make a point about the Federal government, but it didn't change any of the behaviour of the Federal government. But if you measured his success in terms of gaining publicity and getting his message across, he got his message across. There is hardly a country in the world where people weren't aware who Timothy McVeigh was, why he bombed the

Federal building and what his objection was to the Federal government's attitude to Waco, so according to his likes he succeeded. That is
all he was trying to do. He wasn't trying to create a movement. You have
to look at the armed struggle in this sense. The armed struggle was
intended to unite Ireland and force the British to withdraw from
Northern Ireland and it was to get a British withdrawal and a united
Ireland. We don't have a British withdrawal, we don't have a united
Ireland, we have an extremely divided community that votes in a very
polarised fashion – DUP and Sinn Féin – we've never even managed
to build any bridges with our fellow Irishmen, Northern Ireland Protestants. We've never convinced them so far that it would be to their
benefit to join with us in an all-Ireland government. We haven't created
institutions in the Republic of Ireland that win any favour with Northern
Protestants in terms of religion, culture, we've turned our own language,
the Irish language into some like sectarian weapon that largely Protestants don't want to learn, and largely many Catholics don't want to
learn either. And people see our very language as a weapon of one
armed militant group. (…) But if people are calling successful achieving
a few publicity aims and filling a prison system for many years and then
through the heroic and courageous deaths of hunger strikers then gain-
ing a political base, well, that is a very warped sense of success because
the other thing is, it begs the question why didn't we try to gain a political
base? You see one of the issues that interests me is we now have a
polarised situation where we can't convince any Protestants to want to
join a united Ireland, especially with Sinn Féin.[29]

'Republicans weren't able to get their voice across'

The contradictions between the real and perceived effectiveness of IRA
operations partly emerges because the republican analysis has been unable
to interpret correctly the effects that its 'armed propaganda' had on the
different audiences to which it was addressed. The involvement of different
actors in the Northern Ireland conflict makes it possible to distinguish up to
five different strands of public opinion which the violence was going to affect
differently: Northern Irish unionists, Northern Irish nationalists, the public
in Great Britain, the Republic of Ireland and the rest of the world, especially
the United States. In all of these different areas, IRA violence created a
series of obstacles such as those that have been described in previous pages.
These largely coincide with the effects of political violence on public opinion
that previous research has detected. Dowling describes these effects as
follows.[30] First, the boomerang effect: by advocating extreme positions as
expressed in the use of violence, this causes a defensive reaction from
members of the public, so that they end up being more firmly opposed to
positions to which initially they had been more receptive to through the use

of persuasion. Second, the negative credibility implicit in violent actions which obtain media coverage also prevents any massive acceptance of the ideology according to which such acts are justified and which are frequently identified and defined as 'terrorism'. Third, violence tends to feed a sense of fear among certain sectors of the public, giving rise to the increased desire to place their trust in the authorities and agents of the state to guarantee the protection and security which they believe to be under threat. Fourth, violence does not normally attract support for those that engage in it.

All of these consequences can be detected to a lesser or greater extent in the different audiences of IRA terrorism. With respect to the USA, it is true that certain sectors of the media did contribute to an increase in support for the IRA among the Irish community, proving useful for the terrorist group in financial terms. However, this support did not materialise in a wide or unconditional backing from US leaders.[31] Successive US administrations have unequivocally condemned IRA violence and isolated its leaders, as is shown by the refusal to allow Gerry Adams to enter the country because of his links with terrorism until months before the 1994 ceasefire. Shane O'Doherty's testimony shows the negative effects of IRA violence, and explains why the group never carried out any attacks in the USA. In fact, the IRA tried to avoid causing *any* American victims, as can be seen from the following criticism of those republicans who were in favour of indiscriminate attacks in public places, such as the London underground: 'In fact one of my letter bombs famously went off in the British Embassy in Washington and infamously injured an Irish woman from Galway who was the personal secretary to the director of military intelligence there, some colonel guy. She opened his mail and she lost a hand and the republican movement had a fuckin' fit because a bomb went off basically in America but luckily it went off on sovereign British territory in America. But I think I was told categorically under no circumstances was there to be any bombing surrounding Americans. So fuck, how would you have gotten away with bombs in tube stations I don't know because London was full of American tourists.'[32]

The way in which the other audiences mentioned above interpreted IRA violence was very much affected by the prohibitions that both the British and Irish governments imposed on the TV and radio coverage of activities carried out by republicans. At the beginning of the 1970s, the Irish government took already existing legislation, which prohibited the broadcasting of material that had the potential to promote or incite crime or tended to undermine the authority of the state, and added a prohibition on the transmission of interviews with Sinn Féin representatives or any other illegal organisations in Northern Ireland, in other words unionist and republican terrorist groups. In October 1988, the British authorities followed the model put into practice in the Republic of Ireland, imposing similar prohibitions in the United Kingdom. Nevertheless, the restrictions in place in Ireland were more severe, since the words of the silenced voices in the United Kingdom were read by actors. These prohibitions were suspended in the Republic at the beginning of 1994, when the IRA was making final preparations prior to calling its ceasefire, and months later in the United Kingdom, after the truce had actually been announced.

There are conflicting views on the relationship between the effects that these prohibitions had on the political landscape in general and on republican circles in particular. On the one hand, there are those who claim that even if such measures served to limit the publicity that Sinn Féin obtained, the costs outweighed the benefits since the limitations on the freedom of speech were so serious.[33] Similarly, this school of thought considered that such an approach prevented those who 'communicated through the use of violence' from expressing their arguments on radio and television.[34] Alan Protheroe, the BBC's Assistant Director General at the time the legislation was applied, argued that maintaining democracy entailed listening to 'unpopular' and 'even dangerous views'.[35] On the other hand, those who supported the legislation, such as the academic Paul Wilkinson, considered that it was necessary to pay such a price to protect democracy: 'Experience in the Republic of Ireland certainly shows that such a ban can be operated smoothly and efficiently for many years without in any way threatening parliamentary democracy. Few observers pointed out that even in a free society, no freedom of expression is totally unlimited. Most of us believe for example that pornography should be banned from TV and radio. Inviting terrorists on TV to crow about their latest atrocity is the ultimate pornography of violence.'[36]

Despite what some of the detractors of the policy calculated, the draconian restrictions had dramatic and immediate consequences for Sinn Féin, as its head of publicity Danny Morrison explained: 'We monitored the media and discovered that in the three or four month period before the ban there were something like 500 phone calls, ranging from requests for interviews through to asking for information. That dropped to about 100 in the four months afterwards. It's an occasion for opening a bottle of champagne when we get a request for an interview from the broadcasting media at the moment. Broadcasting journalists don't even bother phoning us up because of the internal fights in their organisations, having to go and get clearance and such like. Anybody who goes out of their way to fight for objectivity in the broadcasting media now is considered to be a Provo, there's no question of that.'[37] Other prominent members of the IRA and Sinn Féin share the view that the ending of the media restrictions had an 'enormous' impact on the republican movement since 'for many years the Southern media and Southern politicians had a free run in terms of their articulation as to what was or what was not happening in the Six Counties, as to the nature of republicanism and the integrity of the people who were involved in republicanism'.[38]

There were those who thought that the imposition of such significant restrictions would strengthen the more militaristic elements within the republican movement.[39] As the ending of the violence decreed by the IRA and the testimony of some of those interviewed show, not only was this not the result but, in addition, the republican movement still had to bear afterwards the consequences of its prolonged association with terrorism, showing once again its ineffectiveness as a means of achieving their objectives. As a former IRA activist put it, even after the IRA ceasefire it was quite common for the media to focus on IRA activities and its association with Sinn Féin instead of dealing with other matters of more interest to the party: 'At each and every time that republicans are interviewed, it's a battle for republicans to have to articulate the politics of Sinn Féin, the politics of republicanism as opposed to their position vis-à-vis an individual act or some perception of violent activity or association with armed groups.'[40]

If, as this activist claims, Sinn Féin's representatives continued experiencing a 'hostile' reaction from the media several years after the IRA ceasefire was called and following a considerable reduction in the climate of violence, it is easy to imagine what the situation was when the republican campaign was at its height. His testimony shows that the methods required by a democratic system of political participation, which republicans now ascribe to, are incompatible with the use of violence advocated by Sinn Féin and the IRA in the past. For this reason, another interviewee considered that the media prohibition was 'very detrimental' to the republican movement: 'Yeah, I think it was, because republicans weren't able to get their voice across, not so much within their own community, but to the wider community. People in sort of republican nationalist areas, people knew who they were and knew what they stood for and all the rest of it, but particularly in areas outside, particularly in the South where they weren't that well organised, people didn't know who the republican movement was etc., who the IRA was and all that type of stuff, and I think it was much more difficult because I think then people believed the propaganda that was being put about by the Brits, they didn't know what the republican position was on various issues, so, yeah, I think it was detrimental.'[41]

From this republican's point of view, although when the peace process started the republican movement maintained a 'core committed support' within its community which he didn't think 'would have diminished greatly unless something really catastrophic had happened', this support was never more than 'limited', and therefore 'the question was whether they would have been able to move forward' under such conditions. The media restrictions faced by republicans therefore had an effect in another context beyond that 'core committed support'. This republican activist recognises that most of the nationalist community did not agree with the IRA's use of violence nor would they have voted for a party like Sinn Féin which was in favour of violence, thus influencing the republicans' strategy: 'As censorship increased, as republicans fought, a lot of people weren't attracted to republicanism. One, because, particularly people outside of republican areas who didn't know republicans, so republicans were unable to appeal to those people. All those people saw was the violence. And I think that made it more difficult for republicans to increase their support. But what I'm saying is that I really believe that there was a particular level of support that would have remained and that republicans could have maintained their campaign but the question is, could they have progressed it, and they probably couldn't have. In their view they couldn't have progressed the campaign, that it took something like the peace process to give new energy into the thing and to give a new dynamic into the whole struggle.'[42]

The well-known republican strategist Jim Gibney also admitted that, from the perspective of the British and Irish governments, the media ban was a success. He described the effect on Sinn Féin after this group's disastrous electoral results in 1992, in the following way: 'Sinn Féin faces obstacles on a daily basis which no other party has to confront. Among these is censorship, which, although it has always been applied in relation to the South, this was our first election to be contested in the conditions of institutionalised censorship North and South. For us therefore, the ability to communicate directly through the media to the electorate was severely limited. (...) The SDLP entered this election with the dissenting nationalist voices – Sinn Féin – censored off the media for the previous four years, what party wouldn't like that advantage?'[43]

The opinions of republicans therefore coincide with those of Ed Moloney, a veteran analyst of the Northern Ireland conflict, who thinks that the ban 'removed the organisation from television screens and by so doing isolated it from its voters and potential electorate'. Therefore the restrictions were 'a damaging blow to a party whose political/military strategy depended for success on winning a steadily growing share of Northern Ireland's nationalist vote'.[44] This proved to be the case because by the beginning of the 1980s the republican strategy assumed that combining the use of violence with a greater politicisation of the movement through Sinn Féin would finally lead to John Hume's SDLP, the voice of moderate nationalism, losing its electoral hegemony. This combination of violence and politics was the basic pillar of the 'Armalite and ballot box' strategy. However, the contradictions inherent in this dual strategy which aimed to 'take power in Ireland with the ballot paper in one hand and the armalite in the other' were such that tensions inevitably came to the surface preventing it from succeeding. As the testimony of one former IRA member shows, the group's violence alienated the nationalist electorate, but at the same time Sinn Féin's increased political activity had the potential to alienate those who saw the armed campaign as the only valid form of action: 'Certainly there's some people who wouldn't have voted for Sinn Féin when there was a war on, but there's other people who wouldn't have voted Sinn Féin unless there was a war on, there's an

179

awful lot of Sinn Féin support because of the war. They didn't vote Sinn Féin cause they liked Gerry Adams' face, they voted Sinn Féin because Sinn Féin were actually out there fighting, so there was a hard, a hard element of support for the armed struggle.'[45]

As has been noted, the peace process that led to the Good Friday Agreement in April 1998 is the clearest possible confirmation that this policy was unviable. Its failure finally forced the republican movement to rid itself of what for years was claimed to be an indispensable part of its strategy, namely terrorism. This was confirmed by a former IRA member, who rejected the leadership's continued public claims that violence had been absolutely necessary: 'We didn't need an armed struggle to generate three or four members of parliament and the sad thing is that we had to put the armed struggle away to learn the very simple lesson that people would vote for Sinn Féin-type ideals in the absence of armed struggle, but during armed struggle they wouldn't. And Roman Catholics have a very hard time matching their conscience over voting for killings and murders and bombings and children being killed and civilians being killed and they largely voted SDLP during armed struggle because their conscience, there is a strong Catholicism here, I don't know, it is obviously changing a lot but there has always been a very strong Catholicism and as soon as you remove the equation of armed struggle and remove the problem of people's conscious voting for people engaged in armed struggle there is no problem voting. In fact Sinn Féin are now reaping the rewards of all those who argued "we are going to get more votes when we ditch the armed struggle".'[46]

If, as IRA members admit, their violence inevitably alienated a significant part of the nationalist community on which the group's support had to be based, it is logical that other audiences should also reject the republican approach. As summarised by a representative of the Irish government, the IRA's idea of self-determination was nothing more than coercion. In his opinion, IRA violence would not change the Republic's refusal to coerce unionists into a united Ireland.[47] If this was the position in the Republic of Ireland, one can imagine that the republican propaganda would have fallen on even stonier ground in the case of the unionists and the British. Successive opinion polls carried out during the conflict consistently reflect how the British people have seen Northern Ireland as a far-removed problem, and while many of them have supported the withdrawal of British troops from the area, this does not necessarily mean that they have been in favour of a united Ireland.[48] In the same way, the British public has always seen the Irish question as a burden, although no significant changes in this tendency can be detected as a result of the violence throughout the last three decades. Indeed, the effects of terrorism have often been counter-productive for the IRA, as one of its former members explains: 'I disagreed with the likes of the Birmingham bombings and Guildford bombings. I said they were wrong. I said they were acts of terrorism. I am very lucky to remain alive after that.

Because the contradiction was that you were trying to persuade the English people to support the call for a withdrawal of their troops, but how could you do that there when you are killing them? And people with a very sort of nationalistic notion and the English have a great nationalistic chauvinist notion, they get their backs up. So if you were putting bombs in bars and killing innocent people, they just see that as wanton murder, they don't see what is behind the act. So I disagreed with the likes of the Birmingham bombs and the Guildford bombs, I disagreed with that tactic.'[49]

The perception that Northern Ireland was 'a place apart' has existed long before the Troubles broke out in the late 1960s. Unlike any other British territory, like England, Wales or Scotland, since it was created Northern Ireland's future within the United Kingdom has been a question subjected to the opinion of the people of Northern Ireland. This distinction explains the reaction following a survey carried out in Great Britain in the summer of 2001, which showed 41 per cent in favour of Northern Ireland being part of a united Ireland. In response, the unionist Member of Parliament Jeffrey Donaldson said that this did not worry the unionist community, since Northern Ireland could only leave the United Kingdom if a majority of the population in Northern Ireland so desired, and therefore the views of the rest of the British population were irrelevant.[50] Given the importance of this internal dimension, violence produced the opposite effects among the unionist community to those sought by republicans, the outcome being deepened divisions, as the following testimony illustrates:

> The reason our vote has increased is because our message is getting across. While the armed struggle was on we were censored by the media and we couldn't get a message out. People didn't hear what we were saying, people only heard what the British government said we said. They twisted what we said, they accused us of all sorts of things that we were a bunch of psychopathic killers. I have to have some sympathy for the unionists in this respect. If for twenty five years the British government kept telling them we were nothing but a bunch of terrorists and psychopaths and that this was a crime wave and not a political struggle and that under no circumstances would they deal with us. (...) so we have to break all this down, we have to reach out to these people.[51]

'It reinforced their opinion of us as being sectarian monsters'

An examination of the role of the media in the Republic of Ireland shows how it became an important instrument in shaping public opinion, thus limiting the effectiveness of IRA propaganda. The prohibitions imposed by Irish legislation on media coverage reached the point that in 1983 the state's television and radio corporation RTE (*Radio Telefís Éireann*) was prevented

from broadcasting shouts in favour of Gerry Adams chanted by his supporters when he won the seat for West Belfast in the British parliament.
Years earlier, in 1972, the government had sacked the RTE management
team after the broadcasting of an interview with the IRA leader Sean Mac-
Stiofain. In short, the Irish authorities took very strong action to delegitimise
the political discourse of Sinn Féin and the IRA, aware that the integrity of
the state could not tolerate the slightest challenge from republicans. The
IRA and Sinn Féin thus lost the battle for respectability in the South of
Ireland, where the public was prepared to accept limitations on the freedom
of expression, such as those imposed on the media. To this must be added
the irrelevance of republicans as a political force south of the border throughout the conflict. Before 1997, Provisional Sinn Féin had not won a single seat
in the Irish parliament, and in the elections of that year it obtained a 2.6 per
cent share of the vote, that would rise to 6.5 per cent in 2002. This clearly
contradicts the republican analysis of the conflict, as Albert Reynolds, the
Irish Prime Minister between 1992–94, pointed out when indicating that the
IRA was not in conflict with the British government but rather with the Irish
people, both north and south of the border, an Irish people who longed for
peace and were prepared to accept the existence of Northern Ireland.[52]

The media's attitude to the seemingly interminable Northern Ireland
conflict can generally be described as one of apathy and disinterest.[53] Even
on those occasions when violence caught the media's eye, the consequences
were not always as positive as the republicans would have liked. Ultimately,
republicans view their actions as one more weapon in the battle of wills
between the IRA and the British government in which obtaining the support
of the public was crucial.[54] The IRA itself has recognised that its operations
aimed to achieve a 'political impact and a propaganda impact'.[55] Thus, even
authors who were critical of the way that the British press covered the
conflict have pointed out that the hostile manner in which republicans were
portrayed or interviewed should not have come as a surprise, since 'no state
engaged in military struggle allows genuinely unpartisan coverage of their
opponents' viewpoint'.[56] On many occasions, republicans effectively did the
work of those who they saw as their enemy by perpetrating attacks that were
bound to have a counterproductive effect in the media, as the following
examples highlight.

On 23 November 1988, two pedestrians – Barney Lavery, 67 years old,
and his 13-year-old granddaughter Emma Donnelly (both Catholics) – were
killed by an IRA car bomb in county Tyrone. On 12 April 1989, Joanne
Reilly, a 20-year-old Catholic, died when an IRA bomb exploded without
any prior warning next to the shop where she was working, near a police
station in Warrenpoint. The powerful explosion injured thirty people and
destroyed an extensive residential and commercial area, yet left the police
station virtually undamaged. Annie Bogle, a 74-year-old Protestant, died on
18 October 1993 from a heart attack when an IRA bomb exploded near the

old people's home in which she lived in the small town of Castlederg. Bridie Glennon, a 78-year-old Catholic, died on 14 December 1993 during a bomb warning in which hundreds of people had to be evacuated in the south of Belfast because the IRA had planted a half-ton bomb. The reaction of one of the deceased's family members emphasising that responsibility for her death fell squarely on the IRA's shoulders[57] illustrates well the ineffectiveness, on the republicans' own terms, of such operations. The same can be said of a failed IRA attack on 23 February 1987 in which the only death was that of Willie Johnston, a 65-year-old pedestrian who suffered a heart attack when various mortar bombs exploded next to Newtonstewart police station. As a former IRA activist noted, one of the best known examples of operations that brought negative publicity occurred in Enniskillen in 1987, when eleven Protestants died after a bomb exploded without any prior warning during a remembrance ceremony for the victims of the two World Wars: 'Enniskillen, I thought it was a disaster, to tell you the truth. (…) It was a fuckin' disaster and I think jobs like that pushed the Protestant people further and further away from listening to a republican analysis of this, of what was wrong with Ireland. It reinforced their opinion of us as being sectarian monsters just out to kill Protestants for the sake of killing Protestants because that's all they had seen it as.'[58]

The pages of *An Phoblacht/Republican News* also reflected the negative publicity generated by another example of IRA violence. After the death of Jonathan Ball and Timothy Parry, aged three and twelve years old respectively, when bombs planted by the IRA in wastepaper bins exploded in the English town of Warrington, a wave of revulsion towards republicans swept through both the north and south of Ireland as well as Great Britain. An article written by Hilda MacThomas, a pseudonym used by the wife of a prominent leader of Sinn Féin, stated as follows: 'The week that followed the Warrington bombing starkly illustrated how politicians, the media and the churches have colluded to de-humanise republicans and exclude their viewpoint from the political debate.' She went on to criticise the role played by the British, Irish and Northern Irish media in their coverage of events, as well as the decision of the main nationalist newspaper in Northern Ireland, the *Irish News*, to set up a fund to help the Warrington victims.[59] An editorial in the same edition was highly critical of the authorities in the Republic of Ireland: 'Despite the fact that the border with the Six Counties is a mere 60 miles from Dublin, the ignorance of many people in the city as to the reality of life in the Six Counties is huge. The Dublin government bears a direct responsibility for this. The atmosphere of fear in regard to the Six Counties which it has created through various means, not least political censorship, is responsible for such ignorance.'[60] These examples clearly reflect the open hostility to the IRA in the Republic of Ireland, at times even more so than in the United Kingdom. Mary McAleese, the current President of the Republic of Ireland who was born in north Belfast, criticised RTE, where she worked in the 1980s, for its limited coverage of the hunger strikes and for helping to create an atmosphere in which 'if you did not become apologetic about the IRA, you were in serious danger of being written off as a Provo'.[61]

It has not been uncommon to criticise the British newspapers for their coverage of the situation in the region, even accusing them of failing to explain that the solution for the conflict should come from Britain rather than Northern Ireland.[62] This so-called failure has been a constant feature throughout the conflict, which shows the ineffectiveness of IRA violence since it has been unable to modify the views of the British public, which remain totally at odds with those of republicans. In fact, as the prestigious academic John Whyte has demonstrated, most studies of Northern Ireland conclude that the internal dimension of the conflict is a crucial factor, thus considering endogenous factors to be much more important than exogenous ones. In other words, a solution to the problem was to be found not in Great Britain but in Northern Ireland.[63] Other critics of the role of the media argue that it has represented IRA violence as an irrational and inhuman terrorist phenomenon. One exponent of this viewpoint, Schlesinger, says that this was the result of an effective long-term strategy waged by the British state using sophisticated techniques that he sees as part of a psychological war.[64] Nevertheless, it is not correct to exaggerate the media's role in generating this rejection of IRA's actions, which was practically inevitable, since 'some aspects of the violence you could explain till the cows come home and it would still turn people off', as Michael Farrell, a former member of the civil rights movement who had to leave Northern Ireland following threats from a loyalist terrorist group, has put it.[65]

Republicans have relied heavily on propaganda trying to depict the conflict as a struggle between a national liberation movement and occupying forces, studiously ignoring the pre-eminent role of internal or endogenous factors. Further, in its desire to be seen as a genuine army, the IRA has used typical army terminology such as 'brigades', 'battalions', 'companies' and 'active service units' which are far from the IRA's true state in terms of numbers and organisation. Such delusions reflect the 'fantasy war' idea constructed by terrorist groups which allows its members to consider themselves as soldiers.[66] In this context, there has been no shortage of journalists and academics that have been seduced by the IRA's propaganda. Some have stated that the need to maintain the 'army image' was the reason that the IRA did not take hostages, despite the evidence to the contrary.[67] Others have given greater credibility to public declarations by republicans than to those of British authorities accepting IRA denials after particular atrocities perpetrated by the terrorist group. On many occasions the IRA has denied responsibility for attacks despite having undoubtedly carried them out.[68] One such example is the explosion in the Abercorn café on Saturday 4 March 1972. At 16.30, a bomb exploded without prior warning in a packed coffee shop situated in Belfast city centre. Two people died and many were seriously injured. The IRA issued various declarations denying responsibility, whose truth some accepted at face value.[69] It is unsurprising that republicans should wish to deny responsibility for such a savage attack. In private, however, IRA members have freely admitted that the IRA was responsible, as much research has confirmed.[70]

IRA lies were not infrequent, nor did *An Phoblacht/Republican News* think twice before distorting the truth, something which they constantly needed to do to prevent the morale of sympathisers from being sapped. Thus, in the weekly column entitled 'War news' they lauded the IRA's alleged brilliance and successes in its struggle with 'the enemy'. As a way of example, in its edition of 20 March 1997, the paper reported on an IRA operation in which one of the activists interviewed for this book took part. The 'ambush' was described as 'devastating',[71] although the former IRA member admits that it did not cause 'any real serious injuries, just a few of the Brits had minor injuries'.[72] By contrast, he and another activist were arrested by the police an hour after the attack. This republican was sentenced to eighteen years in prison for attempted murder, being released in July 2000 as part of the early release programme for prisoners introduced after the signature of the Good Friday Agreement. The only thing that was devastating about this attack, then, was the damage it did to the IRA. As Robert Picard has explained, the republican movement has used *An Phoblacht/Republican News* as a propaganda tool to provide unshakeable support for its cause.[73] In this way, an attempt has been made to consolidate the control of a given social group, with republicans' inflated claims of their activities owing much to the propaganda battle in which they were engaged. Danny Morrison, who was in charge of Sinn Féin's Publicity Department and *An Phoblacht/Republican News* during the 1980s, recognised the importance of propaganda when assessing the effectiveness of IRA violence stressing the need to avoid 'counterproductive operations', namely those where civilians got killed and others which generated negative propaganda such as bombs in town centres which were 'completely alienating unionists'.[74]

Such parameters imposed restriction on the IRA's 'propaganda war' reflecting the group's inability to subvert the state and revealing serious tactical and strategic deficiencies. As one activist put it: 'Any operation in which civilians were killed was a disaster, there's no question about that. I know that throughout the entire armed struggle great efforts were always made to ensure that there would be no civilian casualties. For every operation that was carried out, ten would have been called off because of the risk to civilians, but even with that, I think it was impossible. I think one of the lessons of the past thirty years is that it's impossible to avoid civilian injuries.'[75] This was the case even in those instances where the IRA offered prior warnings before carrying out certain attacks, as many activists acknowledge: 'And there was many unintended atrocities committed. And, so it was that aspect of the war that was alienating the support, so that had to be

185

done away with. The bombing campaign was disastrous, the economic bomb-ing campaign. And don't forget like I mean I was lifted. I was arrested the second time coming away from an economic bombing. I mean there was no-one hurt in it, but there was a possibility that people could have been hurt.'[76] Although the IRA has stated that it never intended to cause victims amongst 'non-combatants',[77] the facts show that the group's needs not to limit its actions overrode the alleged protected status of non-combatants. Its activists deliberately caused many civilian victims, despite the fact that ultimately this damaged the IRA, as the following examples show.

In April 1974, eleven people died on an English motorway when an IRA bomb exploded in a coach carrying British army members and their families. Eight of those killed were soldiers. The other dead were Linda Houghton, the civilian wife of one of the murdered soldiers, and their two children Lee and Robert, five and two years old respectively. In May 1977, the IRA murdered Malachy Gregory. This Catholic civilian, married and a father of eight children, was killed on the stairs at work just after his killers had shot at a workmate, who was a UDR member. The circumstances of the crime show that the IRA did not hesitate to kill Gregory even though he was not the original target. In October 1981, two civilians died in London when an IRA bomb exploded next to an army barracks. The forensic expert stated that the person who detonated the bomb must have had a clear view of where it was when it was exploded and therefore knew that there were civilians in the area, and that they would be hit by its full force. In July 1988, Robert Hanna, his wife Maureen and his 7-year-old son David died when an IRA bomb exploded on the road between Belfast and Dublin. The IRA had actually meant to kill a judge called Eion Higgins. A statement issued by the group later admitted responsibility for the attack, stating that its volunteers had made a mistake; they had spotted the judge with his wife and daughter at Dublin airport, just before they were due to travel to Belfast and then somehow confused them with the Hanna family. Nevertheless, those who detonated the bomb knew that the target was a family of three members. Instead of killing the Higgins family, they killed the Hanna family. If the terrorists had hit their target, they would still have killed a woman and a child apart from the person whom they had defined as a 'legitimate target'. In October 1989, an RAF officer, Maheshkumar Islania, was shot by IRA activists in Germany. His 6-month-old daughter also died in the attack and his wife was seriously injured. The IRA later expressed their 'profound regret' for the baby's death. As in the Higgins case, the IRA activists were aware that attacking a 'legitimate target' also involved attacking a child, which according to the republicans' own logic was clearly a 'non-combatant'.

The inherent contradictions in the IRA campaign can be seen from the explanation offered by a republican activist with respect to the Islania attack: 'Because the baby is not part of the war, she's not part of it, her father is because her father chose to be a member of the British army, a member of the Crown forces who are involved in a war against the republican and nationalist people. The child's death was totally unacceptable. Her father is a combatant. What you have to be careful about in all of this when you're trying to find a moral plateau is that you do not deny yourself the right to fight to end the injustice, that you don't end up in a situation where you are so, if you like, moral, so morally contained that you may as well go home and lock the door and stay in the house, I'm talking about a liberation morality that allows you the freedom to stand up for yourself and your people and to end the injustice in which you find yourself and your people find themselves.'[78] Yet this same Sinn Féin leader also stated that 'you have to be careful about it because you could justify anything, all in the name of freedom'.[79] The analysis of the republican strategy contained here shows that the IRA made this very mistake, justifying violence that was, nevertheless, incapable of achieving the group's objectives.

'The more you inflict upon someone the more resistance they exhibit'

Republicans saw IRA attacks carried out in Great Britain as a very effective form of propaganda, especially a series of actions which they called 'spectaculars', targeted at the financial centre of London and Downing Street. Since the 1930s, the IRA had tried to extend and intensify its use of violence in England. Although it did not bring about the desired victory, it was widely supported by activists for the reasons that one of them summarised: 'The IRA's bombing campaign in England in the nineties was more effective than many of the military operations which took place in the North because at the end of the day it was the British government who were in power and the British government who were the people who were going to make the decisions in relation to any change here.'[80] Not all republicans, however, agreed with this glorification of violence in general and the use of so-called 'spectaculars' in particular. In various letters to the editor published in *An Phoblacht/Republican News* throughout 1993, Owen Bennett argued that republicans had lost the battle for the hearts and minds of most of the Irish people, something which posed a serious problem for the movement. He also added that the armed campaign had failed, becoming 'aimless'.[81] Other republicans answered and criticised his letters in the same pages. Thus, the rare phenomenon of a debate in public, albeit a limited one, took place. One of those who took part accused Bennett of effectively executing the British strategy of 'demoralizing and marginalizing activists and supporters within the republican community' by presenting the IRA campaign as counterproductive,[82] while another considered that the criticism would be 'of the greatest encouragement to the enemy'.[83] In the correspondence, Bennett also referred to the extended but, in his view, false belief of his critics that 'IRA spectaculars' were irrefutable evidence that he was wrong. He regarded those arguments as a 'distortion' aimed at avoiding 'the serious questions posed': 'Those who argue for the armed struggle often make political claims in support of it which are extremely unsound. Regardless of the effect it has on Britain's will to remain in the Six Counties, the armed struggle has also had the political effect of isolating the beleaguered northern nationalists from national and international opinion. Even an operation like Bishopsgate cannot alter this reality. Operations like Warrington make the situation worse.'[84]

One reader congratulated Bennett for 'taking the bull by the horns and presenting the harsh realities', since he considered that 'unpalatable it may be, but the central truth of his argument is incontrovertible'.[85] As Bennett maintained, the defence of the armed struggle was based on highly charged 'emotional rhetoric', an approach which dominated republican thinking for three decades when 'sacred cows' had been challenged. Bennett's position was vindicated when the IRA called a ceasefire one year later. As other activists had predicted ten years earlier when criticising the so-called 'armed propaganda', this step had proved to be inevitable, a conclusion which reveals the weakness of the republican position. Such an outcome and the testimonies of IRA activists interviewed plainly contradict the belief that armed struggle was effective. IRA violence, discredited by many observers as terrorism without any legitimacy, was precisely what prevented political progress from being made, despite the fact that this, ultimately, was the republican goal. This therefore underlines the widespread mistake of praising the spectacular nature of each attack, since these are not simply individual or isolated acts, but rather part of a strategy in which the failure to achieve the ultimate aspirations has invalidated the hypothetical usefulness of the means used to achieve them, despite superficially seeming to be effective.

In October 1984, five people died when an IRA bomb exploded in the Grand Hotel Brighton, where the then Prime Minister Margaret Thatcher was staying during the Conservative Party's annual conference. Despite the spectacular and audacious nature of the bombing, coupled with the obvious challenge to the state it posed, it was far from being the success claimed by the republican propaganda machine. Thatcher did not waver in her determination to defeat the IRA as a result of the attack; in fact, quite the opposite happened, as it simply convinced her of the need to introduce new political and security measures that would damage and isolate the group further. It is worth noting that in 2000 the person responsible for the bombing, Pat Magee, who was arrested and convicted shortly afterwards, stated that he felt that it was better that Thatcher had survived, since too many deaths would have been counterproductive.[86] Some fellow IRA activists interpreted this as Magee looking for a way to justify his failure, since the objective had always been to kill the Prime Minister. However, Magee's comments reflect the concerns voiced by certain IRA leaders about the wisdom of carrying out the attack, fearing that if Thatcher died there would be a major clampdown on the group.[87] The IRA attack on 10 Downing Street in February 1991 during John Major's term as Prime Minister, when various mortar bombs exploded in the gardens of the building, can be seen in a similar light. The ability to carry out such attacks did not reflect a strong organisation that, in fact, as analysed in previous chapters, privately accepted that the armed conflict could not dramatically transform the political landscape in Northern Ireland in a way that would advance republican objectives.

These were the issues which led to the strategic shift which culminated in the 1994 ceasefire, a cessation which appeared to have been decided on as early as 1992. This has been noted earlier and was also suggested in the speech delivered by Jim Gibney that year, in which he implicitly announced the IRA's historic decision to abandon the use of violence: 'It is important that we ask ourselves, out loud, does this reality mean that republicans have been deafened by the "deadly sound of their own gunfire"? Does this reality mean that republicans are trapped inside a complex web of struggle from which they can't or don't emerge; hostages to an immediate past because of all the pain, suffering and commitment; to past views expressed, trenchantly, which in time solidified into unyielding principles?'[88]

Gibney, a very close associate of Gerry Adams, explained the meaning of his declaration as follows: 'I also tried to make the point to republicans that whatever we were saying to the unionist community they couldn't hear above the sound of guns being fired and bombs going off and indeed that is the case for everybody else, the British, whoever you want to call them. So I was just trying to say it to republicans, that here is another reality, whatever it is you're saying to people, they can't hear you because people are being killed, bombs are going off, etc.'[89] This realism, which implicitly accepted the need for a way out of the violence and thus pointed towards a future cease-fire declaration, contrasted with the triumphalist way in which *An Phoblacht/ Republican News*, the movement's public mouthpiece, was describing IRA 'spectaculars' at the time. In April 1992, the IRA set off a massive bomb in the Baltic Exchange, in the financial centre of London, killing three people and causing huge financial losses. One year later, another bomb went off in the financial centre; a lorry loaded with explosives exploded in Bishopsgate, causing the death of one person and, as with the Baltic Exchange, substantial financial losses. Although in October 1993, a spokesman for the organisation stated that the armed struggle was not an obstacle to peace, pointing to the British presence as the fundamental problem,[90] in private the IRA was admitting the exact opposite, as the imminent ceasefire confirmed. Given this, the importance of such 'spectaculars' needs to be reassessed, a point accepted by many former activists who have recognised that their transient propaganda value far outweighed their political effects. One of the activists interviewed defined as a 'myth' the claim that a greater number of 'spectaculars' would have improved Sinn Féin's negotiating position during the peace process,[91] a view shared by other republicans:

'You are not going to bring the financial institutions of capitalism to their knees with one bomb. Hitler couldn't do it in the Second World War with quite a number of bombs, you know, the IRA is not going to do it with one bomb. They look like big spectaculars because they are one-offs. Was that going to make a qualitative difference? If you were able to do one of those every other day maybe someone could put forward the argument that yes, over the period of maybe five or six years it would have a massive impact. Logistically it wasn't going to happen and even if it did happen logistically sometimes there is a case that the more you inflict upon someone the more resistance they exhibit rather than them becoming more and more pliable. That sort of stiff upper British lip that was exhibited during the Second World War being a point in case. But it is not about that and there isn't a direct simple equation and correlation between the amount of physical force used and the results that that is going to bring about. The struggle in Ireland is so multi-faceted that there are many factors that you need to bring into that equation.'[92]

'You could only expect one spectacular every now and again. Plus the fact if you are in England you are in totally foreign territory, you don't have the support base. You would have some individual sympathisers but you don't have a support base. Anybody sees anything they'll ring the police, they'll report it, it is only a matter of time until you are caught or you are killed. It was the same here, if anybody was joining the IRA they were never left in any illusions, you were told that this time next year you will either be dead or you'll be in jail, have no illusions about it, there's a very high rate of attrition on IRA volunteers. And a lot of people were getting caught, getting arrested or being killed and that was just it, you maybe learn, ones who would learn and learn quick to be survivors would get a few years out of it but somewhere along the line you'll know, when they want you they are going to put the resources into getting you. So I think if we could have intensified it, we'd have intensified but the practicalities were [that] we couldn't.'[93]

EPILOGUE

In 2003, 22 years after ten republican prisoners died as a result of the hunger strikes, Joe McDonnell, a British Labour MP, assessed this historical event and the subsequent peace process in Northern Ireland thus: 'It's about time we started honouring those people involved in the armed struggle. It was the bombs and bullets and sacrifice made by the likes of Bobby Sands that brought Britain to the negotiating table. The peace we have now is due to the action of the IRA.'[1] In his opinion, the settlement of the conflict meant having to face some 'hard and painful truths', including this one: 'Without the armed struggle of the IRA over the past 30 years, the Good Friday agreement would not have acknowledged the legitimacy of the aspirations of many Irish people for a united Ireland. And without that acknowledgment we would have no peace process.'[2]

This book has shown the error of beliefs like these, errors which have also been expressed in public by members of the republican movement. Precisely because key members of the IRA state that the battle for the legitimacy of the armed struggle is not over yet, it is absolutely essential to demolish the myths that have been built around it. The conflict will only be settled by learning the lessons of the past without reinventing it as some people would like to do; and this is certainly an arduous and painful task, although one that cannot be shirked. Contrary to what McDonnell preached, the British government has, since the beginning of the 1970s, recognised the nationalist aspirations for a united Ireland, and a fundamental element of its Northern Ireland policy since then has been the acceptance of the fact that the unification of the north and south of the island would come about only if the majority of the Northern Irish population gave their assent. This principle, rejected for decades by the IRA, is the pillar supporting the Good Friday Agreement signed in 1998. Statements by some of the former members of the IRA who back this historic document refute McDonnell's opinion on this matter. "My God, I've done 21 years in jail for this, this is not what I fought for!"[3] said one of them, expressing a disappointment that was identical to that of another of his colleagues, who admitted that he felt 'gutted' at having to accept a text that he defined as 'a reality check'.[4] What is successful about an armed struggle that has brought about an Agreement attracting such reactions of frustration, as well as other reactions included in this book, even from those who see the need to support it while renouncing violence? A former prisoner from the organisation offered this response: 'I don't think that the IRA campaign forced the British to the negotiation table. They ended up inside a counterinsurgency programme which was called the negotiation table, but I don't think they were real negotiations.'[5]

The contents of the Good Friday Agreement exhibit the ineffectiveness of a terrorist campaign that has been unable to guarantee the IRA's aims. Renouncing violence has been an obligatory requirement for Sinn Féin to begin casting off the mantle of 'a party apart from the people, proud of our past but with little involvement in the present and only dreams for the future', as Gerry Adams put it some years previously when describing the isolation suffered by his movement.[6] Realism and pragmatism have defeated the ideological absolutism of an organisation that had considered its ultimate objective as being non-negotiable and one which could only be met by maintaining the armed struggle.[7] In spite of the value many republicans attribute to the armed struggle, it cannot be denied that it has not achieved the ends for which the IRA activists justified it; on the contrary, it has given rise to effects that have been highly counterproductive for Northern Ireland. In this situation, there are people who have tried to give meaning to this senseless prolongation of violence using arguments such as those expressed by this former militant: 'I think we had to come through that phase, we had to say "we've tried everything", because had it stopped in 1975, people would say, "we didn't pursue it to the full, let's look at what other ways we can militarily do this, we can do huge car bombs in England, we can do all sorts of things on the continent ...". If they hadn't really been pursued then people would still be saying, "there's another way of doing it", and I would have pursued all those military alternatives, and we've realised that it isn't, we can't get a result.'[8]

However, voices are being raised to highlight the uselessness of the armed struggle against those who defend the necessary suffering it generated. This was acknowledged by one of the leaders of the IRA at the time when some of its activists opted to replace violence with politics: 'The community could very well have been much better off hadn't there been this terrorist campaign. And if you take the kind of apartheid mentality that has developed, that has certainly been a big effect and will have a much longer lasting effect of a negative nature. (...) this so-called war has delayed, deprived this community of moving into the twenty first century. (...) We could have had a much better infrastructure in this society now. If your end gain is forty walls dividing your people and still the different levels of long-term unemployment and all of that, I wouldn't envisage that that would be something that one would be very proud of having achieved. Or if the graveyards are full and the prisons had been full and all of that, that's what one would term achieving something, or if we decided, "right, our war is now concluded because our objectives have been obtained, we now have this and we have that and we have the other", because the current agenda that this leadership are talking about is the agenda that we were on in 1969 and 1970 and, in our opinion, winning. And they have delayed it all of those years by their activity, realised they couldn't achieve their objective, have now come back to our agenda.'[9]

The sophistry used by the IRA and the Sinn Féin leadership to evade the disastrous consequences of terrorism is an attempt to write a self-explanatory history based on the glorification of violence. But the reconciliation that has been proposed as a goal of the peace process cannot be attained through this glorification based on the reproduction of falsehoods, nor from diluting responsibility through adhesion to a subjective morality that sees no wrong in resorting to violence, on the grounds that it was justified because there were no effective alternatives. Should future generations be forced to accept the dangerous romanticism and idealism that have made a myth of the IRA, exalting its terrible consequences on the grounds that justice arbitrarily defined by its leaders called for the bloody price of thousands of victims? Should we underestimate the political immaturity of those who chose to engage in the armed struggle, and the influence that factors such as fanaticism and fundamentalism exerted on its continued existence? What place will be occupied in history by those who, with immense civic and human virtue, have resisted using violence, in spite of having been able to claim the same grievances as those who resorted to the militarism of terror? Should death and dehumanisation be justified as an inevitable component in attaining the goal of freedom for Ireland? Should the lie be perpetuated that it was IRA violence, rather than the peaceful strategies adopted in the 1960s, that was the catalyst for bringing about a much-needed reform to the inequitable situation in Northern Ireland? Should the fact be hidden that those who earnestly sought revolution have finally agreed to take part in a system that they had previously sworn to overthrow with a violence that reinforced reaction and opposition by obstructing political and social changes which might have been construed as concessions to terrorism? Should we ignore the fact that, as the IRA activists themselves admit, their violence split society and hardened the hearts and minds of Northern Ireland's population, polarising them to hitherto uncharted extremes? The statement of one former IRA member answers these questions:

I think that part of the long term process is that we all have to stand up and say that what we done was wrong. That should be part of the healing process. And the legitimising a campaign of violence, I don't think it can be done morally. I can see people trying to analyse it and trying to put it in a context which makes it legitimate, and you can get very close to that, and you can convince a lot of people, 'They done that because they were defending the area or the British were in their country and they shouldn't be there, so...' I don't agree with it. (...) I think [a democratic alternative] could have evolved when the violence stopped. I have to go back to what I was saying earlier on, I think we missed a mechanism that could have been used much more efficiently and effectively and that was the civil rights campaign at the start, that could have been a mechanism for building towards a more democratic, a more egalitarian society, and their long, longer term goals or aims, like republicanism has for a united Ireland etc., could have been closer. (...) I'd have to say that all those years spent in prison by so many people, all those deaths, I don't think it was worth it, when you add all that up, I would say I think it was a net loss.[10]

Although reconciliation is one of the commitments explicitly included in the Good Friday Agreement, as yet there has been no consensus as to the real significance of such an ambitious proposal. Certainly a great many obstacles present themselves in a divided society when it confronts the past, including the difficulty in clarifying the truth about events that happened years previously and which are submerged in a secretiveness that is hard to dispel. However, in an atmosphere as unsettled as this one, still unresolved by Northern Ireland, one essential step can, and indeed must, be taken: the categorical delegitimisation of the IRA's armed struggle. It seems vital to undertake this task, as well as the delegitimisation of loyalist violence, in order to combat the collective amnesia that some people are attempting to impose in order to cloak the effects and results of the destructive terrorism that has been perpetrated. This is a debt contracted by history, whose importance is accentuated by the fact that republican discourse continues to justify IRA violence, as one of its activists points out: 'As far as Óglaigh na hÉireann[11] volunteers would be concerned, their war hasn't ended; as long as the Brits remain here, there is always a major need for armed struggle against them. Morally you have the right to take up arms against them.'[12] The IRA's armed struggle has sent many people to their graves, but history must not allow its abject failure to be buried in oblivion as well.

NOTES

INTRODUCTION

1 G. Ó Danachair (1974), *Provos: Patriots or Terrorists?* Dublin: Irish Book Bureau, pp. 29–30.
2 'Terrorism as a Strategy of Insurgency', Ariel Merari, p. 226, in Conor Gearty (1996), *Terrorism*. Aldershot: Dalmourth, pp. 199–237.
3 This is the view expressed in the IRA's *Green Book*, regarded as the group's internal constitution. Quoted in Brendan O'Brien (1993), *The Long War: The IRA and Sinn Féin*. Dublin: The O'Brien Press, p. 290.
4 'Republicans: "The Greatest Criminals in Ireland"?', paper delivered by Anthony McIntyre at the *All-Ireland Postgraduate Conference*, Queen's University, Belfast, June 17, 1995.
5 Henry Patterson (1997), *The Politics of Illusion: A Political History of the IRA*. London: Serif, p. 10. Other outstanding books on the IRA are Richard English (2003), *Armed Struggle: A History of the IRA*. London: Macmillan; Ed Moloney (2002), *A Secret History of the IRA*. London: Penguin; Malachi O'Doherty (1998), *The Trouble with Guns: Republican Strategy and the Provisional IRA*. Belfast: The Blackstaff Press; M.L.R. Smith (1997), *Fighting for Ireland: The Military Strategy of the Irish Republican Movement*. London: Routledge.
6 Patterson (1997), op. cit., pp. 9–10.
7 'IRA must face up to grotesque reality of its campaign', Fintan O'Toole, *The Irish Times*, April 16, 1999.
8 Interview with Shane O'Doherty.

1 APPRENTICESHIP: 'I DIDN'T KNOW WHY I WANTED A UNITED IRELAND'

1 *Republican News*, February 27, 1972.
2 'Approaches to the Study of Political Violence', Peter H. Merkl, p. 48, in Peter H. Merkl (1986), *Political Violence and Terror: Motifs and Motivations*. London: University of California Press, pp. 17–60.
3 Robert White (1993), *Provisional Irish Republicans: An Oral and Interpretative History*. London: Greenwood Press.
4 'When Terrorists do the Talking: Reflections on Terrorist Literature', Bonnie Cordes, p. 150, in David Rapoport (1988), *Inside Terrorist Organizations*. New York: Columbia University Press, pp. 150–71.
5 Maxwell Taylor (1988), *The Terrorist*. London: Brassey's Defence Publishers.
6 See for example Fernando Reinares (2001), *Patriotas de la muerte. Quiénes han militado en ETA y por qué*. Madrid: Editorial Taurus; and Donatella della Porta

(1995), *Social Movements, Political Violence, and the State: A Comparative Analysis of Italy and Germany*. Cambridge: Cambridge University Press.

7 For arguments supporting these different approaches see Walter Reich (ed.) (1990), *Origins of Terrorism: Psychologies, Ideologies, States of Mind*. Cambridge: Cambridge University Press.

8 Kevin Boyle, Tom Hadden and Paddy Hillyard (1980), *Ten Years on in Northern Ireland: The Legal Control of Political Violence*. London: The Cobden Trust; Kevin Boyle and Tom Hadden (1994), *Northern Ireland: The Choice*. London: Penguin Books, pp. 80–81. Youth was clearly a prominent feature of those who joined the IRA in the early 1970s, as shown by Robert White (1993), *Provisional Irish Republicans: An Oral and Interpretative History*. London: Greenwood Press, pp. 85–86 and Christopher Hewitt (1984), *The Effectiveness of Anti-Terrorist Policies*. New York: University Press of America, p. 13.

9 On this issue, see Bandura's work, especially Albert Bandura (1973), *Aggression: A Social Learning Analysis*. New Jersey: Prentice Hall.

10 Interview with Tommy Gorman.

11 Interview with volunteer Albert.

12 Interview with volunteer Albert.

13 Interview with John Nixon.

14 Interview with volunteer Albert.

15 Interview with Anthony McIntyre.

16 Interview with Anthony McIntyre.

17 Interview with Gerard Hodgkins.

18 Interview with Sean O'Hara.

19 Interview with Tony Catney.

20 Interview with Ronnie McCartney.

21 Interview with Ronnie McCartney.

22 Interview with Ronnie McCartney.

23 Interview with John Nixon.

24 Interview with John Nixon.

25 Interview with Tony O'Hara.

26 Interview with Tony O'Hara.

27 Michael O'Sullivan (1972), *Patriot Graves: Resistance in Ireland*. Chicago, IL: Follett, p. 65.

28 Ibid., p. 61.

29 Interview with Ronnie McCartney.

30 Interview with Jackie McMullan.

31 Interview with Ronnie McCartney.

32 Interview with Rose McCotter.

33 Interview with Brenda Murphy.

34 Interview with Brenda Murphy.

35 Interview with Jackie McMullan.

36 Kevin Bean (1995), *The New Departure: Recent Developments in Irish Republican Ideology and Strategy*. Liverpool: The Institute of Irish Studies, The University of Liverpool, p. 2.

37 Interview with John Nixon.

38 This was one of the organisations that at the end of the 1960s demanded equal civil rights for Catholics and Protestants. The group included some radical elements which organised some demonstrations that were criticised by some sections of People's Democracy – a student-based organisation – because of the instability they generated in an already volatile atmosphere. On this issue, see Bob Purdie (1990), *Politics in the Streets*. Belfast: The Blackstaff Press.

39 Interview with John Nixon.
40 Interview with David O'Donnell.
41 Interview with Eamonn MacDermott.
42 Interview with Eamonn MacDermott.
43 Interview with Gerard Rice.
44 Interview with Tommy McKearney.
45 'The Political Socialisation of Tomorrow's Parents: Violence, Politics and the Media', E. Cairns, p. 124, in Joan Harbison (ed.) (1983), *Children of the Troubles: Children in Northern Ireland*. Belfast: Stranmillis College, pp. 120–26.
46 Interview with volunteer Albert.
47 Interview with volunteer Kevin.
48 Interview with volunteer Kevin.
49 Danny Morrison quoted in 'I don't think violence should be glorified', Mark Lieberman, p. 23, *Fortnight*, no. 280, January 1990.
50 *Where Sinn Féin Stands*. Statement issued subsequent to a meeting of the Caretaker Executive of Sinn Féin on January 17, 1970. Copy lodged at Queen's University Library, Belfast.
51 Henry Patterson (2002), *Ireland Since 1939*. Oxford: Oxford University Press, p. 216.
52 Paul Bew and Gordon Gillespie (1999), *Northern Ireland: A Chronology of the Troubles 1968–1999*. Dublin: Gill & Macmillan, p. 10.
53 Interview with Johnnie White.
54 Interview with Martin McKevitt.
55 Interview with Shane O'Doherty. The interviewee refers to the visits to Northern Ireland in August and October 1969 by the then British Home Secretary, James Callaghan. This visits were complemented with other political measures aimed at addressing the grievances of the Catholic population and with the deployment of the British troops in order to protect this section of the community.
56 Interview with Shane O'Doherty. The SDLP (Social Democratic and Labour Party), formed in 1970 and led until 2001 by John Hume, was the main nationalist party in Northern Ireland while the violence was in place. The party has always opposed violence while supporting the unification of the North and South of Ireland only through peaceful means and if the majority of the population in Northern Ireland gave their consent.
57 For the importance that the media have in creating role models and their influence in aggressive responses see Albert Bandura and Richard H. Walters (1963), *Social Learning and Personality Development*. London: Holt, Rinehart and Winston, pp. 47–108.
58 Interview with volunteer Timothy.
59 Interview with John Nixon.
60 Interview with Gerard Hodgkins.
61 Interview with Brenda Murphy.
62 Interview with volunteer Timothy.
63 Interview with Joe Doherty.
64 Interview with Feilim O hAdhmaill.
65 Interview with Martin O'Hagan.
66 Interview with John Nixon.
67 *Violence and Civil Disturbances in Northern Ireland in 1969* (*Scarman Report*, 1972). Cmd. 566. Belfast: Her Majesty's Stationery Office.
68 Interview with Jackie McMullan.
69 Interview with Jim Gibney.
70 David McKittrick, Seamus Kelters, Brian Feeney and Chris Thornton (1999), *Lost Lives*. London: Mainstream, pp. 50–52.

71 Michael Dewar (1996), *The British Army in Northern Ireland*. London: Arms and Armour, p. 46.
72 Interview with Robert McClenaghan.
73 Interview with Martin McKevitt.
74 Interview with Brenda Murphy.
75 Interview with Breandan MacCionnaith.
76 Interview with John Nixon.
77 Interview with Liam McAnoy.
78 Shane O'Doherty (1993), *The Volunteer*. London: HarperCollins, pp. 11–41.
79 Ibid., pp. 106–09.
80 Interview with Shane O'Doherty.
81 Interview with Paul Little.
82 Interview with Paul Little.
83 Interview with Mickey McMullan.
84 Interview with Brendan Holland.
85 On the radicalisation of People's Democracy, see Purdie (1990).
86 Interview with Brendan Holland.
87 Interview with Brendan Holland.
88 Brendan O'Brien (1993), *The Long War: The IRA and Sinn Féin 1985 to Today*. Dublin: The O'Brien Press, p. 127.
89 'Socialism: the real issue', Paddy Devlin, *Fortnight*, Christmas 1981, p. 11.
90 'Adams on republicanism and socialism', *Fortnight*, September 1983, pp. 8–9. A very coherent criticism of Adams' argument can be read in 'Is the cause of Ireland the cause of Labour?', Bob Purdie, *Fortnight*, November 1983, pp. 14–15. On the ideological tensions between Irish republicanism and socialism, see Henry Patterson (1997), *The Politics of Illusion: A Political History of the IRA*. London: Serif.
91 Interview with Anthony McIntyre.
92 American sociologist Robert White argues that IRA violence cannot be described as sectarian, an argument refuted by Steve Bruce, as can be seen in 'The Irish Republican Army: An Assessment of Sectarianism', Robert White, *Terrorism and Political Violence*, vol. 9, no. 1 (1997), pp. 20–55; 'Victim Selection in Ethnic Conflict: Motives and Attitudes in Irish Republicanism', Steve Bruce, *Terrorism and Political Violence*, vol. 9, no. 1 (1997), pp. 56–71; and White (1997), pp. 120–31.
93 Interview with Paul Little.

2 DEFENDERS?: 'IT JUST GAVE ADDED JUSTIFICATION FOR KILLING SOLDIERS AND POLICEMEN'

1   Interview with Paul Little.
2   Interview with John Kelly.
3   Interview with John Kelly.
4   Interview with Bob Murray.
5   Interview with Ruairi O'Bradaigh.
6   Interview with Johnnie White.
7   Interview with Seamus Lynch.
8   Interview with Seamus Lynch.
9   Interview with Johnnie White.
10 Interview with Seamus Lynch.
11 Quoted in J. Bowyer Bell (1989), *The Secret Army: The IRA 1916–1979*. Dublin: Poolbeg Press, p. 334. Gerry Adams points out that at the beginning of the sixties

the IRA only had 24 members in Belfast since republicans had suffered a 'substantial defeat'. Gerry Adams (1996), *Before the Dawn: An Autobiography*. London: Heinemann, p. 77.

12 Interview with John Kelly.

13 Interview with Anthony McIntyre.

14 Interview with Marian Price.

15 Interview with Marian Price.

16 Anthony McIntyre (1999), *A Structural Analysis of Modern Irish Republicanism: 1969–1973*. Belfast: Faculty of Economics and Social Sciences, The Queen's University of Belfast, unpublished manuscript.

17 'Discarding the fetters of republican myth', Martin McGuinness, *Fortnight*, no. 215, March 3, 1985, pp. 7–8.

18 Interview with Rose McCotter.

19 Interview with Rose McCotter.

20 Interview with Tommy McKearney.

21 Interview with Margaret McKearney.

22 Interview with Liam McAnoy.

23 Interview with Liam McAnoy.

24 'Northern Ireland: From Long War to Difficult Peace?', Ronaldo Munck, p. 86, in Ronaldo Munck and Purnaka L. de Silva (2000), *Postmodern Insurgencies: Political Violence, Identity Formation and Peacemaking in Comparative Perspective*. London: Macmillan.

25 Ibid.

26 Henry Patterson (1997), *The Politics of Illusion: A Political History of the IRA*. London: Serif, p. 11.

27 Quoted in Anthony McIntyre (1999), op. cit. Page not provided in the original.

28 Interview with Eamonn MacDermott.

29 *Violence and Civil Disturbances in Northern Ireland in 1969* (*Scarman Report*, 1972). Cmd. 566. Belfast: Her Majesty's Stationery Office.

30 Frank Burton (1978), *The Politics of Legitimacy: Struggles in a Belfast Community*. London: Routledge, pp. 92–93.

31 Ibid., pp. 97–98.

32 Interview with Shane O'Doherty.

33 'Individuals and Group Goals', Diane M. Mackie and George R. Goethals, pp. 144–66, in Clyde Hendrick (ed.) (1987), *Group Processes*. London: Sage.

34 Interview with volunteer Kevin.

35 'Republican tradition', *An Phoblacht/Republican News*, March 30, 1973.

36 David McKittrick *et al.* (1999), *Lost Lives*. Edinburgh: Mainstream, p. 91.

37 Burton (1978), op. cit., p. 92. By 'Orangees' he refers to Northern Ireland's Protestants.

38 'Toward a Theory of Revolution', James Davies, *American Sociological Review*, vol. 27 (1962), pp. 5–19.

39 Ted Robert Gurr (1970), *Why Men Rebel*. New Jersey: Princeton University Press; and 'A Causal Model of Civil Strife: A Comparative Analysis Using New Indices', Ted Gurr, pp. 293–313, in James Chowning Davies (ed.) (1971), *When Men Revolt and Why: A Reader in Political Violence and Revolution*. London: Collier-Macmillan.

40 Arend Lijphart (1999), *Patterns of Democracy: Government Forms and Performance in Thirty-Six Countries*. New Haven, CT: Yale University.

41 Paul Bew and Henry Patterson (1985), *The British State and the Ulster Crisis: From Wilson to Thatcher*. London: Verso, pp. 11–15.

42 'Community Politics', Bill Rolston, p. 150, in Liam O'Dowd, Bill Rolston and

Mike Tomlinson (1981), *Northern Ireland: Between Civil Rights and Civil War*. London: CSE Books, pp. 148–77.

43 Paul Bew and Gordon Gillespie (1999), *Northern Ireland: A Chronology of the Troubles 1968–1999*. Dublin: Gill & Macmillan, p. 16.

44 'Review Article: The Northern Ireland Problem: Cases, Theories, and Solutions', Arend Lijphart, *British Journal of Political Science*, vol. 5, no. 1 (1975), pp. 83–106.

45 'Relative Deprivation as a Factor in Conflict in Northern Ireland', Derek Birrell, *Sociological Review*, vol. 20, no. 3 (1972), pp. 317–44.

46 Ibid., p. 331.

47 'Social Policy Responses to Urban Violence in Northern Ireland', Derek Birrell, chapter 8 of Seamus Dunn (ed.) (1994), *Managing Divided Cities*. Keele: Keele University Press.

48 This is a view shared by prestigious academics such as John Whyte, John Darby, Richard Rose, R. Moore and J.A. Schellenberg, as summarised by Ed Cairns in 'Intergroup Conflict in Northern Ireland', p. 277, in Henri Tajfel (ed.) (1982), *Social Identity and Intergroup Relations*. Cambridge: Cambridge University Press, pp. 277–97.

49 Dunn (1994).

50 Birrell (1972), op. cit., pp. 323–26 and Lijphart (1975), op. cit., pp. 92–94.

51 See for example J.A. Schellenberg, 'Area Variations of Violence in Northern Ireland', *Sociological Focus*, vol. 10, no. 1 (1977), pp. 69–78; Christopher Hewitt (1981), 'Catholic Grievances, Catholic Nationalism and Violence in Northern Ireland during the Civil Rights Period: A Reconsideration', *British Journal of Sociology*, vol. 32, no. 3 (1981), pp. 364–80.

52 'Deprivation and Political Violence in Northern Ireland, 1922–85', J.L.P. Thompson, *Journal of Conflict Resolution*, vol. 33, no. 4 (1989), pp. 676–99.

53 Interview with Cathal Crumley.

54 Interview with Tommy McKearney.

55 Interview with Margaret McKearney.

56 Birrell (1972), op. cit., pp. 318–19, 328–29; and Richard Rose (1971), *Governing without Consensus*. London: Faber and Faber.

57 Rosemary Harris (1972), *Prejudice and Tolerance in Ulster*. Manchester: Manchester University Press; 'Ardoyne: from quiet suburb to war zone', David McKittrick, *The Sunday Independent*, September 30, 2001.

58 Interview with Margaret McKearney.

59 Interview with Pat McNamee.

60 Joseph Lee (1989), *Ireland 1912–1985: Politics and Society*. Cambridge: Cambridge University Press, pp. 223–24.

61 Henry Patterson (2002), *Ireland since 1939*. Oxford: Oxford University Press, p. 56.

62 F.S.L. Lyons (1973), *Ireland since the Famine*. London: HarperCollins, p. 582.

63 Eunan O'Halpin (2000), *Defending Ireland: The Irish State and its Enemies since 1922*. Oxford: Oxford University Press, pp. 125–26, 248.

64 Interview with Pat McNamee. (Ireland's national police service is known as *Garda Síochána*.)

65 See for example Patterson (2002), op. cit., pp. 128–31, 160–61, 192–99.

66 Bob Purdie (1990), *Politics in the Streets: The Origins of the Civil Rights Movement in Northern Ireland*. Belfast: The Blackstaff Press, pp. 156–57, 245–46.

67 Interview with Danny Morrison.

68 Interview with Rab McCallum.

69 Interview with Seamus Lynch.

70 Interview with Liam McAnoy.

71 Interview with Martin McKevitt.
72 Interview with volunteer Leonard.
73 Interview with Gerard Hodgkins.
74 Interview with Tom Kelly.
75 Interview with Feilim O hAdhmaill.
76 Interview with Joe O'Doherty.
77 Gerard Murray (1998), *John Hume and the SDLP*. Dublin: Irish Academic Press, p. 3.
78 Interview with Martin O'Hagan.
79 Interview with Martin O'Hagan.
80 Interview with Sean Hayes.
81 The *Sunday Times* Insight Team (1972), *Ulster*. Harmondsworth: Penguin Books, pp. 126–42.
82 Adams (1996), op. cit.; and Danny Morrison (1989), *West Belfast*. Cork: Mercier Press.
83 'A View North: Troubles Fiction remains Troubles by Stereotype', Jack Holland, in *Irish Echo Online*, www.irishecho.com/news/article.cfm?id=11359, July 31– August 6, vol. 75, no. 31 (2002). Journalist and author Malachi O'Doherty, who belongs to the same generation as Adams and also grew up in west Belfast during the same period as the Sinn Féin president, has presented a completely different narrative of that time from those who ended up in the republican movement. Malachi O'Doherty (1998), *The Trouble with Guns: Republican Strategy and the Provisional IRA*. Belfast: The Blackstaff Press.
84 Sydney Elliott and W.D. Flackes (1999), *Conflict in Northern Ireland: An Encyclopedia*. Santa Barbara, CA: ABC-CLIO, pp. 680–87.
85 Interview with Gerard Rice.
86 Interview with Carl Reilly.
87 Interview with Raymond Wilkinson.
88 Three weeks later William Marchant was killed by the IRA because he had allegedly taken part in the killing of Marley.
89 Marie-Therese Fay, Mike Morrissey and Marie Smyth (1999), *Northern Ireland's Troubles: The Human Costs*. London: Pluto Press; and Marie-Therese Fay, Mike Morrissey and Marie Smyth (1997), *The Cost of the Troubles Study: Mapping Troubles-Related Deaths in Northern Ireland 1969–1994*. Derry: INCORE.
90 Interview with Raymond Wilkinson.
91 Interview with Thomas Cosgrove.
92 Interview with Thomas Cosgrove.
93 Interview with Thomas Cosgrove.
94 Interview with Carl Reilly.
95 'The Subjective Reality of the Terrorist: Ideological and Psychological Factors in Terrorism', Martha Crenshaw, p. 26, in Robert O. Slater and Michael Stohl (eds) (1988), *Current Perspectives on International Terrorism*. London: Macmillan, pp. 12–46.
96 Interview with volunteer Kevin.
97 Interview with Carl Reilly.
98 McCarthy and Zald have shown how grievances and discontent are very often made up and manipulated by social movements. Quoted in David Snow *et al.*, 'Frame Alignment Processes, Micromobilization, and Movement Participation', *American Sociological Review*, vol. 51 (1986), pp. 464–81.
99 Interview with Carl Reilly.
100 Interview with Carl Reilly.
101 Interview with Carl Reilly.
102 Interview with Carl Reilly.

3 THE CAPTIVE MIND: 'HAVE YOU NOT GOT THE BALLS FOR THE ARMED STRUGGLE?'

1 Elliot Aronson and Judson Mills, 'The Effect of Severity of Initiation on Liking for a Group', *Journal of Abnormal and Social Psychology*, vol. 59 (1959), pp. 177–81.
2 Irish Republican Publicity Bureau (1973), *Freedom Struggle by the Provisional IRA*. Dublin, p. 93.
3 M.L.R. Smith (1997), *Fighting for Ireland: The Military Strategy of the Irish Republican Movement*. London: Routledge, p. 225.
4 Leo Festinger (1957), *A Theory of Cognitive Dissonance*. Stanford, CT: Stanford University Press.
5 Interview with Johnnie White.
6 Interview with Joe Doherty.
7 Irving L. Janis (1982), *Groupthink: Psychological Studies of Policy Decisions and Fiascos*. London: Houghton Mifflin; and Irving L. Janis and Leo Mann (1977), *Decision Making: A Psychological Analysis of Conflict, Choice and Commitment*. London: Collier Macmillan.
8 Irish Republican Publicity Bureau (1973), *Freedom Struggle by the Provisional IRA*. Dublin, pp. 62–63.
9 Group dynamics are a key component of the decision making process of terrorist organisations. 'Group and Organisational Dynamics of Political Terrorism: Implications for Counterterrorist Policy', J.M. Post, in Paul Wilkinson (ed.) (1987), *Contemporary Research on Terrorism*. Aberdeen: The University Press, pp. 307–17.
10 On the importance of legitimacy for groups, see 'Perceived Illegitimacy and Intergroup Relations', Brian Caddick, pp. 137–53, in Henri Tajfel (ed.) (1982), *Social Identity and Intergroup Relations*. Cambridge: Cambridge University Press.
11 As Killian has observed, collective behaviour can not be analysed by simply opposing rational versus irrational. 'Theory of Collective Behavior: The Mainstream Revisited', Lewis M. Killian, pp. 275–89, in Hubert M. Blalock (ed.) (1980), *Sociological Theory and Research: A Critical Appraisal*. London: Collier Macmillan.
12 Interview with volunteer Bobby.
13 Interview with volunteer Bobby.
14 As much research has shown, membership of a group increases personal diffusion of responsibility. See, for example, 'Attributions of Responsibility for Collective Endeavors', Mark R. Leary and Donelson R. Forsyth, p. 169, in Clyde Hendrick (ed.) (1987), *Group Processes and Intergroup Relations*. London: Sage, pp. 167–88.
15 Interview with volunteer Bobby.
16 On the mechanisms of denial commonly used by perpetrators of atrocities, see Stanley Cohen (2001), *States of Denial: Knowing about Atrocities and Suffering*. Cambridge: Polity.
17 Albert Bandura deals with how terrorist groups resort to these mechanisms in 'Mechanisms of Moral Disengagement', in Walter Reich (ed.) (1990), *Origins of Terrorism: Psychologies, Ideologies, States of Mind*. Cambridge: Cambridge University Press, pp. 161–91.
18 As Heskin has pointed out, although not every IRA activist can be defined as a psychopath, it should be stressed that it would be very normal for individuals with such a profile to feel attracted towards a violent and authoritarian organisation like this. Ken Heskin (1980), *Northern Ireland: A Psychological Analysis*. Dublin: Gill and Macmillan, pp. 83–84. The same author deals with the importance of authoritarianism within the IRA in 'The Psychology of Terrorism in Northern

Ireland', chapter 5 of Yonah Alexander and Alan O'Day (1984), *Terrorism in Ireland*. London: Croom Helm, pp. 88–105.

19 Quoted by E. Cairns in 'The Political Socialisation of Tomorrow's Parents: Violence, Politics and the Media', p. 125, in Joan Harbison (ed.) (1983), *Children of the Troubles: Children in Northern Ireland*. Belfast: Stranmillis College, pp. 120–26.

20 Interview with Seamus Lynch.

21 Eamon Collins (1997), *Killing Rage*. London: Granta, p. 4.

22 Interview with Tom Kelly.

23 Interview with volunteer Bobby.

24 Interview with Gerard Hodgkins.

25 Interview with Ronnie McCartney.

26 Interview with Tom Kelly.

27 Interview with Tom Kelly.

28 Interview with Tom Kelly.

29 'Social Psychology of Terrorist Groups', Clark R. McCauley and Mary E. Segal, pp. 235–36, in Hendrick (1987), op. cit., pp. 231–56.

30 Interview with Tom Kelly.

31 Interview with Tom Kelly.

32 Interview with Tom Kelly.

33 Frank Burton (1978), *The Politics of Legitimacy: Struggles in a Belfast Community*. London: Routledge, pp. 88–89.

34 Interview with Sean Hayes.

35 Interview with Sean O'Hara.

36 Ed Moloney (2002), *A Secret History of the IRA*. London: Penguin, pp. 100–01.

37 Interview with David O'Donnell.

38 Interview with David O'Donnell.

39 Interview with David O'Donnell.

40 Interview with Shane O'Doherty.

41 'Attractiveness of Group as Function of Self-Esteem and Acceptance by Group', James E. Dittes, *Journal of Abnormal and Social Psychology*, vol. 59 (1959), pp. 77–82.

42 The workings of this process in other social groups is analysed in Michael A. Hogg and Dominic Abrams (1988), *Social Identifications: A Social Psychology of Intergroup Relations and Group Processes*. London: Routledge, p. 23.

43 Interview with David O'Donnell.

44 Smith (1997), op. cit., p. 135.

45 Interview with Gerard Rice.

46 Interview with Joe Doherty.

47 Interview with Brenda Murphy.

48 Interview with Shane O'Doherty.

49 Interview with volunteer Albert.

50 Interview with volunteer Albert.

51 Burton (1978), op. cit., p. 89.

52 Interview with volunteer Albert.

53 Burton (1978), op. cit.

54 Jeffrey Sluka (1989), *Hearts and Minds, Water and Fish: Support for the IRA and the INLA in a Northern Irish Ghetto*. London: JAI Press.

55 Eamonn Mallie and Patrick Bishop (1987), *The Provisional IRA*. London: Heinemann, p. 288.

56 Richard Kearney (1997), *Postnationalist Ireland: Politics, Culture, Philosophy*. London: Routledge, p. 111.

57 Interview with Raymond Wilkinson.
58 Interview with Gerard Rice.
59 Interview with Thomas Cosgrove.
60 Interview with Gerard Rice.
61 Interview with Breandán MacCionnaith.
62 Interview with Sean Hayes.
63 Interview with Gerard Hodgkins.
64 Interview with Jim Gibney.
65 Interview with Thomas Quigley.
66 Interview with Thomas Quigley.
67 Interview with Paul O'Neill.
68 Interview with Eamonn MacDermott.
69 Interview with Jim Gibney.
70 Interview with Eamonn MacDermott.
71 Interview with Shane O'Doherty.
72 Interview with Mickey McMullan.
73 Interview with Ronnie McCartney.
74 Interview with Martin O'Hagan.
75 Interview with Mickey McMullan.
76 Ibid. The interviewee is referring to the Sunningdale Agreement signed at the end of 1973 which allowed a power-sharing government to be established in Northern Ireland. The IRA rejected this Agreement, which finally failed in 1974, although some of its contents were, from a republican perspective, even more ambitious than those of the Good Friday Agreement accepted in 1998. The disappointing outcome obtained by the IRA after decades of violence was best summarised by Seamus Mallon, SDLP politician and Deputy First Minister of the Northern Ireland Assembly elected in June 1998, when he referred to the Good Friday Agreement as 'Sunningdale for slow learners'.
77 Laurence McKeown (2001), *Out of Time: Irish Republican Prisoners. Long Kesh 1972–2000*. Belfast: Beyond the Pale.
78 Interview with Gerard Hodgkins.
79 Interview with volunteer Albert.
80 Interview with Shane O'Doherty.
81 Collins (1997), op. cit., pp. 176–77.
82 Interview with Gerard Rice.
83 Interview with Gerard Rice.
84 Bandura in Reich (1990), op. cit., pp. 171–72.
85 'Italy: A Systems Perspective', F. Ferracuti and F. Bruno, pp. 308–10, in A. Goldstein and M. Segall (ed.) (1983), *Aggression in Global Perspective*. New York: Pergamon, pp. 287–312.
86 Interview with Martin O'Hagan.
87 'Attributions of Responsibility for Collective Endeavors', Mark R. Leary and Donelson R. Forsyth, pp. 181–82, in Hendrick (1987), op. cit., pp. 167–88.
88 Stanley Milgram (1974), *Obedience to Authority*. New York: HarperCollins.
89 Interview with Marian Price.
90 Interview with Brenda Murphy.
91 Interview with Thomas Cosgrove.
92 Interview with Raymond Wilkinson.
93 Interview with Raymond Wilkinson.
94 Interview with Thomas Cosgrove.
95 Danny Morrison (1999), *Then the Walls came Down: A Prison Journal*. Cork: Mercier Press, p. 289.
96 Interview with Rose McCotter.

97 Interview with Shane O'Doherty.
98 Shane O'Doherty (1993), *The Volunteer*. London: HarperCollins.
99 Interview with Shane O'Doherty. Collins was the IRA leader accused of being a traitor by his former comrades after signing with the British in 1921 the Anglo-Irish Treaty, an agreement which did not guarantee the unification of the North and South of Ireland.
100 Kevin Kelley (1982), *The Longest War*. Kerry: Brandon, p. 153.
101 Gerry Adams (1996), *Before the Dawn: An Autobiography*. London: Heinemann, p. 263.
102 Ibid., p. 216.
103 Eamonn Mallie and Patrick Bishop (1987), *The Provisional IRA*. London: Heinemann, pp. 265–66.
104 Liam Clarke (1987), *Broadening the Battlefield: The H-Blocks and the Rise of Sinn Féin*. Dublin: Gill and Macmillan, pp. 251–53.
105 Interview with volunteer Albert.
106 Anthony McIntyre (1999), *A Structural Analysis of Modern Irish Republicanism: 1969–1973*. Belfast: Faculty of Economics and Social Sciences, Queen's University of Belfast, 1999.
107 Interview with Tony O'Hara.
108 Interview with David O'Donnell.
109 Interview with Brendan Holland.
110 Interview with Breandán MacCionnaith.
111 Interview with Harry McGuire.
112 Interview with Harry McGuire.
113 Interview with Sean O'Hara.
114 Interview with John Nixon.
115 Interview with Ronnie McCartney.
116 Interview with Martin O'Hagan. The expression *Mother Ireland* was very commonly used in Irish nationalism representing Ireland as a mother, thus providing a patriotic reference for republicans.
117 Interview with John Nixon.
118 Interview with Danny Morrison.
119 Interview with John Nixon.
120 Interview with Rab McCallum.
121 Interview with Robert McClenaghan.
122 Interview with Robert McClenaghan.

4 HUNGER FOR POWER: 'WHERE THE HELL DID WE GO WRONG?'

1 The statement is published in Brian Campbell, Laurence McKeown and Felim O'Hagan (1994), *Nor Meekly Serve my Time: The H Block Struggle 1976–1981*. Belfast: Beyond the Pale, pp. 259–64.
2 Richard O'Rawe (2005), *Blanketmen: An Untold Story of the H-Block Hunger Strike*. Dublin: News Island; and interviews by the author with Richard O'Rawe.
3 'Adams pays tribute to hunger strikers', http://news.bbc.co.uk/hi/english/uk/northern_ireland/newsid_1314000/1314592.stm, accessed on May 5, 2001.
4 Interview with Pat McGeown.
5 Interview with Sean O'Hara.
6 Interview with Gerard Hodgkins.
7 Interview with Tony O'Hara.
8 Peter Taylor (1997), *Provos: The IRA and Sinn Féin*. London: Bloomsbury, p. 232.

9 Interview with Brendan Hughes. Both Gibney and Morrison have been very prominent figures in the Irish republican movement for many years.

10 Irving L. Janis (1982), *Groupthink: Psychological Studies of Policy Decisions and Fiascos*. London: Houghton Mifflin, p. 16.

11 O'Rawe (2005), op. cit., p. 233.

12 Interview with Richard O'Rawe.

13 Brendan O'Brien (1993), *The Long War: The IRA and Sinn Féin 1985 to Today*. Dublin: The O'Brien Press, p. 290.

14 Interview with Richard O'Rawe.

15 David Beresford (1994), *Ten Men Dead: The Story of the 1981 Irish Hunger Strike*. London: HarperCollins, p. 128.

16 O'Rawe (2005), op. cit., p. 151.

17 Beresford (1994), op. cit., p. 255.

18 O'Rawe (2005), op. cit., p. 151.

19 Beresford (1994), op. cit., p. 240 and O'Rawe (2005), op. cit., p. 152.

20 Interview with Richard O'Rawe.

21 Interview with Tommy McKearney.

22 Beresford (1994), op. cit., p. 259.

23 Ibid., p. 271.

24 Interview with John Nixon.

25 Beresford (1994), op. cit., p. 273.

26 O'Rawe (2005), op. cit., p. 180.

27 Beresford (1994), op. cit., p. 330.

28 Interview with Brendan Hughes.

29 Beresford (1994), op. cit., p. 329.

30 Ibid., p. 326.

31 Interview with Richard O'Rawe.

32 Beresford (1994), op. cit., p. 333.

33 Interview with Tony O'Hara.

34 Beresford (1994), op. cit., pp. 335–37.

35 Ibid.

36 Ibid.

37 Interview with John Nixon.

38 Beresford (1994), op. cit., p. 336.

39 'Effects of Group Pressure upon the Modification and Distortion of Judgement', Salomon Asch, in H. Guetzkow (ed.) (1951), *Groups, Leadership and Men*. Pittsburgh, PA: Carnegie Press.

40 Elisabeth Noelle-Neumann (1984), *The Spiral of Silence. Public Opinion: Our Social Skin*. Chicago, IL: The University of Chicago Press.

41 Beresford (1994), op. cit., p. 364.

42 Ibid., p. 387.

43 Ibid., pp. 379–80.

44 Peter Taylor (1997), op. cit., p. 248.

45 Ibid., p. 249.

46 Beresford (1994), op. cit., p. 380.

47 Ibid., pp. 380–81.

48 Ibid., p. 380.

49 Interview with Pat McGeown.

50 Séanna Walsh quoted in Campbell *et al.* (1994), op. cit., p. 237.

51 Interview with Mickey McMullan.

52 Beresford (1994), op. cit., p. 418.

53 O'Rawe (2005), op. cit., p. 236.

54 Quoted in Padraig O'Malley (1990), *Biting at the Grave: The Irish Hunger Strikes and the Politics of Despair*. Belfast: The Blackstaff Press, pp. 83–84.
55 Ibid., p. 84.
56 Ibid., p. 80.
57 O'Rawe (2005), op. cit., p. 259.
58 Ibid., pp. 249, 255.
59 Interview with Mickey McMullan.
60 Interview with Mickey McMullan.
61 Interview with Brenda Murphy.
62 *An Phoblacht/Republican News*, November 5, 1981.
63 Interview with Brenda Murphy.
64 Padraig O'Malley (1990), op. cit., p. 60.
65 Brown correctly points out the need to complement Janis's analysis on group-think with the consideration of political factors. Rupert Brown (2000), *Group Processes*. Oxford: Blackwell, pp. 212–19.
66 Ibid.
67 Interview with Danny Morrison.
68 Paul Mitchell and Rick Wilford (ed.) (1999), *Politics in Northern Ireland*. Oxford: Westview, p. 86.
69 John Coakley and Michael Gallagher (1999), *Politics in the Republic of Ireland*. London: Routledge, p. 367.
70 BBC interview with Gerry Adams in 1985. Copy of transcription held at the *Linen Hall Library*, Belfast.
71 Interview with Danny Morrison.
72 Interview with Mickey McMullan. The interviewee refers to the IRA bomb in Enniskillen which killed eleven people in November 1987.
73 'Is Sinn Féin a Victim of its own Design?', Anthony McIntyre in *Parliamentary Brief*, May/June 1998, vol. 5, no. 6, pp. 13–14.
74 'Get on with the business of peace', Danny Morrison, *The Guardian*, October 14, 2002.
75 'Stretching republicans too far', Danny Morrison, *The Guardian*, July 13, 1999.
76 'McGuinness attacks British militarists', *An Phoblacht/Republican News*, November 6, 1997, p. 4.
77 'Strategic republicanism: neither strategic nor republicanism', Breandan O Muirthile, *The Blanket*, January 2002, http://lark.phoblacht.net/strategic.html.
78 'Talking to the Brits', Danny Morrison, *An Phoblacht/Republican News*, January 9, 1992.
79 Interview with Danny Morrison.
80 'Where are the Provos going?', Ed Moloney, *Fortnight*, May 1983, pp. 4–5.
81 Interview with Danny Morrison by Rebecca Rooney quoted in *The progression of Sinn Féin from the 'armalite to the ballot box'*. Dissertation submitted at the Faculty of Humanities of the University of Ulster, Jordanstown, 2002.
82 Danny Morrison (1999), *Then The Walls Came Down: A Prison Journal*. Cork: Mercier Press, p. 291.
83 *Magill*, November 13, 1986, p. 13.
84 David Sharrock and Mark Devenport (1997), *Man of War, Man of Peace? The Unauthorized Biography of Gerry Adams*. London: Macmillan, p. 248.
85 Ed Moloney (2002), *A Secret History of the IRA*. London: Penguin, pp. 292–94.
86 Interview with John Kelly.
87 Interview with Brendan Hughes.
88 Interview with Brendan Hughes.
89 Interview with volunteer Albert.
90 Speech by Martin McGuinness, *Magill*, November 13, 1986, p. 13.

91 'Fertile Ground', *An Phoblacht/Republican News*, June 30, 1983.

92 Interview with Mickey McMullan.

93 Interview with Bob Murray.

94 Interview with Ruairi O'Bradaigh. Leaders like Adams and McGuinness managed to position around themselves other individuals who protected their capacity to exert an enormous influence over the movement implementing a very tight control of the terrorist organisation, as shown by Ed Moloney (2002), op. cit.

95 Ed Moloney (2002), op. cit., pp. 242–43.

96 Ibid.

97 Interview with Tommy Gorman.

98 Interview with Brendan Hughes.

99 Interview with Tommy Gorman.

100 Interview with Ruairi O'Bradaigh.

101 Interview with Brendan Hughes.

102 Interview with Brendan Hughes.

103 M.L.R. Smith (1997), *Fighting for Ireland: The Military Strategy of the Irish Republican Movement*. London: Routledge, p. 182.

104 Interview with Brendan Hughes.

105 Interview with volunteer Mo.

106 Interview with volunteer Mo.

107 'Review of Fourthwrite', Danny Morrison, *Andersonstown News*, March 13, 2000.

108 Interview with Mickey McMullan.

109 Interview with Tommy McKearney.

110 Interview with Brendan Hughes.

111 Interview with Tommy Gorman.

112 Eamon Collins (1997), *Killing Rage*. London: Granta Books.

113 Interview with Marian Price.

114 Interview with Marian Price.

115 Interview with Marian Price.

116 'The Politics of Fear', Gerry Adams, *Irish Voice*, October 25–31, 2000.

117 'Killing republicans – that was not our war', Tommy Gorman and Anthony McIntyre, *Irish News*, October 17, 2000.

118 *Andersonstown News*, October 23, 2000, pp. 1 and 3.

119 Marian Price interviewed by Trevor Byrne in 'Killing for peace', *UTV Insight*, October 26, 2000.

120 Interview with Gerry Adams published in *Andersonstown News*, November 22, 1986 and quoted in Anthony McIntyre, *Armed Struggle: A Strategic Imperative*, p. 32, Belfast, 1991, unpublished. Copy held at Linen Hall Library, Belfast.

121 On this issue see Rogelio Alonso, 'The Modernization in Irish Republican thinking toward the Utility of Violence', *Studies in Conflict and Terrorism*, vol. 24 (2001), pp. 131–44.

122 Interview with Mickey McMullan.

123 'Irish Political Prisoners and Post Hunger-Strike Resistance to Criminalisation', Declan Moen, *British Criminology Conference: Selected Proceedings*, vol. 3 (2000), www.lboro.ac.uk/departments/ss/bsc/bccsp/vol03/moen.html, pp. 6–7.

124 Ibid., p. 15.

125 Ibid.

126 Interview with Ronnie McCartney.

127 'Was it all for nothing?', *Andersonstown News*, September 11, 1999.

128 'This struggle ain't over', letter by Jackie McMullan published in *Andersonstown News* and *An Phoblacht/Republican News*, September 23, 1999.

129 'Was it in vain?', Tommy Gorman, *An Phoblacht/Republican News*, September 9, 1999.
130 'Alternative strategy needed', Finbar Cullen, *An Phoblacht/Republican News*, September 2, 1999.
131 Interview with Tommy Gorman.
132 'Congratulations for Tommy's stand', *Andersonstown News*, October 16, 1999.
133 'Where are the answers?', *Andersonstown News*, October 23, 1999.
134 'Round up the usual suspects', *Andersonstown News*, December 4, 1999; and 'A different kind of split', Seán Mac Riabhigh, *Andersonstown News*, December 18, 1999.
135 Quoted in Mark Juergensmeyer (2001), *Terrorismo religioso. El auge global de la violencia religiosa*. Madrid: Siglo XXI de España Editores, p. 42.
136 Ibid., p. 43.
137 Interview with Harry McGuire.
138 Interview with Marian Price.
139 It is not insignificant that Jim Gibney, a prominent leadership figure, was nicknamed in republican circles as 'God's little helper', God being Gerry Adams. Moloney (2002), op. cit., p. 402.
140 'There is no support for the IRA physical force any more', Tommy McKearney, *The Sunday Tribune*, August 15, 1999.
141 Interview with Brenda Murphy.
142 Interview with Johnnie White.
143 'Provisional Republicanism: Internal Politics, Inequities and Modes of Repression', Anthony McIntyre, p. 187, in Fearghal McGarry (2003), *Republicanism in Modern Ireland*. Dublin: University College Dublin Press.
144 Interview with Brendan Holland.
145 Interview with volunteer Albert.
146 Laurence McKeown (2001), *Out of Time: Irish Republican Prisoners. Long Kesh 1972–2000*. Belfast: Beyond the Pale. The title of the play and the film is *H 3*.
147 Interview with volunteer Albert.
148 Interview with volunteer Leonard.
149 Interview with John Nixon.
150 'Beating the Water: The Terrorist Search for Power, Control and Authority', Andrew Silke, *Terrorism and Political Violence*, vol. 12, no. 2 (2000), pp. 76–96.
151 On the IRA's vigilantism, see 'Rebel's Dilemma: The Changing Relationship between the IRA, Sinn Féin and Paramilitary Vigilantism in Northern Ireland', Andrew Silke, *Terrorism and Political Violence*, vol. 11, no. 1 (1999), pp. 55–93; Liam Kennedy (1995), *Crime and Punishment in West Belfast*. Belfast.
152 Interview with volunteer Albert.
153 Anthony McIntyre, p. 187, in McGarry (2003), op. cit.
154 Laurence McKeown (2001), op. cit., p. 168.
155 Interview with Tommy McKearney.
156 'Critique of the Propaganda War', published in *Congress '86*, vol. 1, no. 2 (1987), pp. 5–8.

5 LOSERS: 'WE HAD GONE AS FAR AS WE COULD WITH ARMED STRUGGLE'

1 Interview with Jackie McMullan.
2 Interview with Jackie McMullan.
3 Interview with volunteer Albert.
4 Interview with Danny Morrison.
5 Interview with Brendan Hughes.

6 Interview with volunteer Kevin.
7 Interview with volunteer Kevin.
8 Interview with Marian Price.
9 Interview with John Nixon.
10 Quoted in 'Hunger-strikers' action "changed the struggle"', Déaglan de Breadún, *The Irish Times*, August 28, 2001.
11 Interview with Brendan Hughes.
12 Quoted in Michael O'Sullivan (1972), *Patriot Graves: Resistance in Ireland*. Chicago, IL: Follett, pp. 225–26.
13 'Ever closer to the brink', *An Phoblacht/Republican News*, September 1970.
14 Peter Taylor (1997), *Provos: The IRA and Sinn Féin*. London: Bloomsbury, pp. 198–99.
15 Liam Clarke and Kathryn Johnston (2001), *Martin McGuinness: From Guns to Government*. Edinburgh: Mainstream, pp. 94–97.
16 'Agitate, educate, liberate', *Republican News*, May 22, 1976.
17 'Revolutionary politics needed to back up military gains', Gerry Adams' speech published in *An Phoblacht/Republican News*, June 23, 1979.
18 *Republican News*, June 18, 1977.
19 'Gerry Adams and the Modernisation of Republicanism', Henry Patterson, *Conflict Quarterly*, Summer (1990), pp. 5–23.
20 Quoted in Eamonn Mallie and Patrick Bishop (1987), *The Provisional IRA*. London: Heinemann, p. 275.
21 Interview with Anthony McIntyre.
22 Quoted in: www.pbs.org/wgbh/pages/frontline/shows/ira/inside/gibney.html
23 *An Phoblacht/Republican News*, November 17, 1983.
24 Quoted in Edgar O'Ballance (1981), *Terror in Ireland*. Novato: Presidio Press, p. 71.
25 Interview with Mickey McMullan.
26 'Memorandum reveals key gaps in SF's public and private positions' and '1997 Sinn Féin offer to incoming Labour Government revealed', Ed Moloney and Lin Solomon, in *The Sunday Tribune*, May 5, 2002.
27 'A blast from the past?', Mark Ryan, *Living Marxism*, February 10, 1996.
28 Interview with Tommy Gorman.
29 Interview with Margaret McKearney.
30 Interview with Mickey McMullan.
31 Interview with Mickey McMullan.
32 Interview with Mickey McMullan.
33 Interview with Joe O'Doherty.
34 Danny Morrison (1999), *Then the Walls Came Down: A Prison Journal*. Cork: Mercier Press, p. 239.
35 Interview with Tommy Gorman.
36 Interview with Eamon MacDermott.
37 Interview with Margaret McKearney.
38 Interview with Tommy Gorman.
39 Interview with Marian Price.
40 Interview with Eamon MacDermott.
41 Interview with Robert McClenaghan.
42 Interview with Shane O'Doherty.
43 Interview with Tony Catney.
44 Interview with Anthony McIntyre.
45 Interview with Paul O'Neill.
46 M.L.R. Smith (1997), *Fighting for Ireland: The Military Strategy of the Irish Republican Movement*. London: Routledge, p. 176.

47 Colm Keena (1990), *A Biography of Gerry Adams*. Dublin: The Mercier Press, pp. 168–69.
48 Interview with Eamon MacDermott.
49 *Fortnight*, no. 279, December 1989 and interview by the author with Peter Brooke.
50 Interview with Eamon MacDermott.
51 Interview with Peter Brooke.
52 Interview with Sean O'Callaghan.
53 Ed Moloney (2002), *A Secret History of the IRA*. London: Penguin, chapter 8.
54 Confidential interviews by the author.
55 Interview with Brendan Holland.
56 Interview with Marian Price.
57 Interview with volunteer Albert.
58 Robert White (1993), *Provisional Irish Republicans: An Oral and Interpretative History*. London: Greenwood Press, p. 172.
59 Gerry Adams in *An Phoblacht/Republican News*, June 23, 1979.
60 Quoted in 'Sinn Féin call to unionists', *An Phoblacht/Republican News*, September 1971. The same argument was put forward in 'The IRA justified', *An Phoblacht/Republican News*, June 1972.
61 White (1993), op. cit., p. 173.
62 Danny Morrison (1999), *Then the Walls came Down: A Prison Journal*. Cork: Mercier Press, p. 241.
63 Interview with Ruairi O'Bradaigh.
64 'O'Bradaigh: Longfordian republican and key figure in Northern peace', *Republican News*, April 5, 1975.
65 'Why I talked to John – by Gerry', *Fortnight*, no. 259, February 1988.
66 Ibid. This was also the position put forward in Sinn Féin documents produced around that time, such as *A Scenario for Peace: A Discussion Paper*, Sinn Féin Ard Chomhairle, Dublin, May 1987 and *Towards a Peace Strategy*, Sinn Féin, Belfast, 1988.
67 Interview with Danny Morrison.
68 Interview with Ruairi O'Bradaigh.
69 Interview with Danny Morrison quoted in White (1993), op. cit., pp. 172–73.
70 Interview with Mickey McMullan.
71 Moloney (2002), op. cit., pp. 255, 329–38.
72 Interview with Tommy McKearney.
73 Interview with Tony Catney.
74 *Northern Ireland: Future Terrorist Trends*, in Sean Cronin (1980), *Irish Nationalism: A History of its Roots and Ideology*. Dublin: The Academy Press, pp. 339–57.
75 Interview with Mickey McMullan.
76 In 1972 up to 496 people were killed, whereas the casualties between 1980 and 1990 amount to a total of 972. Between 1991 and 1999 there were 468 killings. David McKittrick *et al.* (1999), *Lost Lives*. Edinburgh: Mainstream, pp. 1473–93; Marie-Therese Fay *et al.* (1999), *Northern Ireland's Troubles: The Human Costs*. London: Pluto Press, pp. 168–71; and Marie-Therese Fay *et al.* (1997), *The Cost of the Troubles Study: Mapping Troubles-Related Deaths in Northern Ireland 1969–1994*. Derry: INCORE, pp. 46–48.
77 'How the war is being won', *Republican News*, May 14, 1972.
78 'The IRA justified', *An Phoblacht/Republican News*, June 1972.
79 Interview with Danny Morrison.
80 Interview with volunteer Timothy.
81 Toby Harnden (1999), *'Bandit Country': The IRA and South Armagh*. London: Hodder & Stoughton, pp. 289, 290, 306; or Peter Taylor (2001), *Brits: The War Against the IRA*. London: Bloomsbury, p. 354.

82 Ministry of Defence, www.operations.mod.uk/telic/casualties.htm.
83 Tim Pat Coogan (1993), *The IRA*. London: HarperCollins, p. 492. In those years when the IRA was supposed to be involved in the so-called 'major push', the terrorist group was responsible for killing the following British Army personnel: 1988: 22, 1989: 24, 1990: 10, 1991: 5. Moloney (2002), op. cit., p. 338.
84 Interview with Gerard Hodgkins.
85 Interview with Danny Morrison.
86 Interview with Danny Morrison.
87 The document can be read in Eamonn Mallie and David McKittrick (1996), *The Fight for Peace: The Secret Story Behind the Irish Peace Process*. London: Heinemann, pp. 381–84.
88 Interview with volunteer Albert.
89 Interview with David O'Donnell.
90 Interview with Feilim O hAdhmaill.
91 Interview with Rab McCallum.
92 Interview with Danny Morrison.
93 Smith (1997), op. cit., p. 223.
94 Allen Feldman (1991), *Formations of Violence: The Narrative of the Body and Political Terror in Northern Ireland*. Chicago, IL: The University of Chicago Press, pp. 228–29.
95 Anthony McIntyre (1991), *Armed Struggle: A Strategic Imperative*. Unpublished (copy lodged at The Belfast Linen Hall Library, Belfast), p. 72.
96 'Movement is possible', Dr Cahal Daly, *Fortnight*, no. 259, February 1988.
97 Interview with Rose McCotter.
98 Interview with Joe Doherty.
99 Interview with John Kelly.
100 Interview with volunteer Albert.
101 Richard English has also referred to the IRA's failure to understand unionism stressing the divisive effects of republican violence. Richard English (2003), *Armed Struggle: A History of the IRA*. London: Macmillan, pp. 372–73.
102 Interview with John Kelly.
103 These were the words of a Sinn Féin councillor in 1987 quoted in Adrian Guelke (1988), *Northern Ireland: The International Perspective*. Dublin: Gill & Macmillan, p. 212.
104 Interview with Jim Gibney.
105 Interview with Rose McCotter.
106 'IRA strike hard', *An Phoblacht/Republican News*, November 20, 1981.
107 Interview with Jim Gibney.
108 Interview with Liam McAnoy. The interviewee refers to the IRA bomb which exploded in the Belfast Shankill Road on October 23, 1993 in which nine protestants and an IRA terrorist died.
109 Interview with Sean Hayes.
110 Interview with Seamus Lynch.
111 Interview with Seamus Lynch.
112 '"For God and Ulster": The Culture of Terror and Loyalist Death Squads in Northern Ireland', Jeffrey Sluka, p. 147, in Jeffrey A. Sluka (ed.) (2000), *Death Squad: The Anthropology of State Terror*. Philadelphia, PA: University of Pennsylvania Press, pp. 126–57.
113 Interview with Brendan Holland.
114 Interview with Liam McAnoy.
115 Interview with Rab McCallum.
116 McKittrick *et al.* (1999), op. cit., pp. 1473–93; Fay *et al.* (1999), op. cit., pp. 168–71; and Fay *et al.* (1997), op. cit., pp. 46–48. Statistics attribute the Provisional

IRA responsibility for 50 per cent of all the deaths during the conflict. The Provisional IRA and other republican terrorist groups have been responsible for 58.8 per cent of all the killings.

117 'Self-defence', Thomas J. Fox, Letter to the editor, *An Phoblacht/Republican News*, July 31, 1997.
118 See for example McKittrick *et al.* (1999), op. cit., pp. 172–74. This is a point corroborated by English (2003), p. 351.
119 'Shocking statistics of loyalist pipe bombs', Sharon O'Neill, *Irish News*, February 22, 2003.
120 www.irlnet.com/rmlist, May 31–June 2, 2002, May 10–12, 2002, May 24–26, 2002.
121 Interview with Paul O'Neill.

6 WINNERS?: 'THIS IS A PROPAGANDA WAR'

1 'Social Psychology of Terrorist Groups', Clark R. McCauley and Mary E. Segal, p. 241, in Clyde Hendrick (ed.) (1987), *Group Processes and Intergroup Relations*. London: Sage, pp. 231–56.
2 J. Bowyer Bell (1976), *On Revolt: Strategies of National Liberation*. Cambridge, MA: Harvard University Press, pp. 203–04.
3 'The centre cannot hold', *An Phoblacht/Republican News*, January 9, 1992.
4 See for example 'Massive bill on the way', *An Phoblacht/Republican News*, May 27, 1992.
5 Interview with volunteer Mo.
6 'London bombs put Ireland onto election agenda', *An Phoblacht/Republican News*, March 5, 1992.
7 M.L.R. Smith (1997), *Fighting for Ireland? The Military Strategy of the Irish Republican Movement*. London: Routledge, p. 187.
8 Ibid.
9 Gerry Adams (1995), *Free Ireland: Towards a Lasting Peace*. Dingle: Brandon, p. 63.
10 Brian Jenkins (1975), *International Terrorism*. Santa Monica, CA: Rand Corporation, p. 4.
11 See for example 'The Media and Terrorism: A Reassessment', Paul Wilkinson, *Terrorism and Political Violence*, vol. 9 (1997), pp. 51–64; 'Power and Meaning: Terrorism as a Communication Structure', R.D. Crelinsten, in Paul Wilkinson and Alasdair M. Stewart (ed.) (1987), *Contemporary Research on Terrorism*. Aberdeen: The University Press, pp. 419–50; 'Terrorism and Propaganda: Problem and Response', M. Tugwell, in ibid., pp. 409–18.
12 'Terrorism and the Media: A Symbiotic Relationship?', pp. 76–86, in Grant Wardlaw (1989), *Political Terrorism: Theory, Tactics and Counter-Measures*. Cambridge: Cambridge University Press.
13 'The Political Significance of Terrorism', Loren E. Lomasky, pp. 97, 105–6, in R.G. Frey and Christopher W. Morris (ed.) (1991), *Violence, Terrorism and Justice*. Cambridge: Cambridge University Press, pp. 86–115.
14 Wardlaw (1989), op. cit., p. 38.
15 David Miller (1994), *Don't Mention the War: Northern Ireland, Propaganda and the Media*. London: Pluto Press, pp. 250–55.
16 Quoted in Ralph E. Dowling, 'The Terrorist and the Media: Partners in Crime, or Rituals and Harmless Observers?', p. 227, in Yonah Alexander and Abraham H. Foxman (ed.) (1990), *The 1988–1989 Annual on Terrorism*. London: Martinus Nijhoff, pp. 227–46.

17 *The Media and Intrastate Conflict in Northern Ireland*, Robin Wilson, *Democratic Dialogue Discussion Papers*, July 1997.
18 'Terrorism and Media Values: News Selection and the Distortion of Reality', Robert G. Picard, in Alexander and Foxman (1990), op. cit., pp. 219–26.
19 J. Bowyer Bell (2000), *The IRA 1968–2000: Analysis of a Secret Army*. London: Frank Cass, p. 281.
20 Ibid., p. 271.
21 Interview with Anthony McIntyre.
22 'Critique of the Propaganda War', *Congress '86*, vol. 1, no. 2 (1987), pp. 5–8.
23 Interview with Tommy McKearney.
24 Interview with volunteer Albert.
25 Interview with Tommy McKearney.
26 Interview with Tommy McKearney.
27 'Bomb warnings', Mick Kennedy, *Living Marxism*, vol. 50, December 1992.
28 Interview with volunteer Mo.
29 Interview with Shane O'Doherty.
30 Dowling (1990), op. cit.
31 Jack Holland (1999), *The American Connection*. Colorado: Roberts Rinehart; and Andrew J. Wilson (1995), *Irish America and the Ulster Conflict 1968–95*. Belfast: The Blackstaff Press.
32 Interview with Shane O'Doherty.
33 K.D. Ewing and C.A. Gearty (1990), *Freedom under Thatcher: Civil Liberties in Modern Britain*. Oxford: Clarendon Press, p. 248.
34 Article 19, *No Comment: Censorship, Secrecy and the Irish Troubles*. October 1989. London: Article 19, The International Centre on Censorship.
35 Quoted in 'Patrolling the Border: British Broadcasting and the Irish Question in the 1980s', Graham Murdock, p. 110, in *Journal of Communication*, vol. 41, no. 4 (1991), pp. 104–15.
36 Paul Wilkinson, 'Terrorism and Propaganda', p. 33, in Yonah Alexander and R. Latter (eds) (1990), *Terrorism and the Media: Dilemmas for Government, Journalists and the Public*. Washington, DC: Brassey's.
37 Quoted in 'Closing Down the Airwaves: The Story of the Broadcasting Ban', Ed Moloney, pp. 8–50, in Bill Rolston (ed.) (1991), *The Media and Northern Ireland*. London: Macmillan, p. 47.
38 Interview with volunteer Leonard.
39 Michael Farrell, in Andy Pollak (ed.) (1993), *A Citizens' Inquiry: The Opshal Report on Northern Ireland*. Dublin: The Lilliput Press, p. 114; and Ewing and Gearty (1990), op. cit., p. 250.
40 Interview with volunteer Leonard. The interviewee was referring to the general elections in the Republic of Ireland held in 2002.
41 Interview with Feilim O hAdhmaill.
42 Interview with Feilim O hAdhmaill.
43 'Lessons to be learned', interview with Jim Gibney in *An Phoblacht/Republican News*, April 16, 1992, pp. 6–7.
44 Rolston (1991), op. cit., p. 27.
45 Interview with Eamon MacDermott.
46 Interview with Shane O'Doherty.
47 'The fog of war', *The Economist*, p. 47, February 26, 1994.
48 John McGarry and Brendan O'Leary (1995), *Explaining Northern Ireland*. Oxford: Blackwell, pp. 79, 114–20.
49 Interview with Mickey McMullan. On November 21, 1974 the IRA exploded several bombs in two Birmingham pubs killing twenty-one people and injuring over a hundred. On October 5 that year five people died as a result of an IRA

explosion in a pub in the English town of Guildford. On November 7, two people were killed by an IRA bomb in another pub in Woolwich, also in England.

50 'We're Brits and we're proud of it', Jeffrey Donaldson, *The Guardian*, August 22, 2001.

51 Interview with Sean Hayes.

52 Quoted in 'The provocations of the IRA', *The Economist*, Leader, p. 20, March 19, 1994.

53 Robin Wilson (1997), *The Media and Intrastate Conflict in Northern Ireland*, Democratic Dialogue Discussion Papers.

54 Robin Evelegh (1978), *Peacekeeping in a Democratic Society: The Lessons of Northern Ireland*. London: Hurst, p. 38.

55 'Warrington tragedy – what the IRA said', *An Phoblacht/Republican News*, March 25, 1993.

56 Bob Rowthorn and Naomi Wayne (1988), *Northern Ireland: The Political Economy of Conflict*. Cambridge: Polity Press, p. 67.

57 David McKittrick *et al.* (1999), *Lost Lives*. Edinburgh: Mainstream, p. 1341.

58 Interview with Gerard Hodgkins.

59 'Second-class in death as well?', Hilda MacThomas, in *An Phoblacht/Republican News*, April 1, 1993.

60 'Let's work for real peace', Editorial, *An Phoblacht/Republican News*, April 1, 1993.

61 Fionnuala O'Connor (1993), *In Search of a State: Catholics in Northern Ireland*. Belfast: The Blackstaff Press, p. 264.

62 'Northern Ireland and Fleet Street', John Kirkaldy, p. 184, in Yonah Alexander and Alan O'Day (ed.) (1984), *Terrorism in Ireland*. London: Croom Helm, pp. 171–200.

63 John Whyte (1994), *Interpreting Northern Ireland*. Oxford: Oxford University Press.

64 '"Terrorism", the Media, and the Liberal-Democratic State: A Critique of the Orthodoxy', Philip Schlesinger, p. 224, in Yonah Alexander and Alan O'Day (ed.) (1984), *Terrorism in Ireland*. London: Croom Helm, pp. 213–32.

65 Quoted in O'Connor (1993), op. cit., p. 261.

66 'Italy: A Systems Perspective', F. Ferracuti and F. Bruno, pp. 308–10, in A. Goldstein and M. Segall (ed.) (1983), *Aggression in Global Perspective*. New York: Pergamon, pp. 287–312.

67 See how several people were kidnapped by the IRA with the intention of extracting money from them in 'The Provisional Irish Republican Army: Command and Functional Structure', John Horgan and Max Taylor, *Terrorism and Political Violence*, vol. 9, no. 3 (1997), pp. 1–32. Other examples of kidnappings can be found in Liam Clarke (1987), *Broadening the Battlefield: The H-Blocks and the Rise of Sinn Féin*. Dublin: Gill and Macmillan, pp. 213–15.

68 'Bertie talking bollix', Anthony McIntyre, *The Blanket*, April 23, 2002.

69 Liz Curtis (1984), *Ireland: The Propaganda War. The British Media and the Battle for Hearts and Minds*. London: Pluto Press, pp. 268–69.

70 Interviews with the author; Patrick Bishop and Eamon Mallie (1992), *The Provisional IRA*. London: Heinemann, p. 215; David McKittrick (1994), *Endgame: The Search for Peace in Northern Ireland*. Belfast: The Blackstaff Press, pp. 141 and 145; Peter Taylor (1997), *Provos*. London: Bloomsbury, p. 131.

71 'Devastating attacks on crown forces', *An Phoblacht/Republican News*, March 20, 1997.

72 Interview with Raymond Wilkinson.

73 'How Violence is Justified: Sinn Féin's *An Phoblacht*', Robert G. Picard, *Journal of Communication*, vol. 41, no. 4 (1991), pp. 90–103.

74 Interview with Danny Morrison.
75 Interview with Jackie McMullan.
76 Interview with Brendan Holland.
77 IRA statement in *An Phoblacht/Republican News*, July 18, 2002. It should be borne in mind that since the mid-1980s the IRA considered as 'legitimate targets' civilians who may have had a professional relationship with the Army and the police, including civil servants, contractors, cleaners and food suppliers.
78 Interview with Jim Gibney.
79 Interview with Jim Gibney.
80 Interview with Pat McNamee.
81 'Armed Struggle', Letters to the editor by Owen Bennett published in *An Phoblacht/Republican News*, April 8, 1993 and May 20, 1993.
82 'Armed Struggle', Letter to the editor by Thomas O'Connell published in *An Phoblacht/Republican News*, April 22, 1993.
83 'Armed Struggle', Letter to the editor by Pádraig O Foill, published in *An Phoblacht/Republican News*, May 20, 1993.
84 *An Phoblacht/Republican News*, May 20, 1993. In April 1993 an IRA bomb exploded in the financial area of London. One month before, Jonathan Ball and Timothy Parry, who were 3 and 12 years old respectively, died as a result of IRA bombs located in the English town of Warrington.
85 *An Phoblacht/Republican News*, May 13, 1993.
86 *The Sunday Business Post*, August 27, 2000.
87 Sean O'Callaghan, who at the time of the Brighton bomb held an important position in the IRA, confirmed this point in an interview on the documentary *Brighton Bomb*, broadcast by *Channel 4*, on May 15, 2003.
88 *An Phoblacht/Republican News*, June 25, 1992.
89 Interview with Jim Gibney.
90 *An Phoblacht/Republican News*, October 14, 1993.
91 Interview with volunteer Leonard.
92 Interview with Tony Catney.
93 Interview with Gerard Hodgkins.

EPILOGUE

1 'Labour MP faces expulsion', Nicholas Watt, *The Guardian*, May 31, 2003.
2 'Why I stood up for Bobby Sands', John McDonnell, *The Guardian*, June 3, 2003.
3 Interview with Joe Doherty.
4 Interview with Harry McGuire.
5 Interview with Brendan Holland.
6 Henry Patterson (1997), *The Politics of Illusion: A Political History of the IRA*. London: Serif, p. 205.
7 See for example, Jonathan Tonge (2006), *Northern Ireland*. Cambridge: Polity and Kevin Rafter (2005), *Sinn Féin 1905–2005: In the Shadow of Gunmen*. Dublin: Gill and Macmillan.
8 Interview with Rab McCallum.
9 Interview with Seamus Lynch.
10 Interview with Martin McKevitt.
11 Óglaigh na hÉireann is the Irish term used by IRA members to refer to the organisation.
12 Interview with Carl Reilly.

SELECTED BIBLIOGRAPHY

Aughey, Arthur (2005), *The Politics of Northern Ireland: Beyond the Belfast Agreement*. London: Routledge.

Bandura, Albert (1973), *Aggression: A Social Learning Analysis*. New Jersey: Prentice Hall.

Bandura, Albert and Walters, Richard H. (1963), *Social Learning and Personality Development*. London: Holt, Rinehart and Winston.

Bean, Kevin (1995), *The New Departure: Recent Developments in Irish Republican Ideology and Strategy*. Liverpool: The Institute of Irish Studies, The University of Liverpool.

Bean, Kevin and Hayes, Mark (eds) (2001), *Republican Voices*. Monaghan: Seesyu Press.

Bell, J. Bowyer (2000), *The IRA 1968–2000: Analysis of a Secret Army*. London: Frank Cass.

Bennett Report (1979), *Report on the Committee of Inquiry into Police Interrogation Procedures in Northern Ireland*. London: HMSO.

Beresford, David (1994), *Ten Men Mead: The Story of the 1981 Irish Hunger Strike*. London: HarperCollins.

Bew, Paul and Gillespie, Gordon (1999), *Northern Ireland: A Chronology of the Troubles 1968–1999*. Dublin: Gill & Macmillan.

Birrell, Derek (1972), 'Relative Deprivation as a Factor in Conflict in Northern Ireland', *Sociological Review*, vol. 20, no. 3, pp. 317–44.

——(1994), 'Social Policy Responses to Urban Violence in Northern Ireland', in Seamus Dunn (ed.), *Managing Divided Cities*. Keele: Keele University Press.

Brown, Rupert (2000), *Group Processes*. Oxford: Blackwell.

Bruce, Steve (1997), 'Victim Selection in Ethnic Conflict: Motives and Attitudes in Irish Republicanism', *Terrorism and Political Violence*, vol. 9, no. 1, pp. 56–71.

Burton, Frank (1978), *The Politics of Legitimacy: Struggles in a Belfast Community*. London: Routledge.

Cairns, Ed (1982), 'Intergroup Conflict in Northern Ireland', in Henri Tajfel (ed.), *Social Identity and Intergroup Relations*. Cambridge: Cambridge University Press, pp. 277–97.

Campbell, Brian, McKeown, Laurence and O'Hagan, Felim (1994), *Nor Meekly Serve my Time: The H Block Struggle 1976–1981*. Belfast: Beyond the Pale.

Clarke, Liam (1987), *Broadening the Battlefield: The H-Blocks and the Rise of Sinn Féin*. Dublin: Gill and Macmillan.

217

Clarke, Liam and Johnston, Kathryn (2001), *Martin McGuinness: From Guns to Government*. Edinburgh: Mainstream.

Cohen, Stanley (2001), *States of Denial: Knowing about Atrocities and Suffering*. Cambridge: Polity Press.

Collins, Eamon (1997), *Killing Rage*. London: Granta.

Compton Report (1971), *Report of the Enquiry into the Allegations against the Security Forces of Physical Brutality in Northern Ireland arising out of Events on the 9th August 1971*. London: HMSO.

Coogan, Tim Pat (1993), *The IRA*. London: HarperCollins.

Crenshaw, Martha (ed.) (1983), *Terrorism, Legitimacy, and Power: The Consequences of Political Violence*. Middletown, CT: Wesleyan University Press.

——(1988), 'The Subjective Reality of the Terrorist: Ideological and Psychological Factors in Terrorism', in Robert O. Slater and Michael Stohl (ed.), *Current Perspectives on International Terrorism*. London: Macmillan, pp. 12–46.

Davies, James (1962), 'Toward a Theory of Revolution', *American Sociological Review*, vol. 27, pp. 5–19.

——(ed.) (1971), *When Men Revolt and Why: A Reader in Political Violence and Revolution*. London: Collier-Macmillan.

Dewar, Michael (1996), *The British Army in Northern Ireland*. London: Arms and Armour.

Dingley, James (1998), 'A Reply to White's Non-Sectarian Thesis of PIRA Targeting', *Terrorism and Political Violence*, vol. 10, no. 2, pp. 106–17.

Dittes, James E. (1959), 'Attractiveness of Group as Function of Self-esteem and Acceptance by Group', *Journal of Abnormal and Social Psychology*, vol. 59, pp. 77–82.

English, Richard (2003), *Armed Struggle: A History of the IRA*. London: Macmillan.

Fay, Marie-Therese, Morrissey, Mike and Smyth, Marie (1997), *The Cost of the Troubles Study: Mapping Troubles-Related Deaths in Northern Ireland 1969–1994*. Derry: INCORE.

——(1999), *Northern Ireland's Troubles: The Human Costs*. London: Pluto Press.

Feeney, Brian (2003), *Sinn Féin: A Hundred Turbulent Years*. Dublin: The O'Brien Press.

Festinger, Leo (1957), *A Theory of Cognitive Dissonance*. Stanford, CT: Stanford University Press.

Guelke, Adrian (1988), *Northern Ireland: The International Perspective*. Dublin: Gill and Macmillan.

Gurr, Ted Robert (1970), *Why Men Rebel*. Princeton, NJ: Princeton University Press.

Harbison, Joan (ed.) (1983), *Children of the Troubles: Children in Northern Ireland*. Belfast: Stranmillis College.

Harnden, Toby (1999), *'Bandit Country': The IRA and South Armagh*. London: Hodder & Stoughton.

Hayes, Bernadette and McAllister, Ian (2005), 'Public Support for Political Violence and Paramilitarism in Northern Ireland and the Republic of Ireland', *Terrorism and Political Violence*, vol. 17, pp. 599–617.

Hendrick, Clyde (ed.) (1987), *Group Processes and Intergroup Relations*. London: Sage.

Heskin, Ken (1980), *Northern Ireland: A Psychological Analysis*. Dublin: Gill and Macmillan.

Hewitt, Christopher (1981), 'Catholic Grievances, Catholic Nationalism and Violence in Northern Ireland During the Civil Rights Period: A Reconsideration', *British Journal of Sociology*, vol. 32, no. 3, pp. 364–80.

—— (1984), *The Effectiveness of Anti-Terrorist Policies*. New York: University Press of America.

Hogg, Michael A. and Abrams, Dominic (1988), *Social Identifications: A Social Psychology of Intergroup Relations and Group Processes*. London: Routledge.

Holland, Jack and Phoenix, Susan (1996), *Phoenix: Policing the Shadows*. London: Hodder and Stoughton.

Irish Republican Publicity Bureau (1970), *In the '70s the IRA Speaks*. No. 3. Repsol Pamphlet.

—— (1973), *Freedom Struggle by the Provisional IRA*. Dublin.

Janis, Irving L. (1982), *Groupthink: Psychological Studies of Policy Decisions and Fiascos*. London: Houghton Mifflin.

Janis, Irving L. and Mann, Leo (1977), *Decision Making: A Psychological Analysis of Conflict, Choice and Commitment*. London: Collier Macmillan.

Keena, Colm (1990), *A Biography of Gerry Adams*. Dublin: The Mercier Press.

Kelley, Kevin (1982), *The Longest War: Northern Ireland and the IRA*. Dingle: Brandon.

Killian, Lewis M. (1980), 'Theory of Collective Behaviour: The Mainstream Revisited', in Hubert M. Blalock (ed.), *Sociological Theory and Research: A Critical Appraisal*. London: Collier Macmillan, pp. 275–89.

Lijphart, Arend (1975), 'Review Article: The Northern Ireland Problem; Cases, Theories, and Solutions', *British Journal of Political Science*, vol. 5, no. 1, pp. 83–106.

—— (1999), *Patterns of Democracy: Government Forms and Performance in Thirty-Six Countries*. New Haven, CT: Yale University.

Lynn, Brendan (2002), 'Tactic or Principle? The Evolution of Republican Thinking on Abstentionism in Ireland, 1970–1998', *Irish Political Studies*, vol. 17, no. 2, pp. 74–94.

Lyons, H.A. and Harbinson, H.J. (1986), 'A Comparison of Political and Non-Political Murderers in Northern Ireland, 1974–84', *Medicine, Science and the Law*, vol. 26, no. 3, pp. 193–98.

McAdam, Douglas and Paulsen, Ronnelle (1993), 'Specifying the Relationship between Social Ties and Activism', in *American Journal of Sociology*, vol. 99, no. 3, pp. 640–67.

McGarry, Fearghal (ed.) (2003), *Republicanism in Modern Ireland*. Dublin: University College Dublin Press.

McIntyre, Anthony (1991), *Armed Struggle: A Strategic Imperative*. Unpublished (copy lodged at The Belfast Linen Hall Library, Belfast).

—— (1999), *A Structural Analysis of Modern Irish Republicanism: 1969–1973*. Belfast: Faculty of Economics and Social Sciences, Queen's University of Belfast.

McKearney, Tommy (1987), 'Critique of the Propaganda War', *Congress '86*, vol. 1, no. 2, pp. 5–8.

McKeown, Laurence (2001), *Out of Time: Irish Republican Prisoners, Long Kesh 1972–2000*. Belfast: Beyond the Pale.

McKittrick, David (1994), *Endgame: The Search for Peace in Northern Ireland*. Belfast: The Blackstaff Press.

McKittrick, David, Kelters, Seamus, Feeney, Brian and Thornton, Chris (1999), *Lost Lives*. Edinburgh: Mainstream.

Magee, Patrick (2001), *Gangsters or Guerrillas? Representations of Irish Republicans in 'Troubles Fiction'*. Belfast: Beyond the Pale.

Maillot, Agnes (2004), *New Sinn Féin*. London: Routledge.

Mallie, Eamonn and Bishop, Patrick (1987), *The Provisional IRA*. London: Heinemann.

Mallie, Eamonn and McKittrick, David (1996), *The Fight for Peace*. London: Heinemann.

Marx, Gary T. and McAdam, Douglas (1995), *Collective Behavior and Social Movements: Process and Structure*. New Jersey: Prentice Hall.

Merkl, Peter H. (1986), *Political Violence and Terror: Motifs and Motivations*. London: University of California Press.

Milgram, Stanley (1974), *Obedience to Authority*. New York: HarperCollins.

Moloney, Ed (2002), *A Secret History of the IRA*. London: Penguin.

Morrison, Danny (1999), *Then the Walls Came Down: A Prison Journal*. Cork: Mercier Press.

Moxon-Browne, Eddie (1981), 'The Water and the Fish: Public Opinion and the Provisional IRA in Northern Ireland', in Paul Wilkinson (ed.), *British Perspectives on Terrorism*. London: George Allen & Unwin.

Murray, Gerard and Tonge, Jonathan (2005), *Sinn Féin and the SDLP: From Alienation to Participation*. London: Hurst & Company.

Neumann, Peter (2003), *Britain's Long War: British Strategy in the Northern Ireland Conflict, 1968–98*. London: Palgrave.

Noelle-Neumann, Elisabeth (1984), *The Spiral of Silence: Public Opinion – Our Social Skin*. Chicago, IL: The University of Chicago Press.

O'Brien, Brendan (1993), *The Long War: The IRA and Sinn Féin 1985 to Today*. Dublin: The O'Brien Press.

O'Callaghan, Sean (1999), *The Informer*. London: Corgi.

Ó Danachair, G. (1974), *Provos: Patriots or Terrorists?* Dublin: Irish Book Bureau.

O'Doherty, Malachi (1998), *The Trouble with Guns: Republican Strategy and the Provisional IRA*. Belfast: The Blackstaff Press.

O'Doherty, Shane (1993), *The Volunteer*. London: HarperCollins.

O'Malley, Padraig (1990), *Biting at the Grave: The Irish Hunger Strikes and the Politics of Despair*. Belfast: The Blackstaff Press.

O'Rawe, Richard (2005), *Blanketmen: An Untold Story of the H-Block Hunger Strike*. Dublin: News Island.

O'Sullivan, Michael (1972), *Patriot Graves: Resistance in Ireland*. Chicago, IL: Follett.

Patterson, Henry (1997), *The Politics of Illusion: A Political History of the IRA*. London: Serif.

Post, J.M. (1987), 'Group and Organisational Dynamics of Political Terrorism: Implications for Counterterrorist Policy', in Paul Wilkinson (ed.), *Contemporary Research on Terrorism*. Aberdeen: The University Press, pp. 307–17.

Provisional Irish Republican Army (1973), *Freedom Struggle by the IRA*. Dublin: Irish Republican Publicity Bureau.

Purdie, Bob (1990), *Politics in the Streets: The Origins of the Civil Rights Movement in Northern Ireland*. Belfast: The Blackstaff Press.

Rafter, Kevin (2005), *Sinn Féin, 1905–2005: In the Shadow of Gunmen*. Dublin: Gill and Macmillan.

Rapoport, David (1988), *Inside Terrorist Organizations*. New York: Columbia University Press.

Reich, Walter (ed.) (1990), *Origins of Terrorism: Psychologies, Ideologies, States of Mind*. Cambridge: Cambridge University Press.

Rose, Richard (1971), *Governing without Consensus*. London: Faber and Faber.

Scarman, Robert (1972), *Violence and Civil Disturbances in Northern Ireland in 1969*, Cmd. 566. Belfast: HMSO.

Sharrock, David and Devenport, Mark (1997), *Man of War, Man of Peace? The Unauthorized Biography of Gerry Adams*. London: Macmillan.

Sinn Féin (1970), *Where Sinn Féin Stands*. Caretaker Executive, January 17.

Sinn Féin (1971), *Sinn Féin: Yesterday and Today*. Dublin.

Sinn Féin Ard Chomhairle (1987), *A Scenario for Peace: A Discussion Paper*. Dublin.

Sinn Féin (1988), *Towards a Peace Strategy*. Belfast.

Sluka, Jeffrey (1989), *Hearts and Minds, Water and Fish: Support for the IRA and INLA in a Northern Irish Ghetto*. London: JAI Press.

Smith, M.L.R. (1997), *Fighting for Ireland: The Military Strategy of the Irish Republican Movement*. London: Routledge.

Snow, David A., Zurcher, Jr, Louis A. and Ekland-Olson, Sheldon (1980), 'Social Networks and Social Movements: A Microstructural Approach to Differential Recruitment', *American Sociological Review*, vol. 45, pp. 787–801.

Snow, David A., Burke Rochford, Jr, E., Worden, Steven K. and Benford, Robert D. (1986), 'Frame Alignment Processes, Micromobilization, and Movement Participation', *American Sociological Review*, vol. 51, pp. 464–81.

Taylor, Maxwell (1988), *The Terrorist*. London: Brassey's Defence Publishers.

Taylor, Peter (1997), *Provos: The IRA and Sinn Féin*. London: Bloomsbury.

Thompson, J.L.P. (1989), 'Deprivation and Political Violence in Northern Ireland, 1922–85', *Journal of Conflict Resolution*, vol. 33, no. 4, pp. 676–99.

Tilly, Charles (1978), *From Mobilization to Revolution*. Reading, MA: Addison-Wesley.

Tonge, Jonathan (2006), *Northern Ireland*. Cambridge: Polity.

Urban, Mark (1992), *Big Boy's Rules: The SAS and the Secret Struggle against the IRA*. London: Faber and Faber.

White, Robert (1993), *Provisional Irish Republicans: An Oral and Interpretative History*. London: Greenwood Press.

—— (1997), 'The Irish Republican Army: An Assessment of Sectarianism', *Terrorism and Political Violence*, vol. 9, no. 1, pp. 20–55.

—— (1997), 'The Irish Republican Army and Sectarianism: Moving beyond the Anecdote', *Terrorism and Political Violence*, vol. 9, no. 2, pp. 120–31.

Whyte, John (1994), *Interpreting Northern Ireland*. Oxford: Oxford University Press.

Wilkinson, Paul (1997), 'The Media and Terrorism: A Reassessment', *Terrorism and Political Violence*, vol. 9, no. 2, pp. 51–64.

INDEX